What's happening to U.S. banking?...

What's happening to U.S. banking?...

...how you can be protected.

(from the final meltdown)

by Marshall E. Surratt

COMMERCIAL PUBLISHERS
DALLAS

Published by
Commercial Publishers,
2701 Fondren
P.O. Box 8275
Dallas, Texas 75205-8275

Publisher's Cataloging in Publication Data
Surratt, Marshall E.

What's happening to U.S. banking? . .
. . . how you can be protected. (From the final meltdown)

Chapter bibliographical notes. Appendixes. Index.

1. Banks. Savings banks. Savings and loans.
Other financial institutions. What went wrong?

2. Federal and state regulators. Deregulation. Reregulation.

3. Congress and deficit spending. Erratic prices and interest rates. Inflation and loss of value of the U.S. dollar.

4. How to be protected. Individuals and families. Small and large business. Internationally.

Quotations from *Wall Street Journal* by permission of Dow Jones & Co. Other sources also credited.

HG2491 332.1 92-075533

ISBN 0-9635525-0-3

First Printing

Printed in the United States of America

Cover design by Erwin Hearne

To Margaret

Editor's Preface

While we were working on this book the world changed daily before our eyes – not the inexorable turn of events that have resulted from the ordinary daily grinding activity of humankind upon the earth and one another but huge political upheavals. These included the *tearing down of the Berlin Wall; the turning from Communism and separatism of Eastern Europe* that was accomplished with the friendship and aid of the very soldiers they were sworn to resist; *turnovers of governments* too numerous to mention here; *revolutions and attempts* at revolutions; *coups* and failed coups; and *political* and *economic* changes of mind and policy over such disparate matters as *apartheid, nuclear armament, private ownership of property* and a host of others.

These sociological earthquakes made writing about monetary policies extremely risky. More times than I like to remember, monetary policies, governmental philosophies or even boundaries of nations being written about would be radically changed by the time the pages were typed, changing sections of the manuscript that we had just previously completed. But through coups and revolutions, massacres, wars and ever more financial scandals, this book has remained remarkably germane to its purpose.

The more the world changed around us, the more relevant the rockhard facts presented here appeared. And yet, like the householder who can't fix the leaky roof when rain is pouring down, and then does not need a solid roof on bright and sunny days, our own government representatives have maintained a foolish, naive attitude toward the mending of our own fiscal roof.

Never before have we so urgently needed to have a monetary and fiscal system on which we can depend. Never before has the need been so urgent for the people of the United States, and indeed, the world, to *know* how their financial affairs are handled. And once we know, then we can act.

Marshall Surratt knows money and banking; he also knows people up and down the financial scale. The dry and dusty pages of financial reports, bank statements, and statements of profit and loss come alive when they are infused with the flesh and blood of presidents, movie stars, barbers, farmers and the waitress slinging hash.

Knowledge of finance empowers us. Once we know the mechanics of money, we need never be helpless again.

For whatever reason you read this book, you'll be entertained – and you will be enlightened. Please act upon that enlightenment.

Johnnye Montgomery
Midland, Texas

TABLE OF CONTENTS

Introduction

In the 1990s Democrats and Republicans were seeking to blame one another for the severe difficulties of commercial banking, as well as for the failures of savings banks, and for the tremendous losses of the savings and loan fiasco.

What happened to the S&Ls?

What hit the savings banks?

What went wrong with our commercial banks?

Test your memory. Without looking, can you remember whose face appears on the ten dollar bill? The twenty? Who is on the two dollar bill, the hundred, the five hundred? Or even on the one or five dollar bills? How many denominations of currency can you match with faces? (See Appendix B for matchings.)

Who were these people who founded our monetary system? Aristocrats, and rough-hewn pioneers. Self-educated and graduates of the finest schools of their times. They were united in their determination to make the new nation work for the benefit of all the people. In order for our nation to serve the people, the monetary system had to work. No matter what their individual philosophies of government might be, all the founders of our country believed in a sound dollar, one which would keep its value – a dollar which the individual could trust. They knew of the terrible inflation of paper money in France following the rule of Louis IV. They had seen the results of John Law's efforts to pump up the French economy with paper currency. Closer to home, they knew of his Mississippi promotion, the Mississippi Bubble.[1] They heard not only of the beheading of Louis XVI and later of aristocrats and commoners, but also of the utter collapse of France's fiat paper money, ended only when Napoleon became emperor "to save the Republic."[2] They had their own experience with the Continental paper currency, which fiat money became practically worthless, giving us the phrase, "Not worth a Continental."

George Washington – whose well known picture is on the $1 bill – had diverse personages in his cabinet: aristocratic Secretary of the Treasury Alexander Hamilton and democratic Secretary of State Thomas Jefferson. Hamilton, whose portrait graces the $10 bill, and Jefferson, whose likeness appears on both the $2 bill and the five cent coin, argued over redemption of the States' debts as well as the establishment of a Bank of the United States. This bank was to have a monopoly position in which the federal government would be given partial ownership – both proposals of Hamilton. He prevailed on these points throughout the life of the bank – which lasted a few years after Hamilton's own demise at the hands of Aaron Burr in the infamous duel which ended Burr's political career. This wasn't the first time Burr's fate had been affected by Hamilton. His Federalist bid for the presidency had been thwarted by Hamilton's backing of Thomas Jefferson, a Republican-Democrat.

We owe the historic soundness of our currency to these men as well as to Benjamin Franklin, Robert Morris, James Madison and Andrew Jackson. They all agreed on the necessity for a sound dollar, based on silver and gold, with a resulting abiding value.

Philadelphia merchant-financier Robert Morris, Superintendent of Finance under the *Articles of Confederation*, valiantly begged the new states for aid for Washington's army, and pledged his personal fortune to keep supplies and pay available for the struggling troops. Following the war, the optimistic Morris bought up much of undeveloped, stump-lined Washington City and upper New York State on credit. After defaulting on payment, he went to debtor's prison, a heritage of British rule. Revolutionary War hero Henry (Light-Horse Harry) Lee, likewise, went to debtor's prison when his proposed development on the Potomac proved premature.[3] In part due to their painful experiences, the new United States established a system of bankruptcy for the relief of debtors.

When the Civil War emergency created the "greenbacks" – paper currency without gold or silver backing – Robert Morris' portrait was on the $1,000 bill – which likely would not have pleased Morris. Now William McKinley, still another advocate of the sound dollar, looks out on the holder of the $1,000 Federal Reserve Note. That fact you will not likely to observe from experience, since you are not apt to receive any bill above $100. This is due to the withdrawal from circulation of all bills over $100 on orders of U.S. Treasury/Federal Reserve agreement. James Madison, father of the Constitution, opposed fiat paper money, both in his native Virginia and for the new nation. You are not likely to see his portrait either, as his appears on the $5,000 bill. Andrew Jackson, rough hewn product of the western frontier and a founder of the Democratic party, was concerned about "moneyed power" but opposed to inflation and paper money. Jackson's picture is on the more familiar $20 bill.

Benjamin Franklin, a man of many talents and achievements, served in France during the Revolution as representative of the newly declared United States of America. Franklin sought France's military and financial assistance. He knew of the European countries' monetary experiences. Franklin was a sound money man. His picture is on the $100 bill.

Diverse though their individual philosophies, the founders of this country believed in a sound monetary system. We learned early to use the terms "sound as a dollar" and "good as gold." Our dollar and our banks both have been the repositories of Americans' trust since our country's beginning. We could have wars and rumors of wars, famine, pestilence and scandals rocking state and national capitols, but we could rely on our banks and savings institutions, which we equated with the soundness of the dollar. The *Constitution of the United States of America* states that the Congress shall have the power – among other things – "To coin Money, regulate the Value thereof, and of foreign Coin, and fix the Standards of Weights and Measures." Congress would appear to have failed in this – by letting the dollar's value go down, down, down . . .

The 1990s – 200 Years Later – What Went Wrong?

Two hundred years later, we face burdensome savings and loan failures and heavy bank failures. Democrats and Republicans blame one another for the failures and for failing to spend properly on prosecution of wrong-doers in the S&Ls and banks. One thing almost everyone in government today can understand is spending more money (disregarding the fact that such deficit spending makes the dollar ever worth less).

As a case in point, New York's Franklin National Bank is probably causing Benjamin Franklin to spin in his grave. We will discuss its international intrigue, murder, and mayhem later, along with the billion-dollar Eastern savings banks. Bailed out in the 1980s, the large savings banks were again in trouble in the 1990s. We also shall look at the multi-billion-dollar Southwestern bank holding company movement in which all but one of Texas' eleven billion-dollar combinations either failed or had to be bought out. We'll examine the failure of the super-regional Bank of New England Corp. We shall also examine banks and S&Ls – some small, some large – which continue to do very well, maintaining their financial strengths and serving their communities.

Japan's and Germany's financial successes will be considered. The dreams and practices of their people and the dreams and practices of Americans will be compared.

Going After the Cheats, the Chiselers, and the Charlatans

In the 1990s, news reports in U.S. newspapers, TV and radio quoted members of Congress and the Administration on what had been done, not done, and should be done – regarding the S&L and banking situation. *Hearst News Service* quoted then President Bush on going after "the cheats and chiselers and the charlatans" in "the latest salvo in the continuing war of words between the White House and the Congress over who's to blame for the massive wave of S&L failures."[4]

In the Northwest, federal authorities at Seattle were said to have won major convictions against executives and customers of former S&Ls resulting in "sentences of 56 years for nine individuals and restitution amounting to $38 million." Only a few days before this announcement a Seattle newspaper reporter had commented that three years previously it was most difficult to get anyone to pay the least attention to S&L wrongdoings.[5] Just a few days after the announcement by the federal government, a successor S&L also became defunct, went out of business, with deposits sold to a large West Coast bank. About the same time that bank proudly announced an investment in its financial system by Japan's "second largest bank."[6] A year later the West Coast bank, uncertain about its financial situation, solicited a merger into a larger West Coast bank. We shall examine the benefits of mergers, real or imagined. We shall look at certain short-lived super regional banking mergers, as in the Southeast.

Bank fraud by insiders, also fraud by government as in the loss of real value of the people's savings, will be discussed. Federally-owned corporations and entities will be looked into as to their services, profits and losses, and their contributions to the federal debt.

The record of the nearly forgotten peacetime gold standard will be exhumed. We shall look at the gold standard's limit on government spending, and the gold standard's maintenance of the value of the dollar – and of the pound, franc, mark, yen and ruble. We shall consider, with the fall of Communist totalitarianism, what such a standard may be in the future.

Presidential and Congressional commissions on banking will be reviewed, as to what is accomplished by such commissions.

Congressional laws and accompanying regulations on banking will be discussed, including proliferation of regulations upon regulations. The so-called "deregulation" of Garn-St Germain on banks and savings and loans, and some of the terrible effects of legislative fiat which told S&Ls that they were to have all the privileges of commercial banks, will be reviewed.

The sad fact that the Federal Savings & Loan Insurance Corporation (FSLIC) went broke will be examined. That the Federal

Deposit Insurance Corporation (FDIC) and its Bank Insurance Fund also became completely depleted will get attention.

Bank (and S&L) Capital, Assets, and Liabilities

A commercial bank, a savings bank, or a savings & loan association is not allowed to continue in operation when it is without Net Worth. (But of course a government corporation or agency is different. Though the FSLIC was done away after it got into such a negative net worth position.) The net worth of a bank is called its Capital Account. More specifically the capital account consists of Capital, Surplus, and Undivided Profits (Retained Earnings). The capital and surplus portions are supposed to be more or less inviolate. That is, they are not supposed to be impaired, though they may and should be increased. Increases would come from retained Net Earnings (after any shareholder Dividends) or from additional Capital stock sales. Loan Reserve, or Reserve for Bad Debts as it used to be called, is somewhat akin to capital. These days such reserve is usually netted from Gross Loans (Unearned Interest also being deducted) to give Net Loans.

Net worth of an S&L used to be called its Reserve, but nowadays it is generally referred to as Capital. As in all double entry accounting the capital (net worth) of a bank or S&L is the difference between Assets and Liabilities. Somewhat strangely to the general public – and to many bank employees – customer Deposits comprise the major part of bank liabiliities. The bank is liable to its customers for deposits. Loans and Investments are made against deposits and the capital account. Some banks also owe additionally on short or long term Notes.

Among the hundreds of thought-provoking comments from all areas of the nation were questions on what should be done to return to a strong banking system and a strong U.S. dollar. We shall attempt to answer some of these questions in the following chapters – how we may again have strong banks, strong S&Ls and strong credit unions serving the needs of all our communities.

We must also admit that some of the ill services and debts which we of recent generations have bequeathed to oncoming generations may only be solved by our children and grandchildren – as they show us by work and savings a renewal of financial strength as a way of life in these United States. In these last years of the 20th Century peoples in many lands are beginning to enjoy spiritual, economic and political freedoms for the first time in this century. We in these United States should join in this rejoicing.

NOTES

1. Charles Mackay in *Extraordinary Popular Delusions and the Madness of Crowds* included a chapter on John Law's attempt to remedy the financial problems of France caused by wars and other deficit spendings accompanying the reign of Louis IV. Law, a Scotsman of considerable financial abilities, as finance minister of France, found that paper currency would not remedy the country's problems, and sought to bring financial stability by selling shares in the Mississippi Company, promoting France's interests in the new world. Settlements were made as far west as present-day Arkansas. Many were abandoned when the "Mississippi Bubble" burst. The present edition of Mackay's book was published at the instigation of financial statesman Bernard Baruch by L.C. Page and Co. in 1932.

2. Andrew Dickson White, in *Fiat Money Inflation in France*, tells of further paper money inflation through the reign of Louis VI and the French Revolution, until it was ended by the establishment of Napoleon as emperor of France. White graduated from Yale in 1853, studied at the Sorbonne in France and at the University of Berlin. He was minister to Russia and ambassador to Germany. He helped to found Cornell University and was its first president. White headed the American delegation to the Hague Peace Conference.

Fiat Money Inflation in France was printed from an address that White gave in the House of Representatives in 1876, and later to the Union League Club in New York. It was made at the time that the United States was preparing to go back on the gold standard, after the paper currency inflation of the Civil War. White was familiar with the difficulties which France and other European countries had gone through with paper money inflation. The little book has been published several times over the years. The latest edition was published by the Cato Institute, San Francisco, in 1980. White tells of France at the time of the beheading of Louis VI and hundreds of others in the Reign of Terror of the French Revolution. Paper money increased in volume, with value going to near zero in spite of threats of the guillotine for those refusing to accept it. All of this helped bring about the establishment of Napoleon as emperor of France. Napoleon ended paper money inflation and established a pay-as-you-go system. The gold Napoleon coin is a legacy of his reign.

White's warnings sound timely and urgent after a century, as we watch the ever-growing government deficit spending and paper money inflation in the United States. In White's chapter on "*What It Brought*," he stated:

> Even worse than this was the breaking down of the morals of the country at large, resulting from the sudden building up of ostentatious wealth in a few large cities, and from the gambling, speculative spirit spreading from these to the small towns and rural districts.

3. Henry (Light-Horse Harry) Lee, cavalry commander in the Revolutionary War, aide to George Washington, governor of Virginia, father of Robert E. Lee, was further mistreated by a mob in Baltimore during the War of 1812 when he went to the defense of an anti-war newspaper editor. Perhaps going onto two centuries later, we are more tolerant of those who defend the *Bill of Rights*. It was Light-Horse Harry Lee who as a member of Congress composed the resolution on Washington's death which reads in part, "First in war, first peace, first in the hearts of his countrymen."

On May 7, 1992, just over 200 years after the *U.S. Constitution's Ten Original Amendments*, the *Bill of Rights*, were adopted, *Amendment XXVII*, also proposed by the First Congress as part of the *Bill of Rights*, somewhat quietly became Constitutional Law upon approval of legislatures of three fourths of the States. Attributed to feelings of outrage among the American people as to federal spendings and privileges of office, it prohibits members of both houses of Congress from enjoying the benefits of increased salaries they vote themselves until after the next following election of Representatives. (For a graphic picture of salary increases see Appendix M: What Congress Pays Itself.)

4. Dan Freedman, "Bush talks tough on S&Ls," *Hearst News Service*, in *Midland Reporter-Telegram*, June 23, 1990.

5. Steve Miletich, *Seattle Post-Intelligencer,* April 8, 1988.

6. Security Pacific Bank, *Second Quarter Report, 1990*, Los Angeles. One year later, Security Pacific was talking about merging into Bank of America. On April 24, 1992, the merger took place. Two months afterward, Robert Smith, former head of Security Pacific and who had negotiated the merger with BankAmerica, resigned from BankAmerica where he had been given the title of president. Kenneth Howe, staff writer of the *San Francisco Chronicle*, (June 25, 1992) quoted Smith, whose resignation was to take place later, as saying that he had "found my current and anticipated responsibilities at BankAmerica to be less than I want." According to the *Chronicle* he was to receive a "golden parachute worth $2.2 million." The report added that "1,700 employees" out of 91,000 employed at the consolidated banking institution received "pink slips by the end of May . . . the bank had said that 10,000 jobs to 12,000 jobs are likely to be eliminated in the consolidations of operations" of Security Pacific into Bank of America.

With numerous references and quotations from annual and special reports of U.S. and international banks, as well as other public and private reports, end notes for these chapters will generally show the name of the institution before the name of the city in which it is located. For consistency's sake, the name of a publisher will also be given before the name of the city in which the publisher is located, a departure from the tradition of giving the names of cities before the names of publishers.

CHAPTER 1

A Few Years Ago

In the hard times of the late 1920s, in the middle of North Central Texas' blackland farming country, the Citizens State Bank of Princeton, Texas was suffering what appeared to be its death throes. Every day brought a new crisis. The cashier who had been the active officer quit, and young assistant cashier J.W. Neal was left to cope with the daily struggle to find enough spare resources to pay for the cash letter – the checks on his bank's customers from its city correspondent – and wondering what catastrophe would come next. He didn't have long to wait. Less than a week later, almost as if drawn by the smell of blood, the state bank examiner showed up among the normal scattering of customers.

With a curt nod to the apprehensive Neal, the examiner opened the records. He noted the declining deposits of hard-hit farmers and the slow loan repayments. Neal acknowledged his comments. Next came caustic remarks about the bank's depleted cash position. There was nothing Neal could say. The bank was in desperate straits. In the days since he had taken over, it had been all Neal could do each day just to come up with spare resources to cover the checks on Princeton depositors. This was the last straw.

He reached into his pocket and pulled out the keys to the bank vault and the front door – and pushed them over the polished counter to the bank examiner.

"Do you want to close it up?" he asked.

The examiner looked at Neal for a long moment while the clock ticked in the otherwise silent building with its simple oak furniture and plain glass tellers' cages. Outside, the sun blazed on a dusty street, and women passed in gingham dresses and cotton stockings, unaware of the drama going on on the other side of the bank's gleaming window.

Then the examiner pushed the keys back to Neal and came forward to lay his arm around the young assistant cashier's shoulder.

"I'll tell you what, boy," he said, "I believe you can pull this bank through."

Years later, J.W. Neal said he had to pull it through. Bolstered by the strength of a wise state bank examiner's confidence in him and knowing that (in those days before the advent of the Federal Deposit Insurance Corporation) if he didn't pull the bank through, it would mean the ruin of all its depositors, he somehow revived the bank's financial health during the Depression years. Like so many others over the country, the Princeton bank, under the direction of its sole surviving officer and a succession of other competent and public-spirited bankers, became the center of all that was good for the community and its trade area. Neal stayed in banking for a time, eventually moving to a larger bank in McKinney, the county seat, where he was elected county judge.

Half a century later, control of the Citizens State Bank went out of state. It was one of the financial institutions controlled by Herman Beebe, described by Martin Mayer in *The Greatest-Ever Bank Robbery* as the "Louisiana insurance magnate ... who may have been involved with as many as a hundred failed S&Ls and who is one of the the few people in the story to have gone to jail for his swindles." In the 1990s the Princeton bank was struggling to rebuild and to survive. (Just before this book was to go to press the bank was saved from failure – recapitalized by local citizens under local leadership.)

In the 1970s and 1980s most failing banks suffered from incompetency of management rather than from outright dishonesty. Government-created wildly fluctuating prices and interest rates also played a big part. These accompanied ever-increasing deficit spendings by the U.S. Congress. Congress spent more and more and put the United States farther and farther into debt, with debt-created inflation pushing the value of the dollar down and down. Congress at the same time sought to make amends for problems in banks and S&Ls, which problems to a great extent had been created by Congress, by passing more and more laws regarding financial institutions. Multitudes of new regulations resulted. These though, have not assured competent, honest bankers and S&L executives.

In the 1980s many multi-billion-dollar banking institutions and S&Ls went under. (And the remedy of the banking regulators seemed to be to create even larger multi-billion-dollar institutions, that could get into even bigger trouble.) Smaller financial institutions also failed. Government deficit spendings played a big part in this debacle. The Federal Savings & Loan Insurance Corp. (FSLIC) went completely broke and was replaced by a new Savings Institution Insurance Fund (SAIF) under the Federal Deposit Insurance Corp. (FDIC). A new giant federal corporation was created by Congress, the Resolution Trust Corp. (RTC). It was supposed to resolve the problems of the failed S&Ls – with estimated cost to the taxpayers into the hundreds of billions of dollars. The FDIC's old Bank Insurance Fund (BIF) was also hard hit.[3]

On July 20, 1992, the *1991 Annual Report of the FDIC* was

presented to the Congress and to the public. The July date was the earliest that an FDIC annual report had been made in years (some of the annual reports having been nearly 12 months late). The *1991 Report* was also the first to include the new SAIF, which showed a net fund balance of $87 million. The *1991 Report* also admitted that the BIF had a *minus* $7 billion balance. The *1991 Report* for the first time also reported on the FSLIC Resolution Fund, with a *minus* $15 billion balance. The report also told of supposed temporary borrowing powers for the FDIC, with borrowings of $10.6 billion as of December 31, 1991, from the Federal Financing Bank (FFB). (See Chapter 7 for more on the FFB.) The report was over the signature of new FDIC Chairman William Taylor, who had been in office only since October 16, 1991. Taylor, a dedicated public servant, died one month after the date of the report, on August 20, 1992, just ten months after taking office. Most of his career had been in financial institutions supervision with the Federal Reserve System. He was not known to belong to either major political party. In his brief time with the FDIC Taylor appeared to put aside some of the ethereal notions of prior staff members for reshaping the U.S. banking system (as that reported in the previous paragraph). In his short period of leadership of the FDIC William Taylor was willing to face the facts – even those that are most distasteful.

Where are the J.W. Neals and William Taylors, to lead us out of the wilderness of the 1990s? There must be others. They need to be found.[2]

NOTES

1. J.C. Cantrell, Dallas, telephone conversation May 1990. Cantrell, who later headed the Princeton bank, was Collin County judge just before J.W. Neal took that office.

2. Martin Mayer, *The Greatest-Ever Bank Robbery: The Collapse of the Savings and Loan Industry*, Charles Scribner's Sons, New York, 1990. After additional years of out-of-territory control, in December 1992 former Princeton banker Ronald Umphress returned to lead a group of local citizens in recapitalizing Citizens State Bank. The FDIC guaranteed certain loans made by previous management.

3. Letter from Deputy Director Arthur J. Murton, FDIC, Washington, August 7, 1992. In the letter he confirms that, as of the end of 1991, $16.3 billion had been reserved for future bank failures, leaving a deficit of approximately $7 billion in the BIF. Also see *1991 Annual Report of the FDIC*. Also, letter from Edward J. Kane, August 5, 1992. Kane, formerly Everett D. Reese Professor of Banking and Monetary Economics at Ohio State University moved to Boston College in August 1992 as James F. Cleary Professor of Finance. Kane from time to time gives his opion before congressional banking committees.

In the letter he writes: "I believe the present discounted value of losses in the FSLIC mess are well over $200 billion, approaching $250 billion." Kane has suggested to Congress that present reforms in FDIC insurance premiums are insufficient. Among his recommendations is a one-time special "tax" against insured banks to bring the BIF back into reasonable financial condition.

Even after collapse of Boston-based, super-regional Bank of New England Corp. the initials BNE could still be seen high above Springfield, Massachusetts. Third National Bank, which BNE had absorbed, had been in the smaller building in the foreground overshadowed by Monarch Place's BNE. Third National had served Springfield and western Massachusetts for more than a century.

What went wrong?

CHAPTER 2

What Went Wrong?

After the Depression of the early 1930s, the United States enjoyed a period of banking stability unmatched almost anywhere in the world. For more than 30 years, from 1943 to 1974, never a year had passed with even 10 bank closings. The few banks that did fail were small for the most part, and with deposits being protected by insurance, they hardly caused a ripple in the financial community.

Then came the 1980s. In 1985, 1986 and 1987, we saw more than 100 bank closings per year. In 1988 and 1989, the figure rose to more than 200. Even more disturbing than the number of bank failures is the size of failed banks. Recent failures have included multi-billion-dollar institutions, not to mention savings and loan company failures. Though bank closings dropped to less than 200 banks per year in 1990 and 1991, in the latter year deposit dollars of failed banks hit a record $54 billion – more than twice the deposit totals of any previous year.

What went wrong in American banking?

Who is to blame?

Bankers?

Regulators?

Politicians?

News media?

The American people?

Or a combination of all of the above?

Bankers

Stuart M. Andrews, a New York businessman who grew up in Brooklyn and now lives on Long Island, talked about what has happened to American banking. Andrews' first job was a runner with a major New York bank, the Guaranty Trust Co., now Morgan Guaranty. His wife's father was executive vice president of another metropolitan Manhattan bank. He was asked – since most banking failures had been outside the major metropolitan areas – if the banks in the large financial centers are somehow exempt from difficulties. Andrews' reply was "No." Discussing integrity, reliability and trust, for which banking used to be known, he continued:

> Banking has changed. The customer used to look up to his banker. The banker used to look up to his customer. There was mutual respect one for the other. But all this has changed.[1]

Andrews' prophetic statement was before the collapse of the

Bank of New England Corp. and other subsequent billion dollar banking failures.

Regulators

The former chief executive of what was a major Southwestern bank, comments that bankers and regulators are always reacting to the past. In a conversation in his office overlooking downtown Dallas, this able ex-banker said that bank regulatory agencies are only now cracking down on banking as they should have done five to ten years ago. He suggests that now, however, is the time regulatory agencies should instead be loosening up. Examiners and bankers who remain are, at this late date, being ultra-conservative. But loan and collateral values today are more realistic, well below what they were a few years ago. Now, at the very time business should be encouraged, bankers and regulators are reacting to the shakier business climate of five to ten years ago. In addition, he says, Dallas bank failures have left a serious vacuum in banking leadership at a critical time in the city's history.

Politicians

Politicians want to accommodate the American public. They have been on a 30-year spending binge. The last balanced federal budget was more than 30 years ago, in 1960 (though 1969 gave the semblance of being slightly "in the black" – the difference being social security trust funds).

Before 1965 the Federal Reserve System through its 12 district banks backed bank reserves – deposits from member banks – with 25 percent gold. The same was true for Federal Reserve Notes. For every $4 in circulating Federal Reserve notes, $1 was held in gold certificates. As other nations drew against our gold supply, Congress in 1965 abolished the gold requirement for commercial banks reserves with the Fed, then in 1968 did the same for Federal Reserve Notes. Finally in 1971, as the the U.S. gold supply shrank further, U.S. Treasury Secretary John Connally, under the presidency of Richard Nixon, declared that the United States would no longer pay out one ounce of gold to other nations in exchange for 35 U.S. dollars – thus reneging the 1944 Bretton Woods international monetary agreement.

The dollar has since fluctuated against major currencies of the world – and in effect been devaluated again and again under subsequent U.S. administrations.

New problems have arisen regularly, and each year we have tried to fix them by passing additional banking reform acts. Most of the reforms are meant to correct ills brought on by federal deficit spending. Fluctuating interest rates, fluctuating oil and agricultural commodity prices, escalating and then falling real estate values, and the ever-declining value of the dollar are all chickens come home to roost at the doorstep of wild federal spending.

News Media

The failure of the Boston-based Bank of New England Corp. – a multi-state banking concern which had attempted to cover New England – appeared to mean but little to many in the media. The fact that it went "bust" in 1991 was blamed on local economic conditions or real estate, not on management or on government. Little was said about its having tried to grow too fast and too big or of its sorry loans in areas outside of New England. Instead, members of the media explained that we need "50-state" banking companies.

The people of Midland, Texas are known for their optimism and their heavy investiture in the energy business. They ride the tumultuous tides of oil and gas prices year in and year out, happy and expansive in times of high prices, and withdrawn and pessimistic when the energy bubble bursts. Several years ago they changed the name of the chief downtown trafficway where the banks were then located from Iowa Avenue to Wall Street.

Perhaps it was to be expected that when the First National Bank of Midland, the largest independent bank in the state, fell victim to declining oil price expectations (which followed the untimely death of its able chief executive), the bank was pummeled by the press.

A proper role of the media is to present the truth. As more financial institutions have sought regional and national recognition, they have also obtained regional and national publicity, not always favorable. At the same time, financial news coverage has moved beyond New York, Chicago, San Francisco and other major cities to much smaller metropolitan areas.

The Wall Street Journal, with greatly increased circulation, has expanded its news coverage. Now towns such as Midland, Texas can receive negative publicity right up there with the big cities, both locally and nationally. In the case of the First National Bank of Midland, the bad news was unremitting and continuous, with a resulting decline in depositor confidence. No bank can withstand a run on its deposits. No bank keeps all its assets in cash. Otherwise, it could neither make loans nor purchase municipal bonds and U.S. government obligations.

The American People

The American people are somewhat innocent in all this, but they do elect representatives to the councils of local government. They send representatives to state capitols. They send congressmen and senators along with the president and vice president to Washington. If politicians are big spenders, the American public, by sending them back for second terms, is, in effect, applauding the spending.

If some bankers have been neither completely capable nor overly honest, if they instead have sought instant prestige, power and wealth, they may in part reflect the thinking of America of recent years.

Finally, the idea of saving — noted in Japan and Germany — has become a foreign concept to too many Americans.

What went wrong? Who is to blame? We shall examine these questions further.

NOTES

1. Stuart M. Andrews, Hampton Bays, New York. Telephone conversation March, 1990. Prophetically, this was before the collapse of the Bank of New England Corp.

CHAPTER 3

Federal Reserve System, More Congressional Regulations, Federal Deposit Insurance Inhibits Risk or Encourages Risk? Blame the Economy!

Federal Reserve System

In every major country of today's world there is a central banking system. In the United Kingdom it is the Bank of England. In Japan it is the Bank of Japan. In the U.S. it is the Federal Reserve System (or the "Fed"). There are twelve Federal Reserve Banks, with a centralized Board of Governors of the Federal Reserve System, created in 1913 as a compromise between those who would have but one central bank, and those who preferred a number of regional banks.

From time to time, individuals and movements particularly virulent in opposition to the Federal Reserve System, including representatives from both politically economic "left" and "right," have urged the system's abolition. Ernest T. Baughman, scholarly past president of the Federal Reserve Bank of Dallas, has said that there would still have to be some system, or combination of governmental departments to take its place.[1]

The Federal Reserve System seeks to facilitate an even economic growth of the country, through its money supply, credit and other banking functions. Numerous duties and responsibilities have been given the Federal Reserve by law. These include:

1. Setting the Reserve Requirement for commercial banks (and since 1980 for other financial institutions). This sets the theoretical loan and deposit expansion ratios for banks, under our system of fractional reserve banking. Somewhat mysterious – until it is considered – is the fact that commercial banks help to create our money supply – by making loans, which show up as deposits in customers' accounts. Inversely, when loans are repaid, the money supply tends to contract.
2. Setting the Discount Rate (formerly known as Rediscount Rate) for Advances (loans) by commercial banks (and since 1980 other financial institutions). Banks used to discount their

customers' notes, and in turn, rediscount these with the Federal Reserve Bank. Now such borrowing may be by collateral of customer notes, or by other collateral, such as U.S. securities. Borrowing from the Fed is rather unusual. Banks aren't encouraged to be regular borrowers. (Congress in 1991 seemed to suggest that borrowing should be on even stiffer terms for those banks most in need.)

3. Open Market Operations. The Federal Open Market Committee, is composed of the seven members of the Board of Governors of the Federal Reserve System plus five of the presidents from the Federal Reserve banks. The FOMC sets the goals for purchase and sale of government securities in the open market. Such purchases and sales are for the account of all 12 Federal Reserve Banks. By purchase and sale of government obligations, chiefly U.S. securities, monetary growth and interest rates are influenced, especially in the short term.
4. Issuance of Federal Reserve Notes – the primary currency of the United States of today.
5. Regulation of stock market credit (margin requirements). How much, if any, must be paid down, versus what can be borrowed for purchase of securities in the stock markets.
6. Fiscal Agent for United States. The Federal Reserve Banks are fiscal agents for the United States Treasury. Taxes are collected, bonds are sold, funds are deposited in segregated accounts for the U.S. government. The Federal Reserve banks handle subscriptions and redemptions of government securities.
7. Regulation and examination of state member banks. State member banks are also examined by the states that charter them. Other state banks are examined by the Federal Deposit Insurance Corp. National banks are chartered and examined by the Comptroller of the Currency.
8. Regulation and examination of bank holding companies. The Federal Reserve was given the responsibility for approving and regulating bank holding companies under the Bank Holding Company Act of 1956, subsequently amended several times. Many bank holding companies involve but one bank – one-bank holding companies that may be very small or very large institutions. There are benefits as well as some disadvantages for operating under a one-bank holding company. Advantages for a small bank would include making change of ownership and financing, even within a family, easier to accomplish. Leaders of a particular billion-dollar banking company in recent years gave

unofficial thanks to the Federal Reserve for turning down an application of several years ago in which they would have merged their company into another banking corporation through a combined multi-bank holding company. The other – and at the time larger – holding company got into financial difficulties and more than once lost most of its shareholders' investment, while the smaller holding company that was turned down in the merger by the Fed managed to come through relatively unscathed.

9. Check clearings and collections. By far the largest clearings and collections of bank checks, and of S&L and credit union drafts, are via the Federal Reserve System. Other responsibilities of the Fed are detailed in the pages to follow and in Appendix A.

The Federal Reserve System earns interest on federal obligations and federal agency obligations that it holds – but it also pays its surplus earnings to the U.S. Treasury as "interest on Federal Reserve Notes." In 1991 the Fed paid the U.S. Treasury $1.5 billion more than it received.

Monetary Policy vs. Fiscal Policy

In the language of the political economist, *Monetary Policy* is that policy of the central bank, the Federal Reserve System in the United States, that affects the economic life of the nation. *Fiscal Policy*, according to similar theory, is the economic effect of government taxation, borrowing, and spending.

But as we see on the pages to follow, nothing that the Federal Reserve can or will do can offset long-term effects of Congress and the Administration in taxing and spending. See Edward Kane's comments later in this chapter on reducing volatility of interest rates – largely a product of federal deficit spendings – against which Federal Reserve controls can mean but little, and that short-term.

Woodrow Wilson – 1913 – The First 50 Years

President Woodrow Wilson signed into being the Federal Reserve System on December 23, 1913 when a far-sighted Congress passed the Owen-Glass Currency Reform Bill for the purpose of providing a more elastic currency to forestall financial panics such as those of 1873, 1893, and 1907. The Federal Reserve was to consist of twelve district banks that would serve as the central banking system for the United States. Never again would there be the isolation of small banks in small towns with not enough currency to meet the seasonal or sudden demands of depositors – not with a Federal Reserve district bank nearby to supply funds.

The twelve Federal Reserve banks are not owned by the government. Instead, each member bank must subscribe to its stock in the district bank. The seven members of the Board of Governors are appointed by the President of the United States and confirmed by the Senate. Three of the nine directors of each Federal Reserve Bank are appointed by the Board of Governors. One of these three is designated Chairman and Federal Reserve Agent.

During its first 50 years, the Fed served the war bond drives of two world wars and helped supply the credit needs of war industries. It was central to the attempt to ease the post-world war economic recession of the early 1920s as well as the agricultural difficulties that followed. Certain new duties were given by Congress during the Great Depression of the 1930s.

The Depression of the 1930s, the Second World War, the Korean War and the Vietnam conflict created financial strains that the Fed was supposed to alleviate – according to acts of Congress and subsequent implementing regulations.

Responsibilities given the Federal Reserve during its first half century included reserve requirements for commercial banks, the discount rate for banks, open market purchases and sales of U.S. securities, as well as wartime industrial loans.

(The 1933 Glass-Steagall Act's divorcement of commercial banking and investment banking, the use of U.S. securities as collateral for Federal Reserve Notes [the currency we now use], and the 1934 Securities Exchange Act and margin requirements, are also detailed in Appendix A.)

Fiftieth Anniversary of the Fed

In 1964, the 50th anniversary of the Fed, the loose-leaf binder containing the Federal Reserve regulations weighed four pounds, one and one-half ounces. The golden anniversary of the Fed was celebrated with some fanfare that year. The U.S. dollar was still held in high regard internationally then. The federal budget had shown a surplus as late as 1960. We still had gold-backed currency, as well as actual silver dollars, half dollars, quarters and dimes. Young bank officers and depositors could still remember as children being given dimes that they could polish endlessly in pockets filled with marbles and rocks, which would only enhance their gloss. During the savings-stamp drives of World War II, schools all over the country had held regularly scheduled stamp-purchasing days, and students proudly bought one stamp with a silver dime, five with a half dollar, and (wonder of wonders) ten stamps for a beautiful silver dollar, which would often be passed around the classroom for each child to hold and admire before being exchanged for the stamps that would then be carefully pasted in the purchaser's war-bond book. You could buy a bond for $18.75, and if you kept it ten years, you could cash it in for $25.

Seventy-Fifth Anniversary of the Fed

The 1989 diamond anniversary of the Fed received but passing attention. In the interim 25 years, defense and peacetime spending had gone higher and higher, even though the Vietnam war had ended. In addition, Congress had been busy passing laws regarding banking. Never during those years was the federal budget in balance. Our currency's tie to gold was ended; also abrogated was the fixed exchange rate between the dollar and other currencies, which had been law under the Bretton Woods Agreement. Many recent laws have to do with customer protection, such as what banks should tell, or ask, the customer, and often what should not be asked of the customer.

The Monetary Control Act of 1980, which required the Federal Reserve banks to offer their services to savings and loans and credit unions as well as to banks, and consumer protection laws, added to the already bloated package of regulations. By 1989 Federal Reserve Regulations had grown to two loose-leaf binders and weighed 12 pounds, four and one-half ounces – three times the previous weight.

How Powerful Is the Federal Reserve?

Some bankers, many economists, many politicians, and many in the media – as well as a lesser number in the Fed – believe that the Federal Reserve has tremendous powers to cause ease or restraint in the economy. And the Federal Reserve System does have considerable powers for short-term changes or emphases in the economy. Open market operations, discount rate, margin requirements, etc., have temporary effects on economic activities. Some politicians want to say, perhaps even believe, that the Federal Reserve is solely responsible for hard times, high interest rates, and whatever is distasteful to the public.

Impossible for Federal Reserve to Stabilize the Economy Until Government Controls Spending

The fact is that nothing that the Fed can do can overcome the fiscal policy effects of government spendings, especially deficit spendings, and the devaluating effects of inflationary creation of our money supply.

In his 1985 study, *The Gathering Crisis in Federal Deposit*

Insurance, Edward Kane predicted the many difficulties which have come to pass in deposit insurance. He also suggested varying premiums for risks of banks. His concluding two sentences are ever more true:

> If Congress could bring government spending under long-run control, monetary policy would not have to push interest rates over so wide a cycle. Reducing the volatility of interest rates would relieve the car's drivers of the need to take it over quite so dangerous a set of roads.[2]

Consumer Protection?

Admittedly, foolish and short-sighted policies of some banks and S&Ls, such as "redlining" certain neighborhoods against loans while at the same time readily accepting their residents' deposits, were invitations for Congress to act. However, many bills were passed without much thought given to the soundness of banks nor to the national economy.

An Abundance of Banking Regulations

Regulations of the Comptroller of the Currency (whose office charters and examines national banks), regulations of the FDIC, regulations of other federal agencies dealing with banking and regulations of the 50 state banking departments have proliferated in recent years. Every bank is now expected to have a "compliance officer" whose job is to see that his or her particular bank understands and complies with the myriad regulations now intended to govern banks. Much of this concerns consumer protection and reporting, rather than bank soundness. In larger banks, several persons will be charged with such compliance work.

Acts of Congress Affecting Banks and Other Financial Institutions

Acts of Congress on regulating banks and S&Ls have beget even more acts of Congress on banks and S&Ls. Congress has sought to remedy mistakes and problems brought on by their laws by passing additional laws. These laws were supposed to bring safety and soundness to banks and S&Ls. Other bank and S&L related laws were also passed — supposedly for protection of consumers. Many of the consumer protection bank and S&L acts have been like the safe and sound banking acts — little real result except for ever growing confusion. Congress has avoided the real challenge toward safe and sound banking and a safe and sound economy — that which a balanced budget would bring. Instead, an ever greater burden of deficit financed inflation has been the chief heritage of too many acts of Congress of recent decades — with additional spendings in the billions of dollars far in excess of increased governmental income.

Since the mid-1960s, acts of Congress affecting banks and other financial institutions have included:

1964	Housing Act of 1964
1966	Financial Institutions Supervisory Act
1966	Interest Rate Adjustment Act
1968	Housing Act of 1968
1968	Housing and Urban Development Act
1968	Fair Credit Reporting Act
1970	Bank Secrecy Act
1970	Tying Arrangements, amendment to Bank Holding Company Act
1970	Emergency Home Finance Act
1974	Equal Credit Opportunity Act
1974	Real Estate Settlement Procedures Act
1975	Home Mortgage Disclosure Act
1977	Community Reinvestment Act
1978	Financial Institutions Regulatory and Interest Rate Control Act
1978	Housing and Community Development Act
1978	International Banking Act, amendment to Federal Reserve Act
1980	Depository Institutions Deregulation and Monetary Control Act
1982	Garn-St Germain Financial Institutions Act
1983	International Lending Supervisory Act (accompanied IMF expansion act)
1985	Extension of Garn-St Germain Act
1987	Competitive Equality Banking Act
1988	Fair Credit and Charge Card Disclosure Act
1988	Home Equity Loan Consumer Protection Act
1988	International Lending Supervisory Act – strengthening amendment
1989	Financial Institutions Reform, Recovery, and Enforcement Act
1990	Market Reform Act of 1990
1990	Cranston-Gonzales National Affordable Housing Act
1990	Crime Control Act of 1990 (Establishes a National Commission on Financial Institutions, to study problems with S&Ls and to prevent such problems with commercial banks.)
1991	Resolution Trust Corporation Refinancing, Restructuring

and Improvement Act of 1991

1991 Federal Deposit Insurance Corporation Improvement Act of 1991

Regulations Attempting to Deregulate

It should be admitted that many of the Acts of Congress and subsequent regulations have been an attempt to deregulate banks and S&Ls. The infamous quarter-point differential between what banks and thrifts could pay on consumer deposits was eliminated under the Depository Institutions Deregulation and Monetary Control Act – having become near meaningless in the early 1980s when interest rates had gone sky high – even above the Civil War's interest rates! (The 1980 Depository Institutions Deregulation and Monetary Control Act declared that state usury laws were to be overruled by newer and higher federally allowed interest rates.)

S&Ls and Commercial Lending

Carrying deregulation even further, Garn-St Germain in 1982 permitted S&Ls to get into fields hitherto prohibited, especially into commercial lending, with disastrous results.

Interstate Banking and Branching by Federal Takeover

Garn-St Germain also allowed federal regulators to take over failing S&Ls and banks for merger or sale to institutions in other states if the failing institutions had $500 million or more in assets.

Real Estate Loans by National Banks

Real estate lending in nationally-chartered banks was completely deregulated by Garn-St Germain. Early 19th century U.S. banking had relied too heavily on real estate, not only as collateral, but even for capitalization of the "wildcat banks." When Abraham Lincoln's Civil War Congress of 1863 passed the National Currency Act setting up the Bureau of the Comptroller of the Currency to allow for national chartering of banks and for issuance of the new National Currency, the new national banks were not allowed to make real estate loans because of previous unhappy experiences in banking. Not until 50 years later, under Woodrow Wilson, did Congress through Section 24 of the Federal Reserve Act of 1913 allow national banks to make real estate loans, and then only on a very restrictive basis. (The Federal Reserve Act also allowed a national bank to have trust powers where the need for a trust department could be shown.)

More than 25 amendments to federal law were made in the years between 1913 and 1974 – to what national banks could do in the way of real estate lending.[3] By 1974, up to 75 percent could be lent on improved real estate ready for development. Even more could be lent on land with buildings, if properly amortized.

Garn-St Germain – Deregulate!

Garn-St Germain Financial Institutions Act of 1982 (named for Republican Senator Jake Garn and Democrat Congressman Fernand St Germain, then chairmen of the Senate and House Banking Committees), which told the S&Ls that they could get into commercial lending, also told national banks that they could make real estate loans with no restrictions other than what the Comptroller of the Currency might require in the way of rules or regulations. The lengthy paragraphs of Section 24 of the Federal Reserve Act on what could and could not be done in real estate lending were abolished. One short paragraph was substituted, which read:

> Any national banking association may make, arrange, purchase or sell loans or extensions of credit, secured by liens on interests in real estate, subject to such terms, conditions, and limitations as may be prescribed by the Comptroller of the Currency, by order, rule, or regulation.[4]

In addition, the provision that allowed construction loans for residential or farm buildings to be discounted with the Federal Reserve Banks was continued, though never widely utilized.

The Comptroller of the Currency's manual for real estate lending under Garn-St Germain emphasized that the bank should have a firm lending policy for real estate as for other types of lending. No particular limits were prescribed. (The Comptroller's Office had become quite enthusiastic over the idea that a written policy in each national bank was desirable – a type of substitute for regulation and examination.)

Return to "The Old-Time Religion" in Banking

In 1991, then chairman William Seidman of the Federal Deposit Insurance Corporation upset many, including some in the building business, when he advocated a return to the discipline of the "old-time religion" in banking. Seidman seemed to suggest that failures in small and major banking companies and accompanying billions of dollars in losses to the FDIC Bank Insurance Fund would have been avoided had banks still been regulated in their real estate lending. The financial institutions' "Bible," *Pratt's Letter*, quoted Chairman Seidman:

> Many of the loans that have cost the FDIC the most money would have been illegal prior to 1974. Section 24 of the Federal Reserve Act . . . prohibited national banks from making loans where the building contributed less than 25 percent equity and limited overall concentration in real estate lending

> by national banks. These mandatory real estate lending rules were repealed. The FDIC has been paying the consequences ever since.

Seidman added:

> It is time for insured institutions to return to old-fashioned standards of safe-and-sound banking; the restrictions lifted by Congress . . . should be reinstated.[5]

Seidman referred to the margin of 25 percent between loan and value, which would have given a lot of protection to lender banks when deflation knocked down inflated land values.

The complaint of the chief economist for the National Association of Home Builders, who proclaimed Seidman's proposal a "shock," echoed comments from builders in 1989 when the Financial Institutions Reform, Recovery, and Enforcement Act cut back the wide-open 100 percent-of-capital lending authority of S&Ls to a more modest 15 percent of capital for any one borrower, with certain generous exceptions for construction lending.

Comptroller C.T. Conover on Deregulation

In 1984 then Comptroller of the Currency C. T. Conover said, "In fact deregulation of the banking industry is a misnomer. It implies an end of the regulation, examination, and supervision; no one wants or expects that to happen . . . "[6]

As indicated, Comptroller of the Currency goes back to the original National Currency Act of 1863. The Civil War act was intended to help finance the Union war effort, taxes not being popular at the time. This act authorized the chartering of national banks, and the issuing of National Currency by those banks. In addition, there was the Civil War issue of United States Currency, the greenbacks which quickly lost value. Although National Currency has disappeared, we still have the Comptroller of the Currency whose job is strictly to approve, supervise and examine nationally chartered banks.

The era of the 1970s and early 1980s saw a regulatory loosening in chartering of national and state banks. Until this time, new national and state banks seldom had been chartered. In the 1970s, however, alert members of the financial community sensed a change in the wind. New charters were bestowed generously to both independent and holding company applicants. Law firms specialized in bank charter applications. With a properly filled-in application, with properly projected economic growth, prepared by a recognized economist, the charter would almost certainly be approved. Savings and loan associations could also expect the same favorable treatment – if they did the paperwork right.

Federal Deposit Insurance Corporation

The Federal Deposit Insurance Corp., a product of the bank failures of the late 1920s and early 1930s, came into being through a joint effort of leading Democrats and Republicans. Included were Vice President John Nance Garner (who had previously served as Speaker of the House during the administration of Herbert Hoover), businessman-banker Reconstruction Finance Corp. Chairman Jesse H. Jones, senators Arthur H. Vandenberg and Carter Glass, and congressman Henry B. Steagall.

Garner was joined by fellow Texan Jones in supporting the concept of insured bank deposits. Jones had been one of the original board members of the RFC when the corporation was created during Hoover's administration. Like Garner, he had seen the failure of deposit insurance in Texas and seven other states. In Texas such insurance applied only to state-chartered banks and was not based on prepaid premiums, but by assessments on surviving banks at the time of the failure of a bank, or by a guaranty bond.

Glass of Virginia, whose name was on the original Federal Reserve Act, chaired the Senate banking committee. Steagall of Alabama was chairman of the House Banking Committee. Vandenberg, Republican senator from Michigan, had seen the crash of Detroit's two great banking institutions, the Union Guardian and First Wayne groups, aggravated by depression-led unemployment in the motor city. He had also seen the antagonism between Michigan's other U.S. senator, James Couzens, and his former partner Henry Ford.

According to Professor Emeritus Theodore Kennedy of Michigan State University, Vandenberg had also been hit personally by assessment on bank stock that he owned.[7] Bascom N. Timmons, in his book, *Jesse H. Jones, the Man and the Statesman*, says that Garner asked Vandenberg if he still had a copy of the proposed bank deposit bill, and Vandenberg replied that it had never been out of his pocket. Garner then called a recess for the Senate, which was sitting in court on the impeachment of Federal Judge Harold Lauderback, and asked for consideration of the banking bill. Garner had forewarned Vandenberg that he would be able to recognize him easily, since there were not so many Republicans sitting in the Senate in 1933.

The bill was passed over the threatened veto of President Roosevelt, who had predicted that the weak banks could become a burden on the strong.[8] Initially set at $2,500 per depositor, FDIC coverage went up to $5,000 in 1934, and was increased from time to time over the years until it reached $100,000 during hyperinflation and a prime rate above 21 percent in 1980.

Only in recent years have economists begun to pose an interesting question. Does FDIC insurance inhibit risk-taking for banks, or does it encourage risk-taking?

Federal Deposit Insurance Inhibits Risk-Taking?

In the 1977 second edition of the popular college textbook *Principles of Money, Banking & Financial Markets*, authors Lawrence S. Ritter and William L. Silber said:

> But measures that insulate all banks from the slightest chance of failure are also measures that *inhibit risk-taking*, discourage financial innovations, circumscribe management decision-making, and stifle the benefits to the general public that can flow from competitive rivalry. These are high costs to pay, particularly when federal deposit insurance protection has eliminated the widespread distress that bank failures formerly caused.[9]

Federal Deposit Insurance Encourages Risk-Taking?

Only seven years later, in the *1984 Annual Report of the Federal Deposit Insurance Corporation*, Chairman William M. Isaac stated:

> Conceived during the banking collapse of the 1930s, the federal deposit insurance system was intended to restore confidence and stability by protecting small depositors, and this it has accomplished. However, the operation of the deposit insurance system has *encouraged excessive risk-taking* and has subsidized the growth of poorly managed banks at the expanse of sound institutions.[10]

Which of the above is correct? Does federal deposit insurance of accounts inhibit, or encourage, risk-taking? Sadly, it would appear that the 1984 report is more realistic. Perhaps each can be explained as a product of its time. In 1977, only six U.S. banks failed, although 17 had closed the year before. In 1984, 77 banks closed. FDIC disbursements in 1977 had been $205 million. In 1984, they were $2.9 billion. During 1984 was also the near-collapse and bailout of the $41 billion Continental Illinois National Bank & Trust Company of Chicago. A $5 billion loan from the Federal Reserve Bank of Chicago partially offset the deposit run on the bank. Additional interim financing of $2 billion came from the FDIC. Several large banks participated for half a billion.

As further explained by former FDIC Director Irvine Sprague in his book, *Bailout*, the FDIC took $4.5 billion in bad loans from the big Chicago bank, giving back $3.5 billion in cancellation of debt to the Chicago Fed.[11] The FDIC also put another billion dollars into new capital stock and installed new management, headed by John Swearingen, former head of Standard Oil of Indiana. (The first bailout of Continental Illinois National Bank & Trust Co.. 50 years earlier by the Reconstruction Finance Corp., had been at one-hundredth the cost of the later bailout.)

Regulation – Deregulation – Reregulation

In the 1987 official *Fifth Edition Guide to the Federal Home Loan Bank System*, it was stated:

> Despite deregulation, the federal laws and regulations governing savings and loan associations and savings banks fill a book more than three inches thick. The rules tell an institution everything from how it may advertise to how much it may lend its top officers. The rules are numerous and complex and different ones apply to different classes of institutions.[12]

The detailed instructions to savings and loan management did not tell how to determine if a commercial loan was good – when S&Ls were allowed to go into new fields under the 1982 Garn-St Germain Act. Prudent commercial lending, as commercial bankers would also have to testify, and not always successfully, comes from skilled credit analysis and years of experience. Potential hundreds of billions of dollars of losses give moot evidence that S&Ls ran into disaster in their commercial lending. The 1989 Financial Institutions Reform, Recovery, and Enforcement Act was an attempt to re-regulate and salvage what was left.

Robert Morris' Predictions

Philadelphia merchant-financier-patriot Robert Morris served as Superintendent of Finance during the American Revolution. Pledging his personal fortune, he begged the American colonies and European nations to support the war against England – and used every means to get the Continental Congress to give financial backing to George Washington's army. It was during that period of uncertainty, before there was a U.S. Constitution, that interest rates went sky high, as the Continental currency became worthless – giving expression to the term, "not worth a Continental." Morris, who signed both the Declaration of Independence and the Constitution of the United States, predicted that in the years to come it would be too many laws, rather than too few, that we should fear.

How the Swiss View It

Switzerland is noted for its strong banks. The European central banks' bank, the Bank for International Settlements, is located at Basle. T.R. Fehrenbach, author of *The Swiss Banks*, says that the Swiss "take a dim view of high fliers in banking."[13] When a bank gives indication that it may go broke in Switzerland – which would be a rarity – the other banks take it over.

The president of the American-owned subsidiary United California Bank of Switzerland spent some time in a Swiss jail after his bank got into trouble for commodity speculations of depositors' funds. Fehrenbach says that Swiss banking authorities emphasize integrity in banking, rather than a multitude of legislative regulations proclaimed for consumer protection. The Swiss realize that the greatest protection to the consumer, to all bank customers, and to Switzerland's reputation to the world is that of integrity in banking.

In the *1989 Annual Report of Swiss Bank Corporation*, several paragraphs are given to the failure of one of West Germany's largest retail groups, Co Op AG, Frankfurt A.M., following "appearance of press reports representing damaging information on the company. Bankruptcy was averted by quick action taken by a pool of six banks, including Swiss Bank Corporation, to financially stabilize and restructure the company. The former Co Op executives responsible for misleading the creditor banks and auditors have been arrested and investigations are under way concerning fraud, embezzlement and falsification of accounts."

Swiss Bank Corporation reported its loss, and also told of reorganization of a subsidiary bank to prevent losses to other financial companies.

Such is the Swiss way in banking. The report further stated:

> "As far as Swiss Bank Corporation is concerned, the Co Op incident is now resolved."[14]

Oh, that U.S. banks could so easily resolve their problems.

Advice from Professor Kennedy

Professor Theodore R. Kennedy in his letter discussing Senator Arthur Vandenberg's support of the FDIC adds:

> The average American, I believe, understands less about the real operation of a bank than the functioning of the pituitary gland. If you can explain this subject in language the man on the street can grasp, you will confer a genuine benefit on our society.[15]

Blame the Economy!

With failures of gigantic banking companies from such diverse geographic areas as the Northeast and the Southwest, it is amazing that both regulators and bankers should use the same excuse: They blame the economy. Andy Zipser, who has served as staff reporter for both *The Wall Street Journal* and *Barron's*, observes this in a letter to this writer:

My experience in the banking community, however, has been that most bankers fault neither the crooks nor their own ministrations; rather, most tend to blame an impersonal and distant "economy" – one in which they presumably played no part. One consequence: many bankers talk not of a banking disaster, but of a real estate disaster.

This seems to be a textbook example of passing the buck – ironic activity for bankers.[16]

NOTES

1. Ernest T. Baughman, past president, Federal Reserve Bank of Dallas, now living in Oak Park, Illinois. Letters to author, 1989, 1991.

2. Edward J. Kane, *The Gathering Crisis in Federal Deposit Insurance*, MIT Press, Cambridge, 1985.

3. Considering Garn-St Germain and other Congressional "reform" acts for financial institutions, which have brought such disastrous results on the American people, perhaps the best banking act is one that is never enacted.

Such a banking law was the proposed Banking Act of 1956 – or 1957. The date is immaterial, since the bill never passed. The Omnibus Banking Act was one of those multiple provision bills with something for everybody. It had something for the big banks, and something for the little banks. This was an era when financial institutions were generally strong. Commercial banks were serving businesses and individuals in their areas. S&ls were still savings associations, accepting savings and making residential mortgage loans. The few banks which got into difficulties had managements which were patently incompetent, crooked, or both. It was a time of federal surpluses, rather than deficits.

Banking laws in that day were tough. An unamortized real estate loan could be made for 50 percent of the property's value with the further provision that the loan could only be for improved real estate. Had such a provision still been in effect in the 1980s, many billion-dollar bank failures of recent years could not have occurred. By confining loans to 50 percent of value on good property, a loss of half the value would still give the bank protection. The Omnibus Banking Act had a provision which members of the bank examining forces found greatly upsetting. The new law, with its benefits for banks, at the same time would have prohibited any bank examiner leaving his federal job with the Comptroller of the Currency, the Federal Reserve, or the FDIC, to go to work for a bank which might be under his examining authority. The law would apply even if he had never examined the bank where he intended to go to work, or if he were only an assistant examiner with no great authority. Members of the several federal examining agencies were dismayed at the provision which would have prohibited their leaving federal employment to work in commercial banking within a two-year period after termination of employment, or without obtaining special approval from regulatory headquarters.

Although the proposed law had the apparent support of banks of all sizes and seemed inevitable to become law, two assistant national bank examiners decided to strike for freedom. Joe Wallace, who was later to head several banks, and Marshall Surratt, author of this book, composed a joint telegram to the Speaker of the House in Washington, Sam Rayburn. The telegram explained the inequities of the proposed law, which would have tied members of bank examining forces to involuntary servitude under their federal bosses. Rayburn pigeonholed the proposed act in subcommittee where it died with adjournment of Congress. Wallace, Surratt, and many others revere the memory of Sam Rayburn.

4. Section 24 of the Federal Reserve Act, Title 12, Subchapter X, Section 371, Real Estate Loans, 1982 amendment.

5. "Seidman's Bombshell," *Pratt's Letter*, Arlington, Virginia, April 12, 1991.

6. Edward J. Kane, *The Gathering Crisis in Federal Deposit Insurance*, The MIT Press, Cambridge, 1985.

7. Theodore R. Kennedy, East Lansing, Michigan, letter of April 12, 1989. See Appendix F for complete letter.

8. Bascom N. Timmons, *Jesse H. Jones: The Man and the Statesman*, Henry Holt & Co., New York, 1956.

9. Lawrence S. Ritter and William L. Silber, *Principles of Money, Banking & Financial Markets, Second and Enlarged Edition*, Basic Books, Inc., New York, 1977.

10. Federal Deposit Insurance Corporation, *1984 Annual Report*, Washington D.C.

11. Irvine D. Sprague, *Bailout: An Insider's Account of Bank Failures and Rescues*, Basic Books, Inc., New York, 1986.

12. *Fifth Edition Guide to the Federal Home Loan Bank System*, Federal Home Loan Bank System Publication Corporation, Washington, 1987.

13. T.R. Fehrenbach, San Antonio, telephone conversation, May, 1990. Also see his book, *The Swiss Banks*, McGraw-Hill, New York, 1966.

14. Swiss Bank Corporation, *1989 Annual Report*, Zurich.

15. Theodore R. Kennedy, letter cited. See Appendix F.

16. Andy Zipser, Dow Jones & Company, New York, letters of 1989 and 1991.

CHAPTER 4

Deficit Spending, Interest Rates, and Prices

During the late 1950s, when Dwight D. Eisenhower was President of the United States, the State National Bank of Denison, Texas boasted a singular distinction: On a desk behind the tellers' counter, under its ornate oval ceiling, was the Certificate of Deposit register that had been in use when the President was born in the modest Eisenhower home just across the Katy Railroad tracks in 1890. During the nearly seven decades of the bank's existence, which coincided with the life and service of the noted general and president, all the CDs issued by the bank were listed in that thin book, together with interest rates at the time of issue. During that seven decades, interest rates had only once reached the astronomical figure of 10 percent before going back down again to much lower levels.

Everyone, everywhere, knew that interest rates would never again be that high for depositors' funds. On most deposits, no interest was paid. Savings accounts earned four percent at most.

The bank itself was only seven years older than the president. The town of Denison was also rather new when the future General and President was born, having been a creation of the Missouri-Kansas-Texas Railroad for which Eisenhower's father worked. The railroad had established major shops and offices at Denison when it built south through the Indian Territory across the Red River into Texas. By the late 1950s, the bank building had been expanded, with drive-in facilities, architecturally in the same design with the ornate oval ceiling over the lobby and tellers' area.

Unprecedented Deficit Spendings

Unprecedented federal deficit spendings took place during the Great Depression of the 1930s, when the U.S. Government attempted to fight deflation by spending the nation back into prosperity. This adaption of the economic theories of Englishman John Maynard Keynes arguably set the stage for larger troubles down the road. During the same period, various economic reforms, some listed in the previous chapter, took place.

It wasn't until the Second World War engulfed the United States that full economic activity would resume, and even then wartime savings kept interest rates low. In his monumental *History of Interest Rates*, Sidney Homer of Salomon Brothers and Hutzler, investment bankers, stated:

> Skepticism of the ability of the Treasury to finance a war at 2½ percent was widespread. But the amount of savings of individuals and corporations was enormous during the wartime prosperity because incomes were high while expenditures and investments were restricted.[1]

In 1941, yields on long-time U.S. government bonds were less than 2 percent. During the war years, the rates stayed below 2.5 percent. As Homer further stated of the Korean War, which came only a few years afterward but during a time of intense post-World War II economic activity:

> The Korean War in fact broke the grip with which the government had for eight years controlled the market for its own bonds. Although the President [Truman] threw the great prestige of his office behind the demand of the Secretary of the Treasury that government bonds be supported at par, an accord between the Treasury and the Federal Reserve Board was reached in February-March of 1951 which ended the policy of rigid support.[2]

Ending of Gold (and Silver) Backing of the U.S. Dollar

In the years to follow came multiple domestic and foreign spending programs as well as the Vietnam War. Habits of spending of the 1930s became ingrained in Washington and were copied in state capitols and local governments. Whereas deficit financing had but little effect on prices and on interest rates during the depressed economic conditions of the 1930s, such government deficits had tremendous effects on interest rates and prices in the 1960s, 1970s and 1980s.

This was especially true after the 1965 ending of the 25 percent gold reserve for bank deposits with the Federal Reserve, the 1968 termination of the gold reserve against Federal Reserve Notes, and the complete breakdown of the Bretton Woods Agreement in 1971 whereby the U.S. abrogated its promise to exchange gold with other nations. Gold backing for the dollar was terminated, as was the government's agreed fixed-exchange rate of $35 per ounce. Prices of oil, cotton, wheat and real estate proceeded to soar in the late 1970s and early 1980s. The prime interest rate, the rate that major banks charge their best customers, hit over 20 percent in the last year of the Carter administration.

President Jimmy Carter was not solely to blame for such inflationary interest rates and prices. Federal deficit spending overwhelmed the good intentions that Carter had expressed in his campaign pledge to hold down interest rates, — which at the end of his administration were highest since the Civil War. Nor was

Richard Nixon solely to blame for the breakdown of international exchange rates and gold backing for the dollar during his administration. Nor was Lyndon Johnson solely to blame for the end of silver convertibility for the dollar and abolition of gold reserves against bank deposits during his administration. Twenty percent prime interest rate inflation, the breakdown of international exchange rates tied to gold under Bretton Woods, the elimination of gold reserves for U.S. dollars, and the end of silver convertibility, all were associated. All were interrelated with increasing governmental and private deficit spending, based in part on war and defense expenditures of the Cold War, also on various governmental welfare programs, and on private expectations that prices and interest rates would go ever higher.

Value of the Dollar and Freedom to Own Gold

Until the early days of Franklin D. Roosevelt's administration, gold was valued at $20.67 per jeweler's ounce. Gold tended to disappear with the international financial depression, and the President, with subsequent approval of Congress, devalued the dollar until an ounce of gold was worth $35.

Then in 1934, the Gold Reserve Act made the ownership of gold coins and gold illegal. All gold was to belong to the Federal government. Special permission was required for use in jewelry and industry. It wasn't until 1975, after the 1971 revocation of the tie of gold with the dollar, that U.S. citizens were again allowed to own gold. In the 1960s and 1970s, a two-tier system came into being – an attempt by various nations' central banks to exchange currencies at official gold rates, while other gold sales were at higher figures.

In the last years of the Nixon Administration, under Secretary of the Treasury John Connally, gold was officially revalued upward to $42.22 – the free price going above $100 until the official price was abandoned. The dollar was then to "float" against other nations' currencies. Perhaps in part as a legacy of the anti-gold theories of English economist J.M. Keynes, the United Kingdom, the United States and other English-speaking nations were among the last to return to their citizens the freedom to own gold. France and Germany had learned at first hand the extreme hardship of hyperinflation of paper currencies – and the value of gold.

Martin Mayer points out the continuing ill effect from the early 1960s, during the Kennedy Administration, when Congress approved an Interest Equalization Tax on loans of U.S. dollars held abroad to citizens and institutions in the United States. This short-lived tax helped to create the often troublesome Euro-dollars,

dollars held abroad in foreign banks and in foreign branches of U.S. banks.[3]

Japan and the United States – The U.S. Federal Debt

In early 1991, there was rejoicing by some U.S. business reporters, U.S. politicians, and even a few members of the U.S. investment banking community at announcement that certain of Japan's largest brokerage firms had admitted kickbacks to large clients against losses. In late 1991, U.S. investment bankers were also to admit that all had not been quite right with them either, especially in biddings and purchases in the largest U.S. financial market – federal debt issues, debt that would eventually have to be repaid by the American people.

Salomon Brothers, one of the nation's largest and most reputable stock brokerage houses, admitted that bids for U.S. Treasury debt issues were made in excess of what were allowed by Treasury regulations. Salomon's top officials resigned and investor Warren Buffett took over as temporary chairman. Other large U.S. brokers were also questioned by the SEC as to bids on federally sponsored mortgage companies such as Federal National Mortgage Association and Government National Mortgage Association. Big government sponsorship of big finance had become ever more important to big U.S. investment banking. Japan had become important as an investor-creditor in U.S. federal debt issues. When, on occasion, Japanese purchases of U.S. short term debt issues wavered, so had the overall market for U.S. Treasury issues seemed uncertain.

Prices

Crude oil, stable for years at about $3.50 per barrel, shot up to 10 times that amount (and was expected by some to go to $60 to $100 per barrel) when the Organization of Petroleum Exporting Countries (OPEC) stirred up things in the late 1970s. This was also the period of accelerating interest rates. Cotton went up to nearly 90 cents per pound briefly, after years of government support at lower figures. Other agricultural commodities also sought new highs, in part stimulated by exports to the U.S.S.R., (only a short time later to be cut off by President Carter as punishment for the Soviet invasion of Afghanistan). Manufacturing boomed. Real estate prices followed upward for agricultural, industrial, commercial, and residential expansion.

Then it all came tumbling down. Not as low as before, but lower than the period of the late 1970s and early 1980s. City growth continued to expand for a while, accelerated by the banking boom and S&L frenzy – in turn made possible by the new freedoms

Congress had enacted as a "sop" against high interest rates' squeezings of the savings institutions.

Act upon act of government, coupled with private belief that prices and interest rates would never come down again, created economic chaos. At the same time, the dollar continued over the long run to lose value, with neither gold nor silver to back it.

Jesse H. Jones in his book, *Fifty Billion Dollars: My Thirteen Years With The RFC (1932-1945),* detailed the many programs for aiding America during his service with the RFC. This included most of the Great Depression and the Second World War. (And except for strictly relief efforts and unrecoverable war efforts, most of the $50 billions were paid back.)[4]

Jones' 13 years/$50 billion are but a small portion of one-year/$1 trillion federal expenditures of today. Again, the dollar today has no resemblance to its value in years gone by. Nor is there any connection between the wages and salaries of Americans of today and those of their parents and grandparents. Surely we are better off in many material ways. But the decline of the dollar is not a blessing.

More Than Thirty Years Since Congress and the President Balanced the Budget

With the 1990s, more than 30 years have passed since Congress and the President gave the people of the United States a balanced budget.

Dwight D. Eisenhower was President; Sam Rayburn was Speaker of the House of Representatives (Denison was in his district); and Prescott Bush, whose son George was later to become President, was Senator from Connecticut when the last surplus was seen in Washington, during the year 1960.

The three-decade period of deficit spending of the 1960s, 1970s and 1980s was unprecedented in U.S. history. Never before had the country gone so many consecutive years without a balanced budget. Never before had the dollar gone down, down and down in value as it would after 1960. There had been earlier periods with interest rates temporarily sky-high, during the American Revolution and, later, the Civil War, but none would compare with the 20 percent-plus prime rates of the 1980s.

Commodity prices, land prices, wholesale prices and retail prices skyrocketed with inflation of the dollar, chiefly instigated by deficit federal spending. They would then drop precipitously with sudden deflation. U.S. gold reserves had declined so much during the 1960s, as other nations demanded gold for their dollars (U.S. citizens not being allowed to own gold during that time) that Congress and the President eliminated the remaining 25 percent gold reserve requirement for bank deposits with the Federal Reserve Banks and, later, the gold reserve against our currency, the Federal Reserve Notes.

In 1971, the United States abrogated its pledge under the Bretton Woods Agreement to exchange an ounce of gold for 35 U.S. dollars from other nations – and in 1972, the price was set at $42.22 per ounce. In spite of predictions from political economists in and out of government that gold's price would change but little, the price of gold at one time went above $800 per ounce. Later the price dropped into the $300s and $400s, about 10 times previous prices. The U.S. dollar has gone downward, toward one-tenth its previous value. Deficit spending, declining dollars, and upward-fluctuating interest rates and prices have continued over the past three decades.

How About the Local Tax Burden?

Then there are the local taxes. City, school, hospital district, water district, county and state taxes don't contribute directly to the inflation of our money supply and devaluation, but aren't they also a burden?

All taxes *are* a burden on the individual or business paying them; thus the answer must be "yes." State and local taxes have gone up – although not all the same, nor all in proportion to the decline of the value of the dollar. Property taxes have increased. Also, fees on municipal services have escalated, some more than 1,000 percent, over the past three decades. Likewise, sales and income taxes have been instituted, then added to, and added to. All of these come either directly or indirectly from personal income, and are a real burden, especially on those who had hoped to live on fixed-dollar retirement incomes.

At a hotel in a major Southeastern city, the trainee registration clerk remarked that he didn't care what the tax might be (the tax in that city being 13 percent on the hotel or motel bill) since he didn't have to pay it. But such taxes on the outsider, always a selling point for local officials to their electorate, do have to be paid by somebody. And the visitor to the city may have to cut back on his or her visits or business in that city. At the same time in that particular city there was an argument on how to spend the hotel tax – but no discussion on possibly reducing or eliminating it.

As with a few in the U.S. Congress, a few in state legislatures and administrations and a few in local governments were beginning in the 1990s to consider reductions, rather than increases, in government spending.

Trying to Out-Gamble the Government

Financial institutions – commercial banks, savings banks, S&Ls, insurance companies, and other financial institutions – trying to out-gamble the government, with managements unequal to the task, have come to grief. Attempts to out-guess government on prices and interest rates, incompetency and lack of integrity in management, unreal boom and bust conditions, all played parts in the tragic drama. And with all, the dollar has continued to decline in value.

A Return to a Standard of Value

George Donald Pfingst of New Jersey, whose family has long been in the national dental supply business, states:

> I agree fully that the devaluation of the dollar and deficit spending are two of the major causes for the present woes. Probably both developed to take away a real standard of value – to use them for political footballs.

Pfingst hopes this book will help to change [for the better] "some of the banking principles of this country."[5]

NOTES

1. Sidney Homer, *History of Interest Rates*, Rutgers University Press, New Brunswick, New Jersey, 1963.

2. Same reference.

3. Martin Mayer "The Transaction Tax's Evil Twin," the *Wall Street Journal*, July 13, 1990.

4. Jesse H. Jones, *Fifty Billion Dollars: My Thirteen Years with the RFC (1932-1945)*, The Macmillan Co., New York, 1951.

5. George Donald Pfingst, Pfingst & Co., South Plainfield, New Jersey. Letter of October 29, 1990.

CHAPTER 5

The Savings and Loans, The Savings Banks, The Commercial Banks

The savings and loan associations and the savings banks are yet another story.

A quaint custom often chronicled in books and movies of the World War II era was the celebration of the burning of the mortgage. You borrowed from a thrift institution, a savings bank or S&L, at the whopping rate of 4½ to 5 percent, paying as much down as you possibly could and contracting for the shortest period you could afford, so that your house would be paid for before the kids went off to college.

Until recent years a respected but unspectacular industry, the thrift institutions, savings banks and S&Ls performed two basic services. They accepted savings and they made home mortgage loans. Period. The savings banks were mutually owned and centered in the Northeast. Over a period of more than a hundred years, some had become very large institutions, accumulating the savings of thousands of thrifty patrons. The savings banks made mortgage loans and invested in government securities.

Most of these earlier savings banks were insured by the FDIC. The savings associations were also known as savings and loan associations, or building and loan associations, or cooperative banks in Massachusetts, or homestead associations in Louisiana.

Some S&Ls were mutual associations. Others had permanent stock. Although federal insurance of savings association accounts became available in 1934, it was not until 1951 that FSLIC-insured thrifts outnumbered non-FSLIC-insured thrifts. There was no particular need: the local state-chartered S&L was not out to make any big deposit gains, or "share" growth, as it was then called. Members owned shares, or deposits, and had certain voting rights in annual meetings of the associations, somewhat like in the credit unions of today. This was true of both "mutual" and "permanent stock" associations. With establishment of the various federal mortgage agencies – Fannie Mae, Ginnie Mae, Freddie Mac – the S&L associations moved along smoothly, though slowly, known for service to the community as depositories for savings and suppliers of home mortgage funds.

Back then, as now, Congress was tempted to spend more than it took in, and often it did. But deficit spending was only a fraction of what it was to become later. Congress and the federal administration tried to spend the country back into prosperity during the 1930s, doing away with gold coinage and even confiscating the gold coins held by the American people (supposedly to lock it away in underground vaults in Fort Knox). However, the dollar changed but little in purchasing power, and prices remained at depression-level lows, until the much-bigger spending of World War II.

As interest rates began to creep upward in the 1960s, and accelerated in the 1970s, the savings institutions, with their fixed-rate long-term mortgages at 4 and 5 percent, were in a quandary as to how to make ends meet when they had to pay the customer that much or more for deposits.

The concept of "shares" became "deposits," or "Certificates of Savings," or "Certificates of Deposit." Savings had been a means for gradually accumulating funds. A Certificate of Deposit or "CD" could mean a sizeable deposit at one time. At the same time, commercial banks were pushing the new CD – a term hardly known to the general public before that time. (Witness the seldom-used CD register mentioned in the previous chapter.)

After the dollar's gold backing was broken domestically in 1965 and 1968, and internationally in 1971, inflation of the U.S. money supply took off, together with interest rates. (There was no longer any restraint on Congress and its spendings.) By the early 1980s, many thrifts were in a terrible bind, as interest paid on short term deposits greatly exceeded interest earned on old, long-term mortgages.

Nixon Commission – Garn-St Germain

Congress sought to amend this imbalance – largely caused by federal deficit spending – by new privileges for the S&Ls and savings banks. In 1972, President Nixon's Commission on Financial Structure and Regulation recommended that all *qualified* S&Ls and savings banks be permitted, in effect, to become commercial banks. Ten years later, in 1982, the Garn-St Germain Act put the recommendation into law, allowing *all* S&Ls to act like commercial banks, with the further amplification that their *qualifications* would not be questioned.

The *1985 Federal Home Loan Bank Board Savings Association Handbook* explained:

> Garn-St Germain also enlarged the scope of activities savings and loan associations and savings banks could undertake, allowing them to invest portions of their assets in financial services traditionally restricted to commercial banks. Thrifts

may now make commercial, corporate, business, and agricultural loans, offer checking accounts, and issue consumer loans, educational loans, and nonresidential real estate loans, much as commercial banks do.[1]

Garn-St Germain also had other provisions desired by the federal regulators, supposedly strengthening savings institutions and commercial banks. The Federal Home Loan Bank Board (which in 1989 was itself to be abolished) was given new powers to deal with financially troubled institutions. It could overrule state authorities and seize insolvent state-chartered FSLIC-insured institutions, and merge them with out-of-state institutions.

No Commercial Driver's License

Garn-St Germain, in giving the S&Ls the power to act like commercial banks, had in effect handed over the keys of 18-wheelers to the drivers of 6-cylinder sedans with no stipulation that they obtain a commercial license to drive them.

In addition, the S&Ls were not restricted, as were commercial banks, in the amount that an institution could lend to one customer, a fact hardly realized by politicians and public. An S&L could lend 100 percent of capital funds to a single customer. Whereas for over a century national banks had been restricted to only 10 percent (15 percent after Garn-St Germain) of capital funds that could be lent to any one customer, an S&L could lend 100 percent of capital funds to an individual. This was not a problem when savings institutions made home mortgage loans – a customer hardly ever asked for a loan of any great magnitude. But when Congress allowed, even urged, S&Ls to act like commercial banks, and thus earn higher short term loan rates, the S&Ls went all out, extending credit to customer after customer at 100 percent of capital per loan. Thus, when such loans went bad, and many did, the S&Ls were in deep trouble in a very short time. With a loan limit of more than six times that of a national bank (100 percent versus 15 percent), an S&L could get into trouble more than six times as deeply and quickly.

One small Texas S&L went into business in 1981 with an initial capitalization of $1,575,000. More than 300 shareholders had subscribed to its capital accounts. There were no old low-interest loans. Deposit growth came quickly, encouraged in part by the withdrawal of an old-line S&L from the market. In 1983, the collapse of a large area bank allowed additional quick deposits.

Opportunity overwhelmed the inexperienced S&L management and board of directors. As rationalized later, they had to do something with all those funds. Quick earning investment opportunities included "participation loans" with various out-of-territory institutions. Supposed earnings pushed net worth up to $2 million and then above $3 million. One hundred percent participation loans of the complete capital structure were made over and over again – $2 million in an incomplete ski resort in Utah, nearly $3 million in a waterfront development in Florida – many other millions with notorious Vernon Savings (which kept prostitutes on retainer like other institutions kept lawyers and accountants) in various developments. Many of these went sour quickly. The initial $1,575,000 capital account, which in financial statements at one time claimed to be above $3 million, disappeared completely as loans were found to be worthless.

In the end, before the FSLIC finally merged what remained, the S&L had lost $55 million; that is, shareholders lost all $1,575,000, and taxpayers who will have to bail out the FSLIC lost $53 million more on this not-so-large S&L.

The loan limit of 100 percent of capital per loan customer, together with inexperienced management, caused terrible losses for too many S&Ls – and taxpayers.

This weakness in the wide-open S&L lending authority – 100 percent of capital versus 15 percent for national banks – was called to the attention of House Banking Committee Chairman Henry Gonzalez by this writer and very likely by others.[2] The 1989 Financial Institutions Reform, Recovery, and Enforcement Act (FIRREA) reduced the S&L loan limit to that of national banks – with certain exceptions. Unhappily, hundreds of billions of dollars had already been drained from taxpayers' pockets, while S&Ls were allowed, even encouraged, to act like commercial banks, with the much larger loan limits and with managements inexperienced in commercial lending.

At the same time that S&Ls were encouraged to get into commercial lending, they were also allowed to invest in various securities, including "junk bonds" – high yield and high risk and low grade corporate bonds. These were issued by certain Wall Street/Beverly Hills investment houses as part of the leveraged buyout, take-over operations so popular in that era. *Forbes* magazine, in a comparison titled "History Lesson," spoke of convicted junk bond super salesman Michael Milken of Drexel Burnham Lambert and of Samuel Insull, who died eight years before Milken's birth.

Forbes suggested that each was first a hero, then a villain of his time, telling of Insull's Middle West Utilities, which brought electric bills down from 20 cents per kilowatt-hour in Chicago to

2½ cents, as a great engineering success but a failure as a holding company in its junk-grade stocks and bonds.[3]

Whereas commercial banks were restricted in their investments to U.S. government, high-grade municipals, and high-grade corporate bonds – of the top four investment grades – S&Ls were allowed to invest heavily into the lower-rated, speculative municipal and corporate issues, with the rationale that such issues allowed them necessary higher income. Charles Keating and others were subsequently much in the news regarding the Arizona and California S&Ls that they controlled and their junk bond investments. Admittedly, the immediate opportunity for earnings was high – but so was the risk of loss, not only in defaults and bankruptcies of issuing companies but also from market fluctuations in the prices of low-grade bonds.

In addition, some S&L holding companies (Keating's American Continental Corp. and its Lincoln Savings & Loan, for instance) sold their own junk bonds – unsecured subordinated notes of American Continental – to unsuspecting depositors.

Inexperienced boards of directors of S&Ls had little idea of what was necessary for competent commercial lending – the experience that is required, the skill in credit analysis. Neil Bush, son of the U.S. president, admitted that he had very little financial background when he was asked to serve on the board of Silverado Savings in Denver. Neil Bush's background in banking had consisted of six weeks spent one summer in the trust department of a Dallas bank. Too many savings institutions were totally lacking in knowledgeable commercial credit and investment officers and other experienced and skilled personnel.

State Laws and Constitutions to the Contrary

At the same time that S&Ls were declared to be like commercial banks, the federal bank regulators rationalized that in states such as Mississippi and Texas, where there were strict branch prohibitions for banking but none for S&Ls, there should be no restriction on branches for commercial banks. S&Ls and commercial banks had been declared by federal regulators and judges to be equal, state laws and state constitutions notwithstanding. Thus national banks were declared by the Comptroller of the Currency to have the same lack of restriction on branching as S&Ls.

Land Development – All the Way to Campobello

Another generous provision that got the S&Ls into deeper trouble was Congress' permission for them to go directly into land development and do it anywhere. Until Garn-St. Germain, each S&L

had been restricted to its local trade area, and to mortgage lending. Now, no longer would they have to sit on the sidelines on financing customers in developments. S&Ls could participate in the rich land development profits themselves. Again, this was an attempt to let the S&Ls recoup losses occurring in the early 1980s when depositors were paid much higher interest than the old mortgage loans were producing. Some judicious savings associations developed only land that they could sell to developers in their local trade areas, with the understanding that permanent residential loans would come back to them.

However, many others went "whole hog." In 1983, little Madison Guaranty, formerly Woodruff County Savings, of Woodruff County, Arkansas, took on land developments ranging from Arkansas to the famed Campobello Island retreat in Canada, where Franklin D. Roosevelt contracted polio. When the axe fell in Woodruff County, Madison Guaranty president John Latham pled guilty to a felony charge for switching loan documents to conceal the "non-recourse" nature of a "Castle Grande" loan to an insider for more than $500,000. Other clients of Madison Guaranty included former U.S. Senator J. William Fulbright of Arkansas and Jim Guy Tucker, Arkansas lieutenant governor. Fulbright paid off his loan for the purchase of 400 acres of land, although he had been able to sell only 100 acres.

The cost of the Madison demise, according to a news story in *The Arkansas Democrat*, will probably exceed $27 million.[4]

In the 1992 U.S. Presidential race then Arkansas Gov. Bill Clinton was tied in with an owner of Madison Guaranty according to the *New York Times.* The future United States President and wife were reported to have been in a joint real estate venture with James B. McDougal, the governor's former aide and chief owner of Madison Guaranty. Both Clinton and McDougal had served on the staff of Senator Fulbright.

Garn-St Germain, enacted in 1982, sounded like a good idea in the halls of Congress, but it was a tragedy in action. Then the tragedy was compounded in 1985 when the act was extended. Again, for many older S&Ls it was an attempt to bail them out of old low-interest mortgages put on the books before the government went on its big spending spree.

In the 1990s, Democrats and Republicans were trying to blame one other for the S&L fiasco — and accusing one another of failing to authorize more spending for investigators and prosecutors of S&L wrongdoing.

Meanwhile, the dominoes continued to fall.

News reports in financial journals, in the nation's newspapers, on television and on radio quoted members of Congress and the Administration regarding what had been done, what had not been done, and what should be done.

In the Northwest, according to a *Hearst News Service* report, a team of FBI agents and federal prosecutors at Seattle won major convictions against executives and customers of Home Savings & Loan Association in 1987 and Queen City Savings & Loan Association in 1988, resulting in sentences of 56 years for nine individuals and restitution amounting to $38 million.[5]

The Queen City Savings & Loan case was small in comparison to subsequent S&L losses. That particular Federal Savings & Loan Insurance Corp. loss was reported to have cost at least $15 million — a small loss compared to many subsequent S&L failures, which completely depleted the FSLIC insurance fund. *The Seattle Post-Intelligencer* reported that land developer Jerry D. Smith who "ran Queen City, but held no official title" was "convicted of 15 counts of wire fraud, which included conspiracy to defraud federal bank regulators, filing false financial statements and aiding and abetting the submission of a false bank entry."

Smith received a 10-year prison sentence. Former S&L president G. Michael Kirchoff received a lesser sentence. Smith's brother and business associate, Paul D. Smith, was given a probated sentence. The Smiths diverted about $2.5 million in loans from Queen City that were supposed to be used on land development in the Midland/Odessa area of West Texas, and used the money for personal business ventures.[6]

In return for a $9.95 million settlement from International Insurance Co., which carried the fidelity bond on the S&L, the federal government dropped civil claims against 20 Queen City defendants. According to The *Midland Reporter-Telegram*, one of these had arranged the $265,000 in payments from ousted PTL television evangelist Jim Bakker to Jessica Hahn.[7]

Gibraltar Savings of Washington, affiliate of Gibraltar Savings of California, took over Queen City S&L in 1984, reported *The Seattle Times*.[8] In 1990, both Gibraltar associations also fell on hard financial times and were taken over by the new Resolution Trust Corp. (RTC), with $3.9 billion core deposits sold by the RTC to Security Pacific Bank, which was to acquire certain "prime" assets of Gibraltar. Security Pacific in turn had sold an interest in certain of its operations to Mitsui Taiyo Kobe Bank, Ltd., Japan's second-largest bank, and in 1991 sought to end its financial problems by merging into Bank of America.

The cost of S&L failures bankrupted the depleted FSLIC insurance fund, with the taxpayers of America and surviving S&L industry left holding the bag for future S&L failures, estimated initially at $10 to 15 billion and later revised upward to $100 to $300 billion, perhaps $500 billion. The completely bankrupt FSLIC was abolished in 1989, and a new Savings Association Insurance Fund was set up under an enlarged FDIC. The final cost of the S&L fiasco? That could be anyone's guess.

The Savings Banks

Primarily in the Northeastern states, with a few in the Northwest and a lesser number in other states, the savings banks had been organized to encourage thrift among persons of moderate means. Typical savings bank names were "Dime," "Farmers & Mechanics," and "Seamen's."

From early days, state laws and rules for savings banks threw every possible safeguard around savings banks deposits. In some states, the laws designated a list of specific securities that were classed as "equal investments for savings banks and trust funds." Such classifications were to protect the savings of those who were members of the mutually owned savings institutions. Apparently, most of the savings banks remained true to their purpose without becoming captive to the manipulators who took over certain of the S&Ls. But inflation, chiefly Congressionally created, forced higher interest rates. These helped to ruin many savings banks. Lower-earning mortgages and bonds, already on the books, brought in less than was paid on savings accounts and the new CDs. Federal deficit spending and inflation brought disaster for savings banks.

Bailed out and re-formed by the Federal Deposit Insurance Corp. in the early 1980s (savings banks being under FDIC rather than FSLIC), certain of the FDIC-encouraged, new super-savings banks were in deep trouble by the early 1990s, as had been the smaller savings banks from which they had been created 10 years earlier.

Net Worth Certificates

"Net Worth Certificates," part of 1982 Garn-St Germain, were issued by the FDIC to thrift institutions in exchange for notes. Such gave the illusion of higher capital ratios for a while.

These were temporary measures, issued to prop up thrift institutions that had suffered interest-rate mismatches, paying for deposits at higher rates than those they were receiving on investments and loans.

Goldome – Largest Savings Bank Closing Ever

The closure of $11.4 billion Goldome, a Buffalo, New York savings bank, by the New York State Banking Department and the Federal Deposit Insurance Corp. in July 1991 marked the largest savings bank ever to be seized by the FDIC. It had been established 145 years earlier in 1856 as the "working man's bank – Buffalo Savings." In the early 1980s, it expanded dramatically under FDIC auspices. In those years, it combined with the $1.5 billion Union Savings Bank and $3.4 billion New York Bank for Savings, both of New York City, as well as the $1 billion Western New York Savings Bank of Buffalo.[9] Cost to the FDIC on these troubled mergers was $276 million. Goldome, which changed from mutual ownership to shareholder ownership to obtain new capital from stockholders, also acquired two Florida S&Ls, these without FDIC assistance.

Additionally, Goldome got into other businesses, some related (insurance and mortgage) and others not so related (such as plywood).[10] Profitability did not reappear until late in its existence, when in 1989 Thomas A. Cooper, a Bank of America executive, was brought in "to shed assets, refocus on Goldome's traditional mortgage lending and cut costs, including doing away with company limousines and country club membership," according to a *Wall Street Journal* news story.

Though Goldome managed six consecutive profitable quarterly operating periods under the new management, the Federal Deposit Insurance Corp. decided in view of its weakened financial condition to close it. Costs to the depleting FDIC fund were estimated at $930 million – thus with the not-too-successful efforts of nearly 10 years earlier, the FDIC stood to lose more than $1.2 billion on its combined Goldome reformation efforts. Shareholders of Goldome would likely lose everything.

And Yet One of the Most Profitable?

At the same time the FDIC decided to close down Goldome – to take a near-$1 billion additional loss on it and turn over deposits and certain assets to others – *Fortune* magazine cited Goldome among the "World's 500 Largest Service Companies" in profitability in 1990. On another list it was No. 8 in the "Ten Highest Returns on Stockholder' Equity."[11] (In an earlier issue of *Fortune*, Goldome was near the bottom of listings of "most and least" admired companies – according to its previous reputation.) Like some other companies listed – including the federally chartered Federal National Mortgage Association and Student Loan Marketing Association – it had a small capital base, thus allowing Goldome a 29.4 percent return on equity for 1990. But, as stated by Buffalo's mayor, U.S. taxpayers in other parts of the country would wonder why the FDIC waited until Goldome was showing a profit before finally deciding to close it down.

In the 1991 closedown of Goldome, the FDIC would pay KeyCorp of Albany, New York $163 million and First Empire State $40 million to take over New York State assets and deposits. Goldome Savings Bank at St. Petersburg, Florida was turned over to the Resolution Trust Corp. (RTC).

First Empire State

First Empire State Corp. in 1991 was a $5 billion bank holding company headquartered at Buffalo. The 100-year-old Manufacturers & Traders Trust Co. of Buffalo is part of Empire State, as is the East New York Savings Bank of New York City, which First Empire acquired in 1987. First Empire State got 11 Buffalo branches plus the headquarters building and three New York City branches from Goldome. (See Chapter 9, also Appendix O, on this upstate New York banking company.)

KeyCorp

The $23.1 billion KeyCorp styles itself "America's neighborhood bank," and has the slogan of "sticking to the basics." KeyCorp has grown rapidly by acquiring banks from Alaska, Washington and Oregon in the Northwest; Wyoming, Utah and Idaho in the Mountain Area; and over to New York and Maine in the Northeast. KeyCorp received 31 branches of Goldome in 1991 from the FDIC. Speaking of KeyCorp, the *Wall Street Journal* stated that such nationwide banking is what federal regulators have in mind as they lobby Congress to allow banks to "expand beyond existing state and regional barriers; (that) overriding the remaining patchwork of state restrictions would make banks less vulnerable to regional shocks, argues Robert Clarke, comptroller of the currency."[12]

As expressed in KeyCorp's 1990 Annual Report:

> With the unfortunate condition of certain financial institutions, regulatory authorities invited KeyCorp to bid on acquiring these properties, presenting us with unexpected and unique opportunities.

With federal assistance KeyCorp has grown rapidly in size. In 1990 it acquired $3 billion in assets and $2.2 billion in deposits from the RTC in 40 former Empire of America Federal Savings Bank branches in eastern and western New York State, with the right to "put back" assets to the RTC. Total assets for KeyCorp in 1985 were under $8 billion. At the beginning of 1992, after the latest government-assisted acquisitions, assets were $23.1 billion – three times assets of five years earlier. Victor J. Riley, Jr. is chairman, president, and CEO of KeyCorp. KeyCorp's board of directors had included Monoru Makihara, senior managing director of Mitsubishi Corp. of New York, later, Mitsubishi president at Tokyo.[13]

KeyCorp., whose annual reports are full of figures on earnings, expenses, and ratios, is quite proud of its low "efficiency ratio." This is defined as non-interest expenses (salaries, etc.) per net interest and other income. At the same time KeyCorp's goal of earning 1.10 percent on assets, later reduced to 1 percent, has been illusive, as return on assets declined from .93 percent in 1989, to .89 in 1990, to .86 in 1991; acquisitions from the regulators are blamed in part. In 1992 KeyCorp announced an agreement to acquire $4.9 billion Puget Sound Bancorp – and 48 offices of former Security Pacific Bank in Washington state from BankAmerica Corp. Key Corp proudly announced net return of 1.04 percent on assets for of 1992.[14]

Arbitrage Gamble – Seamen's Bank for Savings

In addition to investments in junk bonds and far-away land developments and disastrous attempts at commercial lending, certain of the thrift institutions that had been traditionally most conservative in their investments took yet another gamble in the 1980s: so-called "risk-controlled arbitrage." Described in a front-page report in The *Wall Street Journal* as a "razzle-dazzle 1980s innovation designed to lock in profits through complex combinations of hedging instruments," the system did not always work. *WSJ* reporter Charles McCoy told how the Federal Home Loan Bank at Seattle authorized Far West Federal Bank at Portland, Oregon to experiment with what was promised to make the government "lots of money," but which ended with Far West's demise in June 1991.[15] Then chairman William Seidman of the FDIC is quoted, "A case can be made that this so-called arbitrage will cost the government more than junk bonds."

Other major failures, such as American Savings of Stockton, California and Franklin Savings of Ottawa, Kansas are identified with the arbitrage maneuver. In addition to the thrift institutions leaders, the *WSJ* said:

> The arbitrage cases provided evidence that some large securities firms and other investment bankers sold the thrift industry a bill of goods. And regulators weren't just standing by either; they encouraged the maneuver.

These involved exotic instruments where differences in interest rates, both long term and short term, were supposed to make the S&Ls and savings banks a profit on the difference – and get them out of what government-deficit-created high interest rates had involved them. The supposed interest rate-hedging was likened to a sort of mass psychosis.

Herb Sandler, co-chairman of Golden West Financial Corporation, comments:

> Some of the thrift managers and investment bankers who got involved . . . were simply charlatans, and others were blinded by a consuming belief in their own supposed brilliance.

Risk-controlled arbitrage was tried at already ailing Seamen's Bank for Savings in New York. Jess Hay, chairman of the large mortgage banking firm of Lomas and Nettleton and director of MCorp, and associates R. Ted Enloe and Robert Utley, the latter a former Texas Securities commissioner, tried in 1985 to rescue Seamen's with a $50 million infusion. The *WSJ* told that in 1989 "Seamen's arranged $1 billion worth of interest-rate hedges . . . also increased to about $500 million its holdings of interest-only strips of cash flows from mortgage-backed securities . . . which would also become more valuable if rates rose."

But rates went down, and Seamen's lost. The 100-year-old Seamen's Bank for Savings was closed in mid-1989 – at a loss to the FDIC's depleting insurance fund, this particular loss estimated to exceed half a billion dollars.

Chase Manhattan Bank of New York ($107 billion strong) acquired the $2.1 billion deposit accounts from failed Seamen's Bank "without having to assume Seamen's loans," according to Chase's 1989 Annual Report.[16] By 1991, Chase's assets were down to $98 billion, partly due to its deliberate efforts to downsize – both for better profitability and getting its capital up to better ratios – and to acquire more bargain deposits from failed New England commercial banks as well as thrift institutions.

Franklin National Bank of New York

Since the Great Depression, Franklin National Bank has been the only one of New York City's commercial banks to fail. Although not big by New York standards, Franklin's $3.6 billion 1974 failure was the largest to hit the FDIC in the 30 years of its existence till then. Originally a Long Island institution, Franklin's growth was guided by Arthur Roth, innovative financial leader. Having served the populace well on Long Island, Roth decided to join the big banks on Manhattan Island. He established an ornate office on Manhattan's Fifth Avenue and, as often happens with a new institution, began to pick up accounts not particularly desired by old-time banks.

On July 20, 1972 Lawrence Tisch of Loews Corp., who much later became better known when he moved to CBS television and radio, sold a million shares of Franklin New York Corp. to Italian citizen Michele Sindona at $40 per share. Sindona, with his new interest in Franklin representing 21.6 percent of its shares, pushed the Long Island-Manhattan bank into international banking. The bank became active in the new global currency transactions, with potential high profits but also with high risks. One of Sindona's companies had made a $179 million profit earlier that year against the U.S. dollar, when Richard Nixon's Secretary of the Treasury John Connally announced a 10 percent devaluation of the dollar following the cut of the U.S. tie to gold. From that time on, the dollar fluctuated widely against other currencies. Sindona, from an humble Sicilian background, had become known as banker to the Vatican, at the same time a member of the influential and highly secret Italian Masonic organization, *Propaganda Due*, or *P-2*. Additionally, Sindona was alleged to possess Mafia acquaintances.

David Kennedy, who preceded Connally as U.S. Treasury Secretary under Nixon and who previously had been head of Continental Illinois Bank of Chicago, helped introduce Sindona to American business.

Losses from foreign exchange operations and lack of success in its Manhattan venture created continued difficulties for Franklin National Bank. Joseph W. Barr, Treasury Secretary in the administration of Lyndon Johnson, who had also served as chairman of the Federal Deposit Insurance Corp., was brought in to try to save the Franklin. Losses were too great, however, and the bank was declared insolvent on October 8, 1974, just over two years after Sindona acquired control. What was left of Franklin was sold by the FDIC to European American Bank, a consortium of several banks.[17]

Perhaps Suicide

In 1980, Michele Sindona was sentenced to 25 years in U.S. federal prison in connection with the failure of Franklin National Bank. In 1985 he was extradited to Italy where he received another 15 years for fraud in the failure of Banca Privata Italiana. In 1986 he was given a life sentence for arranging the 1979 murder of Georgio Ambrosoli, Italian bank examiner who had been investigating Sindona's activities. While in prison, Sindona died by potassium cyanide poisoning, perhaps suicide.[18] Four years earlier, his protege, Roberto Calvi, had been found hanging from Blackfriars Bridge in London.[19]

The 1988 *Annual Report of the Federal Deposit Insurance Corporation* disclosed that the preferred shareholders of Franklin had finally been paid, 14 years after the bank closed. Nothing was said of the common shareholders.[20]

Large Banks – Failures – Bailouts

The report also listed the largest bank closing ever for the FDIC, that of the 40 First Republic Banks of Dallas, Houston and other Texas cities, with total assets of $32.7 billion. This far eclipsed the 1983 closing of First National Bank of Midland,with assets of $1.4 billion, which had been the second largest as an FDIC-failed bank, next only to Franklin. The Midland bank's deposits and certain assets were sold by the FDIC in 1983 to Republic Bank Corp. which became First Republic. In 1988, failed First Republic deposits and certain assets went to North Carolina National Bank via an FDIC-created bridge bank, NCNB Texas National Bank. In 1984, slightly larger Continental Illinois Bank of Chicago, with assets of $33.7 billion, had instead gone through an FDIC assisted bailout – all of which we shall discuss later.

New Federal Agencies – Old and New Problems

A huge new federal corporation, the Resolution Trust Corp., was formed under the FIRREA in 1989 to take over ailing S&Ls and the many properties of defunct associations. The Federal Home Loan Bank Board was abolished, and a new Director of the Office of Thrift Supervision created under the Secretary of the Treasury. The completely bankrupt Federal Savings & Loan Insurance Corporation was abandoned, with a reformed Savings Association Insurance Fund (SAIF) placed under control of an enlarged Federal Deposit Insurance Corp., to be administered separately from what at the time was a still solvent commercial Bank Insurance Fund (BIF).[21] Coincident with an S&L's 1990 failure and takeover, that particular S&L was proudly advertising by radio that its deposits were insured by the FDIC – which was at least halfway true under the new law.

The FIRREA had another benefit for big banking companies in the "Oakar Amendment." Named for sponsor Mary Rose Oakar, long-time Democratic member of the House of Representatives from Ohio (and member of the Banking Committee), the amendment allows commercial banks to acquire S&Ls, even across state lines, and operate them as branches of the banking companies.

An early casualty from the Oakar Amendment was a $21 million loss to the new SAIF on September 19, 1991 in connection with failure of Southeast Bank N.A. of Miami, Florida and its affiliate Southeast Bank of West Florida of Pensacola. Certain former S&L deposits had been acquired by these commercial banks in the two-year interim since passage of FIRREA on August 9, 1989. The failing Southeast Banks in turn were taken over by banking regulators and resold by the FDIC to First Union Corp. Out of an initial loss of $178 million, the SAIF was charged $21 million for its part of the former S&L deposits. The FDIC's "loss-sharing" agreement with the First Union National Bank of Florida (a subsidiary of First Union Corp. of Charlotte, North Carolina) concerns the loan portfolio of the over-$10 billion in assets of former Southeast Banks. Eighty-five percent of net charge-offs from former Southeast loans were to be charged to the FDIC during the five years following the 1991 agreement. (More on this in chapter 6.)

Coverage of most S&Ls' deposits by the new SAIF was postponed by Congress in late 1991, until September 30, 1993.

As indicated, some of the billion-dollar savings banks that were already under the FDIC rather than the FSLIC have again gotten into financial difficulties after earlier bailouts.

In the 1990s various proposals were suggested for putting new capital into the FDIC's Bank Insurance Fund, hard hit by continuing bank failures, including super-regional Bank of New England Corp. Proposals were also being made for capitalization of the new Savings Association Insurance Fund.

Hard times for the financial institutions! Hard times for the American people.

NOTES

1. *Savings Association Handbook*, Federal Home Loan Bank Board, Washington, 1985.

2. Henry B. Gonzalez, Chairman of Banking, Finance and Urban Affairs Committee, U.S. Congress, House of Representatives, letter of April 4, 1989.

3. "History Lesson," *Forbes*, December, 1990.

4. Joe Nabbefeld and David Smith, "Madison: S&L Crisis in Microcosm," *The Arkansas Democrat*, Little Rock, June 17, 1990. Also *New York Times*, March 8, 1992.

5. Dan Freedman, "Bush talks tough on S&Ls," *Hearst News Service* as reported in the *Midland Reporter-Telegram*, June 3, 1990.

6. Steve Miltich, "3 found Guilty by Federal Jury in Queen City S&L Case," *Seattle Post-Intelligencer*, April 8, 1988.

7. "FSLIC Receives $9.95 Million in Settlement," *Midland Reporter-Telegram*, May 31, 1987.

8. Peyton Whitely, "Ex-land developer sentenced to 10 years in Queen City case," *The Seattle Times*, July 16, 1988.

9. John R. Wilke and James S. Hirsch, "FDIC Closes Goldome, Splits Bank's Assets, KeyCorp and First Empire State Arrange Takeover; Florida Unit Excluded," *Wall Street Journal*, June 3, 1991.

10. *Moody's Bank & Finance Manual*, Moody's Investors Service, 1990, New York.

11. "The Fortune Global Service 500," *Fortune*, August 26, 1991.

12. John R. Wilke, "Nationwide Banking is getting preview at growing KeyCorp," *Wall Street Journal*, May 31, 1991.

13. KeyCorp, *Annual Report for 1990*, Albany, New York.

14. KeyCorp, *Annual Report for 1991*, Albany, New York. Also, *1992 Report*.

15. Charles McCoy, "Bad Bets: Many Big S&L Losses Turn Out to be Due to a Financial Gamble – 'Risk-Controlled Arbitrage' Was sold by Wall Street and Backed by Regulators – a Sort of 'Mass Psychoses?' " *Wall Street Journal*, August 9, 1991.

16. Chase Manhattan Bank, *Annual Reports for 1989 and 1990*, New York.

17. Luigi Di Fonzo, *St. Peter's Banker*, Franklin Watts, New York, 1983.

18. *Time*, March, 1986, p. 73.

19. Rupert Conwell, *God's Banker*, Victor Gollanz Ltd., London, pub. in U.S. by Dodd, Mead & Co., New York, 1983.

In 1991, members of the Mafia were still being questioned regarding the death of the head of the collapsed Banco Ambrosiano, Roberto Calvi – called "God's Banker" because of his ties with the Vatican. *Wall Street Journal* of July 31, 1991 quoted British *Reuters* wire service which in turn quoted Mafia informer Francesco Marino Mannoia in Italian newspapers, that Calvi "was killed on the orders of Pippo Callo, a member of the Mafia's so-called cupola, or board of top family leaders, for embezzling money from Mr. Callo and Licio Gelli, former head of the illegal Lodge P-2." Gelli is quoted in the *Corriere Della Sera*, "I can say that Calvi never took anything from me."

According to Penny Lernoux, Gelli had made much of his fortune in South America, under Juan and Isabel Peron in Argentina, where he established a P-2 Chapter in Buenos Aires. See Penny Lernoux, *In Banks We Trust*, Anchor Press/Doubleday, Garden City, 1984.

20. Federal Deposit Insurance Corporation, *1988 Annual Report*, Washington D.C.

21. *FDIC 1991 Annual Report*, Washington. Also, *Financial Audit* by U.S. General Accounting Office, 1992.

Comptroller General Charles A. Bowsher wonders about the sufficiency of provisions in the congressional acts that set up funding for the new SAIF, primarily premiums on S&L deposits plus U.S. Treasury allowances. He fears that $32 billion projected in receipts by the year 2000 will not be sufficient if S&Ls continue to fail in numbers. He allows that projections of troubled S&Ls vary considerably between various federal agencies, committees and boards.

With the FDIC's long-established Bank Insurance Fund (BIF) continuing to decline – reluctantly announced as a *minus* $7 billion dollars as of the beginning of 1992 – the Comptroller General has reason to be concerned about both bank and S&L funds. With the First Republic-NCNB (NationsBank) transaction continuing to be upped in cost to the insurance fund, up from $2.5 billion to $2.9 billion to $3.4 billion, the MBanks-BancOne transaction up from $2.6 billion to $2.8 billion, the Texas-American-Team Bank transaction up from $989 million to $1.1 billion, plus additional large and small troubled bank costs, the adequacy of projections and funds is to be questioned. Of course, neither the Bank Insurance Fund nor the Savings Association Insurance Fund will fail – Congress can instead appropriate more and more, against taxpayers' debt and debt.

CHAPTER 6

Bank Holding Companies, Even Bigger Banking Companies

From a banker whose formerly strong bank sold out to a multi-bank holding company that merged with still another holding company, now in bankruptcy:

> Shortly after we were acquired by the holding company we were sent a $6 million loan participation. After a few days had passed we received a phone call regarding the loan. When we replied that our loan committee was looking at it, we were told, "That loan was not sent to you for your committee to look at. You were given it so that you can return a check for $6 million." We later learned that the loan was already in default when it was sent to us.

From another banker (now with the federal Resolution Trust Corp.) whose strong bank was also sold to a holding company that had extensive losses before selling to a larger interstate holding company that continued to have losses from its acquisitions:

> They hired MBAs by the dozens, gave them short periods of training, turned them loose on commercial loan desks, with disastrous results.

Comparable to the public utility holding company expansion enthusiasm of a half century earlier was the multi-bank holding company expansion enthusiasm of the late 1970s and early 1980s. It was the thing to do. Boston's Bank of New England Corp. acquired the Connecticut Bank & Trust Co. and other New England banks. California-based Bank of America, which had been the largest banking institution in the United States and in the world, was encouraged to take over what had been the largest bank in the adjacent Pacific Northwest, ailing Seafirst Corp. and subsidiary Seattle-First National Bank. This again made BankAmerica Corp. (holding company for Bank of America) the biggest in the land, albeit temporarily. Financial journals and financial regulators favored the strength of bigness. A plausible argument was that geographical size and diversity, as well as financial statement bottom-line footings, added stability to the financial system.

In the Southwest, Dallas banks had long been dominant – with the city's two largest, Republic National and First National, and the Mercantile also prominent in leadership. This didn't seem quite right to the leaders of Houston, a larger city and a seaport. So in the port city, First City National Bank, itself a product of amalgamation of the ultra-conservative First National Bank of Houston, with newer, but also conservative City National, changed that image and began to acquire banks from other cities into its holding company system. Bank of the Southwest, previously Second National, likewise shed its conservative character and began to acquire banks from across the state into its new Southwest Bancshares multi-bank holding company. Texas Commerce, which chiefly grew out of the Jesse Jones-controlled National Bank of Commerce, was more judicious in its holding company growth, reflecting the Jones tradition.

From New England, conservative Everett Ware Smith, who had been vice chairman of New England Merchants National Bank, predecessor of Bank of New England Corp., moved to Cleveland, Ohio, serving two banks there, heading Cleveland Trust Company, later Ameritrust. (Sadly, certain of his successors at Cleveland also sought to diversify, geographically and otherwise, with less than satisfactory results. One even complained of the bank's having too much capital, which, after losses was not true when it sold out to rival Society Bank in 1991.)

Out of Connecticut Bank & Trust, Walter Connolly moved up to lead Bank of New England Corp. at Boston, in an aggressive expansion program that ended only when regulators determined the company was in deep trouble.

On the West Coast, the historic figure of A.P. Gianini was difficult to replace at Bank of America. Several successors attempted to keep its prime position, and the opportunity to cross state lines — by taking on Seattle's ailing Seafirst — seemed to be advantageous. But Bank of America slipped, no longer largest in the world, nor in the United States. (In recent years, Bank of America has closed 10 percent of its branches.) Fifteen years earlier, A. W. (Tom) Clausen, then president of Bank of America, had said at a national conference of Robert Morris Associates at San Francisco that the necessity for liquidity in banks — the ability to meet depositors' withdrawals and to make new loans and investments — is not just textbook theory — it is a real requirement. He said that quality of loans and investments is most important — this before "quality" became such a byword in finance, business, and the media. He told the meeting of bank loan and credit officers — again before problems surfaced in the savings banks, in the S&Ls and in the commercial banks — that financial statements of customers should be studied and understood, not just checked for form. At the 1975 meeting, Clausen warned bankers to do their own homework on participation loans that they purchased from others.[1]

(In the years to come, Seafirst, Continental Illinois, and other big banks buying participation loans from notorious Penn Square Bank were to remember his warning.) Loan participations, accepted without understanding what the loans represented, were also to bankrupt many savings associations when under Garn-St Germain the S&Ls tried to become commercial banks.

Clausen also stated, a decade and a half earlier, that each generation of bankers needs to be re-impressed with these truths. This West Coast banker who was to serve as president of the World Bank before briefly returning to Bank of America said that bankers are also hindered by inertia – guilty of red tape and archaic forms and lazy thinking – just what they accuse government of doing. Clausen also recommended back then that minorities should be given opportunities in banking.

In 1992 the Federal Reserve approved BankAmerica's acquisition of Security Pacific Bank, which put BankAmerica again into second place in size of U.S. banks. Several years earlier a West Coast investment banking company had suggested that Security Pacific acquire BankAmerica. Instead, First Interstate made a long, unsuccessful overture toward acquiring BankAmerica.

Seeking to Stay in Second (if Not First) Place

BankAmerica's 1991 earnings were $1,124 million, just under J.P. Morgan's. (However, this did not include Security Pacific's $775 million loss. Merger with Security Pacific was completed in 1992.) As of year end 1991 BankAmerica had $115.5 billion in assets. Security Pacific had $76.4 billion in assets.

Through the Oakar Amendment (Chapter 5), BankAmerica Corp. in 1992 also picked up for a bargain $103 million the $3.4 billions in assets (mostly cash) and deposits of government operated Sunbelt Savings of Texas from the RTC. The RTC and predecessor S&L regulators who had arranged the aggregation of busted Texas S&Ls into Sunbelt took the loss on assets. BankAmerica also signed a contract with owner Ronald O. Perelman to acquire $7.5 billion First Gibraltar Savings of Texas for $110 million. As part of the "Southwest Plan" federal regulators in 1988 had given Perelman $5.1 billion to cover losses, plus tax breaks, when he took consolidated First Gibraltar. Perelman contributed $314 million.

In the Security Pacific merger BankAmerica Chairman and CEO Richard M. Rosenberg hoped for eventual savings of $1.2 billion annually – primarily from reduced costs of personnel. Quoted in the End Notes to the Introduction to this book is the report by Kenneth Howe of the *San Francisco Chronicle* that Robert Smith, former head of Security Pacific, resigned from his new position as president of Bank of America one month after the merger. According to the *Chronicle* he was to receive a "golden parachute worth $2.2 million."

In 1991 BankAmerica earned .99 percent on assets, down from 1.04 percent in 1990, and 1.14 percent in 1989. This was before the Security Pacific merger and before the latest RTC acquisitions.

In the 1991 *Annual Report*, BankAmerica Chairman Rosenberg stated: "We are not interested in achieving size for its own sake." He mentioned the traditions of A. P. Gianini, who built a great institution by service to customers. A few years ago Bank of America announced a 10 percent reduction in number of branch offices, this before the Security Pacific acquisition. Certain Security Pacific offices will also be closed. There will also be reduction in number of employees for the combined institution. The announced goal in connection with the consolidation was that 60 percent of the costs savings would come from reduction in personnel expense. As with KeyCorp, BankAmerica Corp. also told of holding down the expense to revenue ratio, with the percentage's going down over the previous two years. Over the same years, however, the earnings on assets ratio also decreased.

In the Texas acquisition are many former S&L branches which gave little service except to accept deposits. The federal government as owner or sponsor of the S&Ls was not interested in making loans. BankAmerica Corp. will have a tremendous challenge to keep costs down, perhaps eliminate jobs, but at the same time attract talented lending personnel. Without profitable loan business, additional offices and overhead, and deposits – even at bargain acquisition prices – may add only mediocre earnings.

There were eleven billion-dollar bank holding companies in Texas in 1984. Some merged with one another – supposedly to gain strength – and then went under. Only one was still operating under the same ownership in the 1990s: Cullen/Frost. Two were merged with out-of-state institutions. Some were still being refinanced with FDIC assistance under new ownership. Some of the largest no longer existed, having failed and been replaced by out-of-state entities under FDIC guidance and assistance.

Failure of Dallas' Three Leading Banks

The two largest Southwestern banks had been Republic National Bank and First National Bank (InterFirst), both of Dallas. Long-time CEOs of the two banks, Fred F. Florence at the Republic and Nathan Adams at the First National, were joined by Robert L. Thornton at the Mercantile National Bank at Dallas, competitors and yet co-workers for the betterment of Dallas and its trade area.

Typical of the cooperation was the successful operation of the Texas Centennial Exposition at Dallas in 1936 – remarkable in that Dallas had not existed when Texas Independence was declared in 1836 – also remarkable in that the exposition took place during the midst of the Great Depression.

Florence, Adams and Thornton were the executive committee of the exposition.[2]

All three men had died before the boom and bust of the 1980s. Their successors were not able to keep their banks alive in the environment of holding company expansion and boom-and-bust conditions.

By the mid-1980s Texas Commerce and First City, both of Houston, were threatening to become the Southwest's largest, reinforced by their multi-bank holding companies. In order to continue to be the largest in both the lead bank and in the overall holding system, Republic and InterFirst agreed to merge in mid-1987. InterFirst had already grown in number of banks and assets by acquiring First United of Fort Worth, celebrating the merger via a 30-mile chartered train trip from Dallas to Fort Worth. Republic's acquisitions included what had been Houston National Bank – one of the banks rescued by Jesse Jones 50 years earlier.

The merger of Republic and InterFirst was announced as leading to greater efficiencies and taking care of weaknesses. Combined assets of the two Dallas bank holding company systems totaled more than $38 billion for the 100-plus subsidiary banks at the beginning of 1987. The combined First Republic system lasted just over one year. An admission of difficulties but hope for survival was given in the interim March 31, 1988 *First Quarterly Report*, over the signature of Albert V. Casey, newly elected chairman of the board and CEO of First Republic (formerly head of American Airlines and one-time U.S. Postmaster General and still later chairman of the RTC):

> The Corporation had experienced significant declines in the sources of funds during the first quarter . . . our goals are to return to profitability as quickly as possible and to build a strong and much-needed banking institution in Texas.[3]

In 1990, two years later, in the Bankruptcy Court for the Northern District of Texas, the Fourth Amended Disclosure Statement, submitted to creditors of bankrupt First RepublicBank Corporation, stated:

> In early 1988, First RepublicBank Dallas, N.A., and certain other of the Texas subsidiary banks experienced substantial declines in deposits and other funding sources. News stories in the *Wall Street Journal* and other periodicals detailing the

> deposit outflow seemed to fuel an even greater drain on deposits. The declines created significant liquidity problems, and coupled with the prospect for continuing losses, caused management . . . to discuss funding with the Federal Deposit Insurance Corporation.[4]

Thus, on July 19, 1988 the consolidated 40 banks of First Republic, largest banking company in the Southwest, were all declared insolvent by federal and state regulators by reason that the large Dallas and Houston banks had deficit net worths and all subsidiary banks' stocks had been pledged to the loan to the Federal Deposit Insurance Corp. with a loan to the Federal Reserve Bank of Dallas also owing. The FDIC notified the other regulators that its loan would not be renewed and the dominoes tumbled. Besides the cross pledge of stocks, there were interlocking deposits.

Long-established smaller banks that had thrown in their lot with what had been a $40 billion dollar banking system went down the drain with the biggest of them (though the holding company itself was not taken over). Small and large shareholdings were devastated. Federal regulators then declared that the bankrupt banking system was now one big bank, regardless of the Texas Constitution, (which prohibits branch banking outside the county) so as to allow interstate sale of the whole package under the $500 million assets minimum of the Garn-St Germain Act of 1982. An FDIC-sponsored Bridge Bank, NCNB Texas – a new subsidiary of North Carolina-based NCNB Corp., a banking company smaller than First Republic – was to receive deposits and such assets as it chose.

The North Carolina corporation was also allowed to receive income tax benefits from the failed Texas bank, although the corporations were separate entities, and the North Carolina bank was not required to take on bad loans from the Texas bank. A proposed new banking company that Albert Casey would have created was turned down by the FDIC in favor of the already existing NCNB, 1,000 miles away.

Initially, NCNB Texas operated as a bridge bank of the FDIC. Investment by the North Carolina company was to come later. Initial estimate of loss by the FDIC was $2.5 billion. In 1990, the FDIC estimated its loss in First Republic at $2.9 billion, more than 62 percent of the total 1988 failed-bank costs. A year later the FDIC's estimate of loss on the "First Republic transaction" had been raised to $3.4 billion.[5]

In the FDIC-assisted takeover, NCNB Texas National Bank was allowed to choose those loans and other assets, including banking houses and other facilities, which it deemed economically viable. It was also allowed to collect less-than-desirable loans on behalf of the FDIC for a fee. Subsequently, NCNB (NationsBank) received additional S&L deposits from the RTC as well as nine banks of National Bancshares out of San Antonio, with estimated cost to the FDIC of $263 million on the failed San Antonio company. See Chapter 9 for more on NationsBank and its record of service and earnings. Also see Chapter 9 on what happened to Detroit in the 1930s vs. what happened to Dallas in the 1980s.

In Houston, First City National Bank, a combination of long-established First National Bank and somewhat-newer City National, shed the conservative legacy of F. M. Law of the First National and Judge J.A. Elkins of City National to go on an expansion campaign in the late 1970s. Local and distant banks were brought into a holding company. A more aggressive lending policy took effect. When the Houston bank and certain other banks got into trouble, First City was not shut down as had been First Republic at Dallas. Instead, the subsidiary banks retained their identities in a reorganization.

The FDIC allowed A. Robert Abboud and brokers Donaldson, Lufkin and Jenrette (whom we'll see along with parent Equitable Life in Chapter 10) to put in $500 million new capital, along with $1.5 billion from the FDIC. Old shareholders lost 99 percent of their investment. At the same time that the reorganization took place in 1988, a book by New First City Chairman Abboud, *Money In the Bank: How Safe Is It?*, was published by the Bank Administration Institute. Directors of the First City banks were given copies to display on their desks or lend to friends or would-be bank customers.

The book contained some good information. It also recounted Abboud's career at First National of Chicago with his brief stay at Occidental Petroleum under the imperious Armand Hammer (whom we'll see in connection with Financial General – First American Bankshares in Chapter 8). In the book Abboud also told of his experience at First Chicago in international lending toward which he then attempted to guide New First City, when other U.S. banks were pulling back internationally.

In less than four years First City was again in trouble, partly on loans, international and otherwise, made during Abboud's tenure as chairman before his resignation in 1991.[6] In 1992, the wealthy Coca family of Madrid sued First City for $1.2 billion – over a $140 million international real estate loan which Abboud had approved. Other loans were made to Drexel Burnham Lambert – noted for its junk bonds – and to Federated Department Stores – part of the unsuccessful HLT buyout by Canada's Campeau. Efforts to seek out large national and international loan customers helped to pull First City down.

FDIC-Created New First City Taken Over Anew By FDIC

Criticisms were levied at federal regulators in the latter part of election year 1992 because so few banks had been closed. Earlier predictions of failures had not been met. Thus four days before Election Day of the First Tuesday of November 1992, on Friday evening next to Halloween, 20 First City banks created four years earlier under FDIC sponsorship, with assets of $8.8 billion were closed by the Acting Comptroller of the Currency, the new Texas Banking Commissioner, and the Acting Chairman of the FDIC. These were replaced by 20 newer, New First City Bridge Banks owned by the FDIC. (Top positions in both the national bank examining office and the FDIC had been unfilled since earlier in the year. The U.S. Senate had refused to consent to continuation in office of the previous Comptroller, and the FDIC had been without a Chairman since the death of William Taylor.)

Two First City banks, the flagship Houston bank and the second largest First City Bank at Dallas, were declared to be insolvent by the respective regulators, the Comptroller of the Currency and the Texas Banking Commissioner. The FDIC then determined that the other 18 First City banks should share in the deficiencies under "cross-guarantee" provisions of the 1989 Financial Institutions Reform, Recovery, and Enforcement Act. (Reference to FIRREA was not made in the FDIC's Press Release of 10-30-92. It was given to this writer after inquiry of the FDIC at Washington.) Two more First City banks, the sixth largest at San Antonio and the 11th largest at Austin, were then determined as likewise in deficit capital positions after the cross-assessments. The FDIC announced that depositors in the particular four First City banks would lose 20 percent of their deposits in excess of the insured limit of $100,000. Depositors in the other 16 better-capitalized banks would be paid in full. Estimate was that 5,000 depositors would lose $260 million in the four banks.

Congress' FDIC Improvement Act of 1991 had mandated that future bank closings were to follow the least costly means – and though these provisions were not fully in effect, regulators very likely were reacting to Congressional and public pressure. Too, Washington's thinking may have been that First City with $8.8 billion in assets was not a major banking system. Whereas with First Republic, MCorp, and Texas American all banks had been consolidated into one "bridge bank" – State Constitution to the contrary – with the First City closings 20 bridge banks were created for the

20 First City banks.

In telephone conversations with representatives of the FDIC's Washington headquarters the question was posed by this writer as to whether the 20 bridge banks could be sold interstate, with the $500 million minimum of Garn-St Germain. After consultation amongst themselves a return telephone call allowed that the FDIC might have to consolidate certain banks if interstate sale is most desirable in those particular cases. As indicated, in the past State Constitutional prohibitions have not meant much to Washington regulators – and in Texas the banking industry had given in and obtained a state-wide banking law – based not on Constitution but on federal judges and regulators.

In 1992 as in 1988 federal regulators appeared reluctant to give consideration to First City banks' being reacquired by local interests. Instead, companies and groups who had been involved in other bailouts or acquisitions were mentioned, those who had previously dealt with the FDIC and FSLIC and other still-existent, defunct, or successor federal regulatory agencies.

Veteran First City banker C. Ivan Wilson had replaced Robert Abboud as head of the banking company and had energetically sought to recapitalize the banking company and to sell off local banks to local interests. Wilson was removed by the FDIC. Installed in his place was Washington, D.C. banker Edward G. Harshfield. Harshfield had previously been with New York's Citicorp.

Dennis E. Nixon, president of successful International Bank of Commerce at Laredo, says, regarding First City and other similar federal bailouts-takeovers, that the regulators have made it nearly impossible for private investors to strengthen weakened banks. Instead banks are allowed to fail – at the expense of the Bank Insurance Fund and the bank's shareholders and other creditors, and even depositors. Thus the regulators have a "self fulfillment of their prophecies of failure."

First City's second FDIC takeover cost, initially estimated at $500 million, was completely revised when bids from prospective purchasers totaled $60 million in excess of that amount. The earlier $1.5 billion costs would remain – plus losses to two sets of shareholders, also to bondholders and other creditors, and even to depositors – less the $60 million excess. See chapter Endnote 6 for the latest episode on First City, with effects on communities served and bank employees.

Jesse Jones and Houston

Texas Commerce Bancshares came through better than most. Shareholders sold out to Chemical Bank of New York in 1987 without too great a loss on their investment. Chemical added $248 million additional capital to the Texas subsidiary's reserve for local losses in late 1989, but in 1990 and 1991 had a profit on its Texas Commerce investment. Texas Commerce kept rather well to the Jesse Jones tradition. Jones had gone to Washington in 1932 to join the Reconstruction Finance Corp. (RFC), which was to subsequently strengthen banking, business, insurance and agriculture, and help finance the defense plants of World War II. Before going to Washington, Jones had already given his attention to Houston's banks. When the hard times of the early 1930s hit his home town, Jones saw to it that no Houston bank failed. His own National Bank of Commerce in good shape, he invited the heads of the banks of Houston to his Houston penthouse office for a Sunday meeting in 1931, for workouts of Houston's two ailing banks, the Houston National and Public National. The former, controlled by Texas governor and oil man Ross Sterling, was in financial trouble when oil dropped to 10 cents a barrel. Jones urged the other banks to form guaranty funds, with utilities and certain other business leaders joining in the effort to protect Houston banks and depositors.

When the president of South Texas Commercial Bank (which was in sound condition) hesitated, Jones called that bank's chairman, Captain James A. Baker, prominent Houston attorney and grandfather of U.S. Secretary of the Treasury and Secretary of State James A. Baker III. Baker, who was also Jones' personal attorney, was at his Maine retreat. He approved their bank's cooperation.[7]

When no other Houston bank would save the Public National Bank, Jones allowed that his National Bank of Commerce would take it over.

Fifty years later, Texas Commerce, which had hoped to remain a separate company so as "to forestall acquisition by money center banks," did merge with New York's Chemical Bank but under favorable conditions.[8]

Financier and oil man Jack Brown, who served on the Midland bank's board, explains how Texas Commerce came through better than most.

"We had Ben Love (head of Texas Commerce, carrying on the Jesse Jones tradition of bank soundness)." Brown also said that [other] ". . . bankers got into things they didn't understand."

Under Love's successor, Marc Shapiro, Texas Commerce has continued to operate banks in each community as separate banks — not only abiding by the Texas Constitution but gaining the goodwill of the community by having local boards of directors and local chief financial officers. Chemical Bank gives financial support, but allows Texas banks to serve their communities, rather than merely being satellites and conduits for deposits to the holding company. In 1990, Chemical's net earnings were $291 million. Texas Commerce contributed $104 million of this. In 1991 Manufacturers Hanover Corp. of New York merged into Chemical. Net earnings for the year were but $154 million. Texas Commerce contributed $126 million of the $154 million.

First Interstate

As the name implies, First Interstate Bancorp (FI) of Los Angeles sought to be more than just a California banking company. The name was even franchised. Mentioned earlier was FI's unsuccessful effort to take over giant Bank of America. When Oklahoma's largest bank, billion dollar First National Bank & Trust Co. of Oklahoma City, failed in 1986, the FDIC sold certain assets along with deposits to FI. FI also acquired Allied Banks of Texas, without federal assistance. FI took a $180 million write-down on its Texas assets. In 1990, in a reversal of policy, FI began selling off acquisitions. In 1991, the Oklahoma City bank was sold to strong Boatmen's BankShares of St. Louis for $86 million, less than 1.2 times the Oklahoma City bank's net worth. Deposits of renamed Boatmen's First National Bank were $680 million at the beginning of 1992, third in size among the banks in Oklahoma City. Boatmen's was seeking to move from the former palatial quarters to a more modest structure across the street. Oklahoma City, with 33 percent downtown office vacancy, was in the depressed class with Dallas, which had 32 percent of downtown properties vacant in late 1992.[9]

FI also sold off banks in Iowa, New Mexico and Colorado, and its overseas branches, and slimmed assets more than $8 billion, from $59 billion at the beginning of 1990 to $51 billion at the beginning of 1993. In only three of the six years from 1986 through 1992 did FI show a profit, with return on assets of .57 percent in 1992. The *1991 Annual Report* began with a statement from Chairman of the Board Edward M. Carson: "Our geographic diversification, which has caused disappointing financial results over the past few years, should now, as we look to the future, provide the stability that we are all determined to achieve." In 1992 FI still had operations in 13 states (more states than any other bank). The report also told of a new program to assess the abilities of FI's loan officers and of continuing education for its staff – commendable for any bank.

Letters of Credit

Letters of credit traditionally were financial letters issued by commercial banks to aid customers' purchases, sales or storage of commodities or other products. Extremely useful in international and domestic trade, they simply smooth commercial transactions. A bank acceptance is a draft issued under a letter of credit, accepted by a commercial bank for future payment. There were also travelers' letters of credit, which enabled customers of banks to issue drafts on their home banks when traveling internationally. The latter have been generally superseded by travelers' checks and credit cards, and by the wire transfer of funds between banks of different nations.

Originally, commercial letters of credit were solely for exporting, importing and storing goods. But over the years, letters of credit were allowed to be used as a bank's guarantee to a third party that a bank's customer would make good on a loan. And, in too many cases, banks have been left holding the bag.

Banks were willing to issue these "standby" letters of credit because they could charge large fees and thought they never would have to make good the loans. But time has proved otherwise. One sizeable bank, the $200 million Abilene National Bank, later MBank-Abilene, was in part brought down by entanglement of letters of credit issued before its acquisition by MCorp, which in turn helped to pull down MCorp.

Letters of credit can be proper commercial banking instruments. When misused, they can also lead to abuse and loss, both for customers and banks.

Southwest Bancshares, which grew out of long-established Second National Bank of Houston, later known as Bank of the Southwest, shed the conservative image exemplified by C. M. Malone of the Second National. Seeking not to be second to anyone, Southwest merged with Mercantile of Dallas. Mercantile had likewise moved away from the banking practices of its founder, Robert L. Thornton, Dallas civic leader and mayor.

As with the First and Republic merger, the Southwest and Mercantile merger failed to add strength, even though renamed MCorp with "M" signifying "Momentum." Momentum Place, the MCorp headquarters skyscraper in downtown Dallas, appears to be an example of (Professor C. Northcote) *Parkinson's Law* – that the final palatial structure is often a memorial to the previous live institution. Momentum Place was completed just before the takeover of the lead bank and most of the subsidiary banks by the regulatory authorities in 1989. The adjacent office buildings previously filled by the former Mercantile Bank's customers and tenants are today starkly vacant.

After a nine-month stand-off between the regulators and management of MCorp a threatened bankruptcy of MCorp by creditors allowed the Comptroller of the Currency to declare 20 of the 25 MBanks as insolvent on March 28, 1989. Certain MBanks, including those along the Texas-Mexico border, were exempted because of their financial strength and because there had been no cross-pledging of assets as with First Republic. Consolidating the 20 into one, again overriding the Texas Constitution so as to qualify the banks into a minimum of $500 million in assets for an interstate sellout under Garn-St Germain, the FDIC formed an $11 billion Deposit Insurance Bridge Bank three months later. On June 28, it was awarded to healthy Banc One Inc. of Columbus, Ohio.

Like NCNB of Charlotte, North Carolina, the Ohio bank got preference over large money center banks, perhaps in part because of stronger financial ratios of the Ohio and North Carolina banks as compared to major banks of New York, Chicago, San Francisco and other money market centers.

Both NCNB and Banc One then picked up ailing S&Ls' deposits in several states, Banc One getting the $2.7 billion deposits of Dallas-based Bright Banc Savings from the RTC.

In his "Management Report to Shareholders" at the annual meeting of Banc One stockholders on April 17, 1990, Chairman John B. McCoy said of the acquisition of the former Texas MBanks deposits and assets:

> . . . we knew we would not even submit a bid unless we had credit guarantees from the FDIC similar to those NCNB (North Carolina National Bank) had negotiated in buying the failed First Republic Bank.[10]

Speaking of the Texas acquisition, and perhaps eventually other acquisitions as well, McCoy added:

> . . . had to be 50 percent of book value, we had to have the ability to put all the problem loans to the government, there could be no viable thrift competitors and no retail bank competitors except the number one bank in the state. That, in a nutshell, is our deal in Texas.

Details of Banc One's initial $34 million investment and the FDIC's initial $416 million investment in the former MBanks are given in Appendix H. In 1990 the FDIC estimated its total costs attributable to the 20 failed MBanks at $2.6 billion. (In 1991 the estimate was increased to $2.8 billion.) Surviving bankrupt MCorp and the FDIC continued to spar in the courts.

Texas American Bancshares was an outgrowth of the former very strong, very conservative Fort Worth National Bank. Founded by

K.M. Van Zandt and associates, it was the epitome of ranching and commercial stability. In the 1980s, carried away with the euphoria of growth of its new holding company, it suffered loan losses and sought guidance, and possible bailout and merger, from the federal regulators. On April 28, 1988 the holding company admitted that its three largest banks – Fort Worth, Dallas and Houston – were insolvent.

A tentative bailout by bank owner and sports principal Carl R. Pohlad of Minneapolis was announced. A year later an announcement was made that this would not be concluded, and an offer by Ronald Steinhart, head of new Deposit Guaranty Bank of Dallas – an amalgamation of several small FDIC-distressed properties – was allowed by the FDIC to be consummated. Acquisition was of deposits and of some loans and other assets, under the name Team Bank. FDIC costs from the Texas American failure are estimated at $1.1 billion as of 1992.

National Bancshares Corporation, like Texas American, was an outgrowth of an old, established and sound institution, National Bank of Commerce of San Antonio. The lead bank and the other banks adopted the abbreviated NBC Bank name. The NBC Banks also fell on hard times and considered a merger with Texas American Bancshares, hoping for FDIC assistance. It wasn't done.

Under FDIC guidance, NBC then looked for a possible bailout with Carl Pohlad of Minneapolis or with Equitable Bank of Pittsburgh. When nothing else worked out, in 1990 the regulators declared a majority of the NBC banks insolvent and sold deposits and prime assets to NCNB Texas, as it had done with the Southwest's largest banking system, First Republic. The North Carolina-based holding company, which also has acquired deposits of several S&Ls from the Resolution Trust Corp., is now by far Texas' largest banking institution. Estimated cost to the FDIC on the NBC takeover: $263 million.

Smallest of the billion-dollar holding companies, BancTexas' lead bank traced its history to the long-established, ultra-conservative National Bank of Commerce of Dallas, which had merged with Empire State Bank, founded by able banker Michaux Nash. National Bank of Commerce was long headed by the Adoue family. Jean Baptiste Adoue Jr. served as mayor of Dallas. A long-time tennis player, ultra-conservative Adoue had done his civic duty by playing tennis with Franklin D. Roosevelt's ultra-liberal third-term running mate, Henry Wallace. Adoue did not live to see the changes in his bank. As one of the staff of the BancTexas days stated; "We are rather high rollers."

FDIC assistance was provided for two takeovers of BancTexas, with certain sound "country banks" sold off. First FDIC assistance was in a 1987 recapitalization in which the FDIC contributed $150 million with the Hallwood Group, New York firm, underwriting an offer of $50 million.

Three years later the remaining holding company lead banks were again declared insolvent, and deposits and some assets were sold to Hibernia Corp. of New Orleans' new Texas subsidiary, Hibernia Bank of Pflugerville, operating out of the town of Pflugerville, Texas (population 750). In 1990 the FDIC estimated overall BancTexas cost to the FDIC at $254 million. In 1991, Hibernia, facing losses in its expanded Louisiana empire, sought to sell its nearly new Texas operation.

In 1992 Hibernia sold its Texas operation to Comerica of Detroit for $58 million – a loss of $17 million from what Hibernia had invested in its FDIC assisted venture in Texas. (Hibernia was partially compensated by dividend income received during its Texas operation.) More is told of Comerica – formerly Detroit Bank & Trust – in Chapters 9 and 14. The Detroit bank's long-time able head, Joseph Dodge, represented the United States in the rebuilding of the banking systems of Germany and Japan after World War II. Comerica's management does not take on other banking systems unless these make economic sense – rather than simply following Washington regulators in their attempts to push particular programs, super-regional or otherwise.

The Texas Exception – Cullen/Frost

The one banking institution of Texas' 11 billion-dollar holding companies that did not sell out, did not seek FDIC assistance and did not collapse is Cullen/Frost. Headquartered in San Antonio, long that city's largest bank, Frost National has been in business more than 100 years, and is now led by a fourth-generation member of the Frost family. Joined by the Cullen family at Houston, and the Kempner family at Galveston, Cullen/Frost pulled through the difficult years of the 1980s when every other holding company in Texas either gave up its ownership or went under financially. Only Cullen/Frost exceeded the state average in the number of its member banks that showed a profit in the difficult year of 1987, when all other holding companies performed below average. In earlier years when other big Southwestern banks were seeking to acquire the largest number of offices and to make the biggest loans, Frost withstood the temptation to run with the herd. As the new century approaches, Frost appears ready to go into still another century of service.

Bank of New England Corp.

Bank of New England Corp., Boston, was to be the example of what a super-regional, interstate banking system could do for staid New England. At the beginning of 1989 (December 31, 1988), financial figures showed $32 billion in assets, up from $30 billion a year earlier, and double the $16 billion of five years earlier.

Shareholders' equity was $1.6 billion, 5.1 percent of assets, highest in dollars ever, and higher in percentage than in any of the preceding three years. Non-performing assets were only 1.68 percent of total assets, an apparent improvement from 1.76 percent the previous year.

The corporation showed net earnings of $282 million, highest ever, at .94 percent of assets, a desirable ratio for a large banking institution. One year later, December 31, 1989, the bottom had dropped out. Super-regional Bank of New England Corp. announced a $1.1 billion loss for the year. Assets were under $30 billion at the beginning of 1990 and continued to fall throughout the year. Shareholders' equity was only $458 million, compared to $1,641 million a year earlier. Non-performing assets were more than five times what had been reported a year earlier, $2,203 million, compared to $419 million of a year earlier.[11]

During its last year, Bank of New England struggled to keep its credibility in the world-currency and interest-swap markets, with off-balance-sheet liabilities greater than reported assets. More than $30 billion in foreign obligations was finally wound down. These are part of the heritage of the failure of Bretton Woods and the ending of fixed exchange rates.

In early 1990, the corporation board fired chairman Walter J. Connolly, former Hartford banker, who had engineered the big interstate bank merger. A year later, in early 1991, federal regulators closed what remained of Bank of New England Corp. after additional heavy losses were reported and capital had completely disappeared.

Ex-chairman Connolly was quoted by Joanne Johnson of the *Hartford Courant* as saying the merger was a mistake, that he was "terribly sorry" about the crisis that led the FDIC to seize the three remaining banks, and that the wisdom of merging the Connecticut and Massachusetts banks in the first place would have to be questioned.[12]

Outsiders can wonder if problems had been present at Bank of New England Corp. all along. But if so, these were ignored or covered up by an apparently never-ending economic boom in New England.

During the one-year interim, ex-Boston banker Lawrence K. Fish returned to New England to try to lead Bank of New England Corp. out of the wilderness. He sold the Rhode Island bank Old Colony-Newport National – to Citizens Finance, a subsidiary of the Royal Bank of Scotland. He sold leasing and credit card operations to the Bank of Tokyo, Japan. No new capital stock was sold; the corporation appeared to be in a failing position. An offer by Springfield and Western Massachusetts citizens to buy back Bank of New England Corp. West was turned down.

With continuing losses and after threatened runs by depositors, in early 1991, all of the Massachusetts system and the Connecticut and Maine banks were taken over by the FDIC.

Connecticut Bank & Trust Co., founded in 1832 at Hartford, had gone through growth times and hard times of the 19th and 20th centuries. The more-than-150-year-old bank perished in the interstate holding company

Surely the economy was difficult in the 1980s and 1990s. But Merchants National Bank at Boston, founded in 1831, like Connecticut Bank & Trust had survived at least three financial panics of the 19th century – as well as the Great Depression of the 20th century. It was management that failed at the Bank of New England.

The Third National Bank at Springfield, founded during the Civil War in 1864, was likewise lost. Stodgy old Third National's inconspicuous brick building on Main Street in Springfield had been vacated when Bank of New England-West moved into multi-story Monarch Place in 1987.

In 1991, building owner Monarch Capital was also having financial trouble.[13] The initials "BNE" had appeared on all four sides of the building tower.[14]

Also during 1991, the Federal Deposit Insurance Corp. (FDIC), perhaps bowing to criticisms for its previous cross-country sales of failed bank holding companies, allowed Rhode Island-based Fleet/Norstar Financial Group, Inc. to acquire the remnants of Bank of New England Corp. In a joint venture with Wall Street buy-out specialists Kohlberg, Kravis, Roberts & Co., the Providence banking company obtained deposits and such assets as Fleet/KKR might choose from the remnants of the holding company's banks in Connecticut, Massachusetts and Maine. The depleting FDIC Bank Insurance Fund was to take the loss – in billions of dollars as would be determined – initially estimated at $2.5 billion.[15]

Bank Holding Companies

A holding company can serve a useful and proper purpose. A

holding company may also abuse its functions.

The Board of Governors of the New York Stock Exchange in 1926 employed J.B.M. Hoxsey, vice president of the Bell Telephone System at Atlanta, to report on whether holding companies and investment trusts should be listed on the exchange. According to Matthew Josephson in *The Money Lords*, Hoxsey said that "holding companies such as Insull's in utilities and the Van Swearingen's in railroads were . . .

> ". . . necessarily bad . . . a mere exploitation of what may be termed the surplus earnings of the operating companies during periods of prosperity, and a temptation to rape the subsidiaries for the benefit of the holding company."[16]

Samuel Insull, mentioned elsewhere in this book, and Mantis and Oris Van Swearingen leveraged utilities and railroad operations to the extreme. The empires collapsed when times got tough. This was also to happen some 60 years later in some of the bank holding companies when they became overly dependent upon their subsidiary banks for survival.

No More Credit from the Bank

The head of a long-established, family-owned Southwestern distributing company recalls that, as with his father before him, he used to call on the long-established bank in his city for credit needs. On occasion, the company might need up to $500,000 to carry a particular job, so for several years the business maintained a half-million dollar line of credit with the bank. The company's financial record continues to be excellent, going back nearly 100 years under the same ownership.

In years gone by, as with his father before him, the head of the business would visit the head of the bank at least once a year to review the company's progress and possible credit needs. Likewise, the banking leader would visit their firm to show appreciation for their business and to see how they were getting along.

The banker is now dead. The bank, without his leadership, also died, a victim of his successors' attempts to build a widely geographic multi-bank holding company. The federal regulators awarded deposits, and some assets, at a loss of several billion dollars to the bank insurance deposit fund — to an out-of-state institution.

The distributing company head says the new owners were wise in that they kept a couple of old-time bankers who have some knowledge of what is going on in his business. But to get a loan commitment is now uncertain. Thus, he doesn't depend on the new banking institution for credit, although he still maintains the company deposits there. Instead, he carries credit for customers out of his own resources, necessarily at a smaller volume than in years gone by. (He requests that his name not be given, as he might have to ask the out-of-state bank management for some future credit need.)

C & S/Sovran and NCNB

During 1991 the not-yet-two-year-old super-regional Southeastern bank holding company, C&S/Sovran, decided its merger of Citizens & Southern Bank of Atlanta, Georgia, and Sovran of Richmond and Norfolk, Virginia, was a mistake. Whereas in 1989 each company had been reporting good earnings and assets, by mid-1991 the merged six-state-and-District of Columbia super-regional holding company admitted it had problems. An officer in the Atlanta office of what had been C&S indicated these came chiefly from Washington's real estate market. (Not even federal spending could keep the national capital's real estate market booming forever.)

But with the blessing of bank regulators in Washington, it was proposed to merge the troubled $50 billion C&S/Sovran (the 12th largest in the nation) into the $65 billion NCNB Corporation under the name "NationsBank."

A problem facing Atlanta civic leaders was the relocation within their city of C&S headquarters, from downtown to a more uptown site. Consolidation of C&S/Sovran into NCNB would solve this quandary, as headquarters would be in North Carolina.

Southeast and First Union

At the same time, super-regional bankers and national regulators proposed to bail out ailing $13 billion Southeast Banking Corp. of Miami by merger into $32 billion First Union Corp. of Charlotte, North Carolina with FDIC assistance. The Federal Deposit Insurance Corp. offered to cover 85 percent of Southeast's bad loans, up to five years (from the depleting FDIC bank insurance fund). At the same time, First Union would close 119 Florida branches and lay off 2,800 employees. NCNB passed the opportunity of absorbing Southeast to negotiate instead the takeover of C&S/Sovran with the new name of NationsBank. First Union, operating in North Carolina and Georgia and with limited office in Nashville, Tennessee would have a larger presence in Florida through the FDIC-assisted takeover of Southeast. Although First Union already had some loan problems according to the *Wall Street Journal*, from "earlier acquisitions" with FDIC backing, it was not expected to add to these from the Southeast acquisition.[17] Reported in the previous chapter was the first (Oakar Amendment) loss of $21 million to the new SAIF, part of an initial $178 million charge to the FDIC on the Southeast failure.

Even Bigger Banking Companies

The preferred solution, according to national regulators, politicians and many in the media, for lack of success in super-regional banking ventures, would appear to be for even-larger, super-regional banks.

Going Along Pays Off Well

In 1992 the owners of Team Bank, whose major deposits and selected assets had been acquired less than two years previously out of ailing Texas American Bancshares of Fort Worth, announced that they had agreed to sell their largely FDIC-created institution to Banc One Corp. of Columbus, Ohio. Banc One, which had earlier received deposits and selected assets from all of the MBanks which the regulators were able to declare insolvent, announced it would pay what amounted to 2.2 times Team's year-end book value.

The Team stockholders included Ronald Steinhart, the New York investment banking firms of Goldman Sachs & Co., Dillon Read & Co., and Allen & Co., and the Harvard Endowment Fund (Aeneas Group). At $782 million, they stood to receive "nearly three times the $270 million put up between February 1988 and February 1990," according to The *Wall Street Journal*. The *Journal* said:

> It also vindicates Mr. Steinhart's early backers, such as Goldman Sachs & Co., and the Harvard University Endowment Fund, which bet on him at a time when Texas banks were pariahs on Wall Street. Not only had most of the state's major banks collapsed by then, but Mr. Steinhart himself had served as president of one of the biggest casualties, InterFirst Corp. of Dallas, shortly before it cratered.[18]

In its short time operating the former Texas American banks, Team's management, in addition to having no bad loans (the FDIC taking these), had cut operating costs in the new branches, including the former venerable Fort Worth National Bank. Staffs were pruned drastically and quarters reduced in size. Even so, for the 56 branches Team acquired, the *WSJ* reported that for 1991 "return on assets was a lackluster 0.76 percent; 1 percent is considered good."

As recounted earlier, Carl Pohlad of Minneapolis had kept the FDIC waiting for more than a year on the Texas American banks acquisition before he finally pulled out of the deal. Team, formerly Deposit Guaranty, was then allowed to step in, with some priority given them as a local group.

For Banc One, the Team acquisition would also be a big entrée in trust business in Texas, Banc One standing to gain $5.3 million in trust assets from the acquisition. In its earlier acquisition of failed MBanks, there were no trust assets. Ailing MCorp sold its trust division in 1990 to Ameritrust Corp. of Cleveland, Ohio. (It, in turn, was taken over by Society Bank of Cleveland in 1992.)

Going along with the federal regulators in their goals of ever larger super-regional banking systems would appear to pay well to the short-term owners of Team Bank, including several Wall Street investment banking firms. The astute Allen & Co., Dillon Read & Co. (Treasury Secretary Nicholas Brady's old firm), and Goldman Sachs would profit well. Whereas Goldman waited many months in its futile efforts toward facilitating a merger of First Interstate and Bank of America, earning only consultation fees, the brokerage firm would nearly triple its investment on what it had helped purchase from the FDIC in the Team acquisition.

Through its Team acquisition Banc One would also move from 12th to 10th place in size of U.S. banking companies, as well as increase its presence in Texas. Previously, only North Carolina-based NationsBank had been favored by two major acquisitions of failed Texas banking companies, First Republic and NBC. Banc One would now also have two such systems to build on in Texas. (Both NationsBank and Banc One had also been allowed to acquire various failed Texas S&Ls.) Profit to the owners of Team on the sale to Banc One would be about $457 million. Loss to the FDIC insurance fund on the Texas American bank failures, estimated at $989 million in 1990, was increased to $1.1 billion in 1991.

Suits by the FDIC and RTC Discourage Local Ownership

Directors of banks and S&Ls should exercise reasonable, prudent, oversight of the management of financial institutions. But the unfortunate fact that a bank or S&L may have financial problems is not an automatic reason for bank or S&L regulators (sometimes a year or more later) to come after members of boards of directors. To attempt collections of multi-million dollar claims just because some of the former board members may be well-off – at least before the FDIC's and RTC's hired law firms hit them for all they are worth – is not necessarily right. Gretchen Morgenson in *Forbes* says: "It's time for Congress to call off this witch-hunt and face up to its own responsibility in causing the disaster. What did Congress think would happen when it handed Uncle Sam's credit cards to a lot of people and didn't put proper restriction on how they used them?'' Such was the effect of Garn-St Germain and other disastrous acts of Congress.

As *Forbes* sums it up: ''In the name of recovering money for the taxpayer two government agencies are destroying the livelihoods of innocent people and scaring bankers into closing their loan windows.''[19]

The threat of multi-million-dollar liability suits has caused many bank and S&L directors to quit their jobs or to shy away from new elections to bank and S&L boards of directors. This particularly has hit locally owned financial institutions. The most-recently-approved, super-regional, federally sponsored banking companies would appear immune to such treatment.

NOTES

1. A.W. Clausen, ''The Banking Environment,'' keynote address to the Annual Fall Conference of Robert Morris Associates, San Francisco, November 3, 1975 (from notes of the author).

Gary Hector in his book on BankAmerica blames Tom Clausen as well as successor Samuel Armacoast for many of the giant West Coast bank's problems. See Gary Hector, *Breaking the Bank: The Decline of BankAmerica*, Little Brown & Co., Boston, 1988.

Also see *1991 Annual Report* and *2nd Quarter 1992 Report*, BankAmerica Corp., San Francisco. Also, David LaGesse, '' Bank, thrift to merge,'' *Dallas Morning News* September 22, 1992.

2. Kenneth B. Ragsdale, *The Year America Discovered Texas; Centennial '36*, Texas A&M University Press, College Station, 1987.

3. First RepublicBank Corporation, *First Quarter Report Statement* of newly elected chairman Albert V. Casey, Dallas, March 31, 1988.

4. *Fourth Amended Disclosure Statement* of Bankruptcy Court for the Northern District of Texas, Dallas, In Re: First RepublicBank Corporation and IFRB Corporation, Debtors, May 19, 1990.

5. For estimated loss of $2.9 billion on First Republic, see John O'Keefe, ''The Texas Banking Crisis: Causes and Consequences 1980-1989,'' *FDIC Banking Review*, Winter, 1990, *Federal Deposit Insurance Corporation*, Washington, D.C. Later figure of $3.4 billion in *Annual Report*, Federal Deposit Insurance Corporation for 1990, dated October 15, 1991.

In mid-1992 another group that had hoped to acquire First Republic deposits, Lone Star Partners, brought suit against NationsBank, seeking up to $4 billion damages. The suit said ''NationsBank should be forced to give up control of former First Republic assets,'' according to a report by David LaGesse in July 25, 1992 *Dallas Morning News*. The suit alleges that Hugh L. McColl III, son of NationsBank's chief executive Hugh L. McColl, Jr., was an employee of Bear Stearns & Co., which investment banking firm also represented then NCNB, now NationsBank. The late, former U.S. Senator John Tower of Texas had been a member of the Lone Star Partners. According to the *Dallas Morning News*, attorney Carl David Adams said the goal of John Tower and partners had been ''to keep First Republic out of foreign hands.'' Included in the suit was the name of Dresdner Bank of Frankfurt, Germany, which had committed $500 million for the Lone Star bid, but which was also identified in news reports as a partner of NCNB. NCNB reported that Dresdner did not participate in the purchase. July 28 *Dallas Morning News* reported a counter-suit by NationsBank Corp., attorneys for the North Carolina bank claiming the suit by Lone Star

Partners as "nothing more than part of a scheme to unjustifiably extract money from defendants by threatening to publicize false allegations."

6. *Annual and Quarterly Reports*, First City Bancorporation, Houston, 1989, 1990, and 1991.

A. Robert Abboud, *Money in the Bank: How Safe Is It?*, Bank Administration Institute, Homewood, Illinois, 1988.

Jim Fuquay, "First City collapses once more," *Fort Worth Star Telegram*, October 31, 1992. Christi Harlan, "U.S. Takes Over at First City Bancorp., Texas, Regulators' Step Squelches Effort to Recapitalize Without Federal Help," *Wall Street Journal*, November 2, 1992. David LaGesse, "20 First City banks seized by regulators, *Dallas Morning News*, October 31, 1992. Mark Wrolstad, "Era ends for big Texas banks," *Dallas Morning News*, November 1, 1992, Telephone conversation with Dennis E. Nixon, International Bank of Commerce, Laredo, Texas, November 3, 1992. Also, *FDIC News Release*, PR-150-92 (10-30-92). Telephone conversation with FDIC, Washington, November 1992.

In early 1993 the FDIC announced sale of the $9 billion assets of 20 New First City Bridge Banks. The five largest at Houston, Dallas, Beaumont, El Paso and Midland went to New York based Chemical Bank's Texas Commerce subsidiary. Frost of San Antonio received San Antonio and Austin banks. Little Rock, Arkansas' First Commercial and Oak Park, Illinois' FBOP Corp. received banks at Tyler and Lufkin and at Madisonville. Other banks were sold to existing Texas commercial and savings banks, but except for the bank at Alice, none went to local interests. The FDIC admitted that its two month earlier estimate of $500 million loss may have been a miscalculation, as bids totaled more than that amount with a $60 million surplus. Part of the excess would go to some of the depositors who had suffered losses in the closings by the regulatory authorities. Bank analyst Frank Anderson of Stephens, Inc. was quoted in January 28, 1993 *Wall Street Journal*: "The first question that comes to mind is, if the FDIC cut such a good deal, then why were they so quick to pull the plug on First City's plan?" Robert Brown, chief financial officer of First City Bancorp., who with associates had been working on selling certain First City banks with recapitalization of the others, said the FDIC's miscalculation was even bigger than officials are conceding. An early estimate was that 1,700 jobs would be lost, just in the Chemical acquisition. The Texas Commerce subsidiary would not assume real estate properties and commercial loans in the Dallas and Houston banks and would be covered by a five-year loss sharing agreement with the FDIC. Objections from the U.S. Justice Dept. under the new Clinton administration, that banking competition would be lessened and lending to small businesses and others would be more difficult, caused Texas Commerce to agree to sell the banks at Midland and Beaumont, save that it would retain indirect consumer loans and trust operations. The El Paso bank would go to St. Louis' Boatmen's Bancshares. (See February 12 and 24, 1993 *Dallas Morning News*.)

7. Bascom N. Timmons, *Jesse H. Jones: The Man and The Statesman*, Henry Holt & Co., New York, 1956.

8. Harry Waddell, "Editor's Column," *ABA Banking Journal*, February, 1984. Quotes from letters from Marshall E. Surratt, and from Ben Love, then chairman and CEO of Texas Commerce Bancshares, regarding Jesse H. Jones. And, Walter L. Buenger and Joseph A Pratt, *But Also Good Business: Texas Commerce Banks, and the Financing of Houston and Texas,* 1886-1986, Texas A&M Press, College Station, 1986. Also, Jack E. Brown, Midland, conversation, November, 1990.

9. First Interstate Bancorp, *1991 and 1992 Annual Reports*, Los Angeles. Also, Steve Brown, "Office vacancies downtown hit all-time high of 32 percent," *Dallas Morning News*, October 14, 1992. And telephone conversations with Dan Bush and Stacy Martin, *Daily Oklahoman*, October, 1992. Also, Boatmen's Bancshares, Inc., *1991 Annual Report*, St. Louis.

10. Banc One, *1989 Annual Report*, Columbus, Ohio

11. Bank of New England Corp., *1989 Annual Report*, Boston.

12. Joanne Johnson, "Connolly, ex-BNE head, admits merger was a mistake," *Hartford (Connecticut) Courant*, January 12, 1991. Information on Rhode Island bank sale from John Kostrzewa of the *Providence Journal*, telephone conversation, August 27, 1992.

13. Carolyn Robbins, "Towering Troubles," *Sunday Republican* (Springfield, Massachusetts), January 27, 1991.

14. William J. McMordie, Agawam, Massachusetts, letter of March 4, 1991.

15. Nancy Piccin and Jo Ann Moriarty, "Fleet bid wins assets of BNE R.I., company to take over bank," *Springfield Union News*, April 23, 1991. In the same issue, staff writer Christopher Geehern told of a New York group, Private Capital Partners, Inc. that hoped to provide new capital to keep Monarch Capital and Monarch Life alive and in Springfield.

16. Matthew Josephson, *The Money Lords, the Great Finance Capitalists 1925-1950*, Weybright and Talley, New York, 1972. The quotation from J.B.M. Hoxsey is from *Time*, February 8, 1937, at U.S. Senate hearing on railroads.

See other references to Samuel Insull and Middle West Utilities in this book. The Van Swearingen brothers, who had developed attractive Shaker Heights in suburban Cleveland and downtown Union Station and Terminal Tower, in their heyday controlled the Missouri Pacific Railroad, Texas & Pacific Railroad, and related lines. The Missouri Pacific was to fall into receivership for many years, finally coming out and eventually being purchased by the Union Pacific Railroad.

Dan Cordtz took 'A look at America's real estate moguls down through the ages,' in *Financial World*, November 12, 1991, beginning with Robert Morris, and including John Jacob Astor, Jay Cooke, Henry M. Flagler, Carl J. Fisher, Oris and Mantis Van Swearingen, and William Zeckendorf.

17. Martha Brannigan, "First Union Flexing Its Muscle in Florida. Bank Scores by Acquiring Assets of Southeast, American Pioneer," *Wall Street Journal*, September 23, 1991.

18. See Gabriella Stern and Michael Allen, "Banc One Corp. Agrees to Buy a Dallas Bank," *Wall Street Journal*; Mitchell Schnurman, "Steinhart fashioned a gem from Texas banks' rubble," *"Fort Worth Star-Telegram*; and David LaGesse, "Team Bank sale sign of industry recovery," *Dallas Morning News*, March 24, 1992

In 1991 the Texas legislature changed the state law to allow state-wide branch banking, though the Texas Constitution still prohibited it. This, in effect, allowed the state-chartered banks to do what the federal regulators and judges had by regulation and ruling declared to be the law for national-chartered banks, state constitution to the contrary.

A word of bitterness regarding the heritage from dealings with the government's bank regulators, from a retired officer of a large bank (who asked to remain in anonymous):

"It is odd how employees pension fund, bondholders, and shareholders lost so heavily, the public also taking a big loss – and two years later the new owners could sell out for half a billion dollars profit. It is also an irony that ex-officers should pay 5 percent to an attorney to get their lump sum pension when senior executives paid nothing to get much larger settlement funds."

19. Gretchen Morgenson, "What did pop expect to happen when he gave the kid his credit card?", *Forbes*, September 28, 1992.

CHAPTER 7

Credit Unions, Farm Credit, Other Federal Credit, Fractional Reserve Banking, Bank For International Settlements, Brokered Deposits

The Credit Unions

In the olden days, when commercial bankers thought of hard times, or had time to spare, they used to rail against the savings and loans as unfair, or potentially unfair, competition. After Congress through Garn-St Germain declared the S&Ls to be like banks, with such disastrous results and failures, commercial bankers decided the S&L menace was more chaos than competition. And since they had to have *someone* to complain about, they took up the threat of credit unions.

They also argued that credit unions, theoretically nonprofit, cooperative in nature and exempt from federal corporation taxes, should not try to expand into larger ventures, if they wanted to keep their tax-exempt status.

Fortunately for their own continued success, credit unions have pretty well stuck to that which they do best, serving their members; although in 1990 some non-federally insured Rhode Island credit unions did get into trouble, having followed the path of some of the S&Ls by making loans outside their expertise. Often employees of a particular business or government agency, credit union members are known to one another. They pool their savings. They borrow when need be. Oftentimes the loans are paid through payroll deductions. With dedication nearly a religion, credit union leaders have seen to their cause, and since 1970 have been federally insured through the National Credit Share Insurance Fund. "Corporate credit unions" coordinate check (or share draft) clearings, also pool funds and facilitate borrowings by the local credit unions. The National Credit Union Administration Central Liquidity Facility supplies liquidity needs of credit unions.

In Texas, credit unions even own a bank, the Town North National Bank of Farmers Branch.

Some communities have community-wide credit unions, often outgrowths of previous industry or military base credit unions, which continued after the industry or military base left the area.

In the *1989 Annual Report* of the National Credit Union Administration, Chief Economist Charles Bradford reported with some pride that the capital ratio of the federally insured credit unions of the United States is considerably higher than the standard for commercial banks. He also stated that "credit unions are not engaged in some of the risky lending and investing activities of banks."[1]

By 1992, 80 percent of the depositors in the failed Rhode Island credit unions had been paid from a special state sales tax, and others were continuing to be paid, according to John Kostrzewa of the *Providence Journal*.

The credit unions should be proud. They have done well in doing that when they know best, not seeking to preempt others' turfs, as the S&Ls did so disastrously.

Federal Housing Administration (FHA)

Nearly as old as the Federal Deposit Insurance Corp. (FDIC), and the now defunct Federal Savings & Loan Insurance Corp. (FSLIC), the Federal Housing Administration (FHA) was created by Congress under the National Housing Act of 1934. Original purpose of the FHA was to insure mortgage loans for single family homeowners. Like every federal agency, FHA has mushroomed over the years. Congress has added, and added, to the FHA's responsibilities – in subsidized housing, in multi-family housing, even in hospitals. The FHA itself has been under the administrations of several federal offices. It is now part of the U.S. Department of Housing and Urban Development (HUD). As with most supposed business ventures of the federal government, the FHA has been operating at a loss. Like most other federal insurance operations, the FHA's insurance trust funds were at a danger point in the early 1990s.

For all its insurance operations, the FHA lost $4.2 billion in 1988 and $3.9 billion during 1989, according to HUD's report issued in 1991. The report of independent accountants Price Waterhouse stated that FHA's Mutual Mortgage Insurance (MMI) Fund's equity of $1.0 billion (insurer of single family mortgages) is "not sufficient to protect against adverse economic conditions."

At least there is some equity in that fund, compared to a *deficit* of $6.4 billion in FHA's GI Insurance Fund, incurred "primarily relating to its multi-family coinsurance programs." These deficits were reported to have come chiefly through "several FHA lender/coinsurers in default of their obligations for GNMA securities backed by multi-family coinsured mortgages." Congress allows the FHA insurance funds to borrow from the U.S. Treasury, supposedly to be repaid from future net insurance earnings. U.S. taxpayers most likely will pay off these deficiencies, just as they will pay off

FSLIC and other ill-fated federal insurance ventures.

General Accounting Office on the FHA

During 1991 the U.S. General Accounting Office sent a report to HUD Secretary Jack Kemp titled, "Monitoring of Single Family Mortgages Needs Improvement."[3] The conclusion was that the FHA had depended too much on private mortgage companies in underwriting single-family mortgages, and that such procedures needed tightening. No doubt such was true. But even more costly to the entire FHA insurance program was the enlargement of FHA insurance to cover multi-family projects, hospitals and subsidized housing designed to benefit citizens but extremely costly to those who also pay taxes. Promoters of such projects gained from these programs. Perhaps some residents did. Taxpayers did not.

Farm Credit Agencies

The farm credit agencies are still another story. Long considered models for federal sponsorship of private agricultural credit, the Federal Land Bank System goes back to 1917. This was the system of local farm land banks making long-term real estate loans to farmers and ranchers. The Intermediate Credit Banks were established in 1926 and strengthened in the 1930s when the Banks for Cooperatives were also organized.

In 1988, the Federal Land Bank of Jackson, Mississippi got into financial difficulty and had to be liquidated, shattering a record of stability that had stood for 71 years. A former farmer-borrower customer described the Jackson Land Bank in its last days as having splurged on a palatial headquarters building – a "small *Taj Mahal*," he called it. He also said the Jackson bank gave little consideration to its farmer customers as the bank itself got into financial trouble, unwilling to renew farm mortgages, putting both farmers and the bank out of business. Description of the Jackson bank's imposing building fills a requisite of *Parkinson's Law* – an institution achieving expensive indulgence just at the time that it is failing in purpose – and like the *Taj Mahal*, a burying place.

FDIC examiners and liquidators were brought in to assist in the liquidation of the Jackson bank, but the disaster was largely ignored by the news media. With the bank's over-extension attributed in large part to falling land values, Congress, seeing the handwriting on the wall, stepped in to approve a combination of land banks and intermediate credit banks, and proposed to cut the remaining number by half. Such refinancing was to be via a new Farm Credit System Assistance Corp., with assessments on existing farm credit associations.

The Banks for Cooperatives were also urged to consolidate.

The overall Farm Credit System (FCS) consolidation effort was not received with much favor in some areas of the country. Some local associations brought suit, while others attempted to leave the system.

Wildly fluctuating land prices since the 1970s have made farming and agricultural lending difficult. For example, in Iowa one of the best farming areas of America, choice farm land had sold as high as \$3,000-\$3,400 per acre before dropping to \$700-\$800 per acre, and more recently recovering to \$1,200 per acre, according to Iowa real estate expert Don Hebert.[4]

Such fluctuations, along with whipsawing of interest rates and commodity prices, cannot but make lending extremely difficult to gauge – with repayment equally precarious. The farmer and livestock producer finds it next to impossible to hedge against such conditions.

Fifty years of federal farm subsidies have made international trade cumbersome, too. Thus, the farmer or rancher of the 1990s must have unusual business sense as well as agricultural know-how. See Commodity Credit Corp. (CCC), also in this chapter.

U.S. farm subsidies cost taxpayers \$6-\$26 billion per year.

Net loans of Farm Credit Banks, Banks for Cooperatives and FCS Direct Lenders were \$66 .3 billion in 1990.[5]

Properly operated, and exclusive of subsidies and price supports, agricultural credit programs could be useful to farmers and ranchers. Production loans from both local agricultural credit associations and local commercial banks can be re-discounted through the regional credit banks so as to provide additional agricultural credit. Seldom have commercial banks taken advantage of this facility.

After years of bargaining, the conveners of the General Agreement on Tariffs and Trade (GATT) appeared uncertain of success in attempts to bring the United States, developing countries and the European countries together on tariff agreements – chiefly because of agricultural subsidies. The United States is not alone in subsidies of its farm products. The European nations trying to unify economically are not unified on abolition of their subsidies of farm products. At least they have not been willing to join world-wide in a free market in agricultural commodities.

Farmers Home Administration

Established during the Great Depression, the Farmers Home Administration (FmHA) is supposed to be lender of last resort for farmers unable to get credit otherwise.

As with every well-intentioned government agency, the FmHA grew beyond its original purpose, even to offering industrial loans, and in 1989 its Business and Industrial Loan Program had accumulated losses of 32 percent of funds advanced. More than $6 billion dollars had gone into this particular category of FmHA loans and grants over the years. The program has since been discontinued. Total Farmers Home Administration loans and grants had exceeded $156 billion through 1989.[6] As pointed out by *Farm Journal*, "FmHA has far outgrown its original mission to provide temporary credit to promising, but disadvantaged farmers. At last count it supplied 30 percent of the nation's farm operating loans."

Farm Journal also quoted Gene Severens, a small farm advocate with the Center for Rural Affairs: "FmHA has become the lender of last resort for every farmer in America. That's not a proper public purpose that taxpayers should support, even if they can afford it."[7]

In the 1990s it has become obvious that the taxpayers cannot support many of the government programs that Congress has saddled upon the taxpayers – as evidenced by failure to balance the budget in 30 years.

New England's Outstanding Farm Credit Banks

While some of the other Farm Credit Banks were in trouble and when the super-regional company Bank of New England Corp. was beginning to show danger signs, New England's Farm Credit Banks of Springfield (actually located in smaller Agawam, Massachusetts) continued to serve the local farm credit associations and cooperatives and their customers in the New England states, and New York and New Jersey.

The Farm Credit Bank of Springfield and the Springfield Bank for Cooperatives operate with the traditional Yankee thriftiness, making loans to farms and fishermen and cooperative agricultural associations. Members of the Springfield Bank for Cooperatives chose to keep it independent of the federal mergers. The 1989 *Annual Report*, signed by Chairman Donald S. Clarke of the Farm Credit Bank, Chairman Norman P. Harvey of the Springfield Bank for Cooperatives and President James A. Person, showed $1.5 billion in loans to farmers and others by the Farm Credit Bank and related associations, total assets of nearly $2 billion and net worth of $228 million. The Springfield Bank of Cooperatives reported net loans of $128 million (after $565 million participations sold), total assets of $274 million, and net worth of $41 million.

In the annual report for the Springfield Farm Credit Banks a prophetic note was given, this a year before the Bank of New England failure:

> The directors and management of the Farm Credit Bank of Springfield and the Springfield Bank for Cooperatives have witnessed excellent community-oriented commercial banks in the Northeast merge with their big city cousins during the past 10 years. Unfortunately, many of these banks have lost their identity and commitment to community as a result of consolidation. The directors of the Springfield Banks have chosen to build upon what they believe to be one of the great strengths of Cooperative Farm Credit in the Northeast – an organization structure that is both close to the customer and efficient in its operation. Farm Credit System institutions in the First District have chosen to make modest adjustments to organization structure, practice prudent cost control, create efficient management structures, emphasize quality, and focus on the customer. The directors and management of the two banks at Springfield remain fully committed to quality, service, and the farmers and cooperatives who own these institutions.[8]

Federal Financing Bank

Still another federal agency, or corporation, is the Federal Financing Bank. Hardly known to the public, the name is seldom seen in print. Created in 1973 to finance other federal agencies such as Farmers Home Administration, Tennessee Valley Authority, Rural Electrification Administration, Foreign Defense Security Sales, Low Rent Public Housing, Export-Import Bank, U.S. Postal Service, Student Loan Marketing, and Navy Ship Leasing, the Federal Financing Bank was originally intended to have been off-budget.

Officials of the U.S. Treasury also serve as officers of the FFB. The original intention expressed by Congress in 1973 was that the bank was to have a line of credit with the U.S. Treasury but was to borrow primarily in the open market. As it turns out, very little effort was given to borrowing in the financial markets. Instead, the bank has relied on its apparently unlimited line of credit with the U.S. Treasury. Agencies discovered that they could pass on guaranteed obligations to the Federal Financing Bank and not infringe on their own budgeted allotments from Congress.

Through the fiscal years from September 30, 1987 through 1988 and 1989, total dollars receivable from various agencies and corresponding dollars owed by the FFB declined – from $158 billion to $136 billion, but at the end of September, 1990, both were up to $173 billion. In the year ended September 30, 1990 a new borrower appeared, the Resolution Trust Corporation (RTC), the bailout agency for the S&Ls and the bankrupt Federal Savings and Loan Insurance Corp. (FSLIC). From owing nothing a year earlier, the RTC went to the second largest debtor to the FFB, as of September 30, 1990 $41 billion, behind the Farmers Home Administration's $52 billion. By January 31, 1991 the RTC had surpassed the FmHA in its debt through the FFB, $56 billion for the RTC versus $52 billion for the FmHA. The RTC was also preparing to borrow additional billions in its own name, bonds to be sold directly in the public market.

Financial Statements for the FFB from 1987 to 1990 are detailed on the next page.

FEDERAL FINANCING BANK

STATEMENT OF FINANCIAL POSITION AS OF SEPTEMBER 30, 1990, 1989, 1988, & 1987 (IN THOUSANDS)

Assets	1990	1989	1988	1987
Funds with U.S. Treasury	$339,396	$376,467	$880,668	$444,065
Loans Receivable, net	173,404,268	136,186,540	146,329,826	157,547,345
Accrued Interest Receivable	4,796,938	4,440,554	4,321,694	4,740,237
Accounts Receivable	2,070	4,787	4,864	2,714
Total Assets	$178,542,672	$141,008,348	$151,537,052	$162,734,361
Liabilities and Accumulated Deficit				
Borrowings	$173,473,847	$136,183,392	$146,546,133	$157,537,929
Accrued Interest Payable	5,091,327	4,842,801	4,756,772	5,129,458
Debt Prepayent Premium	2,024,497	1,899,605	1,481,238	165,605
Other Liabilities	851	1,918	1,052	991
Total Liabilities	$180,590,522	$142,927,716	$152,785,195	$162,833,983
Accumulated Deficit	$ (2,047,850)	$ (1,919,368)	$ (1,248,143)	$ (99,622)
	$178,542,672	$141,008,348	$151,537,052	$162,734,361

Source: Federal Financing Bank, Washington DC[9]

The Federal Financing Bank charges its other federal agencies one-eighth of one percent above what it pays the U.S. Treasury. As noted above, contrary to original purpose, the Bank abandoned the original concept of borrowing in the general financial markets. Instead, it borrows directly from the U.S. Treasury. (It has also borrowed $15 billion from the Civil Service Retirement fund.) The Department of Defense guaranteed financing through the bank of military items for the Philippines, Turkey, Morocco and Kenya. Presumably, these will be repaid by those countries, though at a slight subsidy per Congressional provisions explained below.

As indicated, by January 1991 the new RTC was the biggest borrower from the bank, having achieved that status in just a year's time, after its establishment in August, 1989. A portion of the RTC bailout funding will be repaid by sales of assets of defunct S&Ls. But, undoubtedly, a large portion also will be paid by U.S. taxpayers. Additional RTC debt is already helping to further devalue the dollar and to add to the already heavy burden of daily interest due on the federal debt.

Add to this that in 1991 Congress told the FDIC that it could also borrow from the Federal Financing Bank, supposedly on a temporary basis, to help keep afloat the depleting FDIC Bank Insurance Fund.

During some years, the FFB operated at a profit, from the one-eighth of one percent differential charged the agencies over the bank's cost of borrowing through the U.S. Treasury. However, Congress decreed that the Rural Electrification Administration (REA) and the Defense Security Assistance Agency (DSAA) should be exempt from the provision that the repayments of debt be at the market value of agencies' debts. Instead, REA and foreign defense debt repayments are credited at par value. These subsidies to the REA and DSAA more than offset the Bank's earnings in recent years, pushing the FFB to a *deficit* net worth of $2 billion for the fiscal year ended September 30, 1990. A deficit seems to be typical of most federal operations.

Commodity Credit Corporation (CCC)

Early in his administration, Franklin Roosevelt's "New Deal" Secretary of Agriculture Henry Wallace attempted to raise agricultural prices by plowing under every third row of cotton and by killing six million little pigs. When these efforts met with little success, a big Mississippi cotton planter, Oscar Johnson, appealed to Roosevelt to take other measures. Thus, on October 17, 1933 the Commodity Credit Corporation was incorporated under the laws of Delaware by Jesse Jones and other members of the board of the Reconstruction Finance Corp. It was first in a series of corporations and agencies to operate under the ownership of the RFC. Jones agreed with Roosevelt and Johnson to set an initial price of ten cents per pound for cotton, a penny above its selling price of nine cents. Thereafter, the CCC during its life under the RFC "made loans to farmers that topped the government's help to railroads and was second only to the amount dispensed to banks and other financial institutions."[10]

Once in 1938 when Congress was not in session and Roosevelt was not in Washington, the CCC needed $150 million to make cotton and wheat loans to farmers. Jesse Jones took it upon himself to authorize the financing, although the law said nothing along that line. Later, in 1939, Jones appeared before the Senate Banking and Currency Committee asking for an increase in authority to do what he had already accomplished. Newly elected Republican Senator Robert A. Taft, after questioning Jones, said, "Mr. Jones, you have violated the law."

"No, Senator," replied Jones, "I have not violated the law. I have construed the law and administered it according to my best judgement under the circumstances, and if you think the increases I have asked should not be voted, vote against them. What I did was what I felt sure the Congress would have authorized me to do had it been in session. I felt that it was my responsibility to meet the situation, and did, always having something to go home to when my services are no longer required."

Taft voted for the millions that Jones requested. Jones always got along well with members of the Congress by being candid with them. Just before Roosevelt's death, after Wallace had been removed from the ticket as Vice President to be replaced by Harry Truman, the dying President nominated Wallace to be Secretary of Commerce and head of the RFC and the many agencies which Jones, then Secretary of Commerce, held. In deference to the President, Wallace was approved as Secretary of Commerce by the Congress; however, all other responsibilities and powers were taken away from him.

The CCC survived Roosevelt, Jones and Wallace by many years. It is still with us, re-chartered as a federal corporation in 1948 under the Department of Agriculture. Published reports detail price support efforts on grains, from barley to wheat, on milk, tobacco, cotton, beet sugar and cane sugar and other commodities. In 1987, taxpayers contributed $25.8 billion of the $35 billion in commodity price supports for the previous year's crop. CCC net outlays for 1990 were only $6.45 billion – in part due to drought on wheat production. Net costs for 1992 are projected at $10.6 billion.

Comptroller General Charles Bowsher suggested that the CCC write down $5 to $8 billion in receivables from less developed countries and others.[11] The CCC has become a big-time money loser.

Export-Import Bank

Still another financing operation for the Federal government is the Export-Import Bank of the Unites States. Created in 1934, it is "the U.S. Government agency that facilitates the export financing of U.S. goods and services." According to the bank's own description:

> By neutralizing the effect of export credit subsidies from other governments and by absorbing credit risks that the private sector will not accept, Eximbank enables U.S. exporters to compete fairly in overseas markets on the basis of price, performance, delivery and service.[12]

The bank's loans and guarantees cover up to 80 percent of the export value. The bank even provides working capital.

The Export-Import Bank also loses money for the taxpayers of the United States. The *1989 Annual Report* showed that 33.6 percent of its loans were under reserve for losses. The bank had a net worth of *minus* $4.2 billion. The *1989 Annual Report* is commended by Comptroller General Charles A. Bowsher in that the management of Export-Import Bank had taken the initiative to change its previous inadequate accounting system to conform to generally accepted accounting principles that "should assist the Congress in the oversight of the bank."[13]

Whether Congress will be willing to be less generous in subsidizing U.S. exporters in the costly attempt to "neutralize" the export subsidies of other countries remains to be seen. In ongoing GATT negotiations, the United States and the countries of the emerging European Economic Community are finding it hard to agree on reducing agricultural production subsidies.

With few exceptions, federally owned banking and financial institutions are money losers. Their losses are paid by additional inflationary federal borrowings or more directly by taxpayers' dollars.

Federal Reserve System

In addition to its regulatory powers (listed previously) the Federal Reserve System is a profit maker for the government. As holder of U.S. Treasury and government agency securities, the 12 Federal Reserve Banks earn interest on those obligations, a total of

$19,262,265,500 in 1991. But at the same time the Federal Reserve banks paid the U.S. Treasury $20,777,552,288 in 1991 as interest on Federal Reserve Notes, the currency that we use. In some years, the balance is slightly reversed. In effect the Federal Reserve passes on most of its surplus earnings to the federal government.[14]

At the same time, the Federal Reserve is an unintentional creator of continued inflation of the money supply in that it acquires portions of the deficit-created federal debt against which it issues circulating Federal Reserve Notes and bank credit. Since Congress abolished the requirement for gold reserves against Federal Reserve members' deposits in 1965, and gold reserves for Federal Reserve Notes in 1968, and after the United States government abrogated our promise to back the U.S. dollar internationally with gold in 1971 there has been but little to hold back federal deficit spending and inflationary creation of our fiat money supply. Inflation of the money supply has resulted in an accelerating decline in the value of the dollar.

In 1991 some in government suggested that the depleting FDIC Bank Insurance Fund should borrow from the Federal Reserve — more inflation to cover weaknesses in what was originally intended to be a self-insured system for deposit accounts.

Fractional Reserve Banking — Gold and Silver — The Bank for International Settlements

The worldwide system of fractional reserve banking continues to mystify not only the general public but many supposed economic experts. The fact that commercial banks should create deposits by making loans seems not only mysterious but sinful to many people, perhaps tied in with the bad connotation of usury or excess interest charges. (See Appendix A for more on fractional reserve banking.)

Fractional reserve banking has been abused, and usurious charges have been made, particularly when gold or silver reserve requirements were eliminated. The Federal Reserve System and the various central banks in other countries have often been unwilling accomplices to the inflation of the money supply accompanying deficit government spending. Government notes and bonds issued to cover year after year of deficit budgets accelerate the abuse of the fractional reserve banking system when the central bank issues currency or bank credit to cover these deficit government obligations.

The central bank for the central banks of Europe, the Bank for International Settlements (BIS), still looks to gold, even does its bookkeeping in a unit called the *gold franc*. It also keeps most of its reserves in gold. Year after year, without being too antagonistic, the BIS has urged the U.S. to change its ways of federal deficit spending – without much success.[15]

Brokered Deposits

Brokered deposits are not necessarily deposits from stock brokers, although some of the large brokerage houses have offered their customers' funds to banks and S&Ls for the highest dollar rates. Deposits have also come from professional brokers of funds, again seeking high rates, plus the security of FDIC, and formerly FSLIC, insurance. Brokered deposits, usually in the form of CDs, offer no continuity and little loyalty to the bank or S&L. They are "hot" funds, ready to leave at maturity if higher funds are available elsewhere or if rumors indicate the bank or S&L may be in trouble. It is nearly impossible to make loans based on such deposits, although some banks tried, with disastrous results.

At the same time high rates from financial institutions in limbo, kept alive by the regulators until federal insurance funds could be found to close them, attracted deposits from out of territory and penalized stronger local institutions that would not pay as much for deposits. Usually the regulators have discouraged brokered deposits; however, on occasion, as with the S&Ls, when they were reluctant to close the door of ailing financial institutions they allowed and encouraged such elusive funds, supposedly on a temporary basis.[16]

In a 1991 letter to the author, Ernest T. Baughman, former president of the Federal Reserve Bank of Dallas, emphasizes the "excessive growth rates and associated bad loans and investments in many S&Ls and some banks" caused by money brokers collecting "hot deposits through the use of CDs." He suggests this type should not be insured – or the amount be limited in proportion to capital or total liabilities or to annual increase.[17]

NOTES

1. Charles Bradford, Chief Economist, 1989 *Annual Report of National Credit Union Administration*, Washington. Also, John Kostrzewa of the *Providence Journal,*, telephone conversation, August, 1992.

2. Federal Housing Administration, *Annual Report for Fiscal Year 1989*, Washington, 1991.

3. General Accounting Office, Report to the Secretary of Housing and Urban Development, *Federal Housing Administration Monitoring of Single Family Mortgages Needs Improvement*, Washington, 1991.

4. Don Hebert, real estate broker, Coralsville, Iowa, telephone conversation and letter, August, 1990.

5. Farm Credit Administration, *1990 Annual Report*, McLean, Virginia.

6. Farmers Home Administration, *A Brief History of the Farmers Home Administration*, Washington, 1990

7. Marcia Zarley Taylor, "What Went Wrong at Farmers Home?" *Farm Journal*, February, 1989.

8. Springfield Farm Credit Banks, *1989 Annual Report*, Springfield (Agawam), Massachusetts.

9. Federal Financing Bank, Washington, reports of 1989, 1990, 1991.

10. Bascom Timmons, *Jesse H. Jones: The Man and The Statesman*, Henry Holt & Co., New York, 1956.

11. Commodity Credit Corporation, *1988 Annual Report*, Washington. Also, letter from Sarita G. Schotta, Deputy Administrator, Management, Agricultural Stabilization and Conservation Service, U.S. Dept. of Agriculture, September 14, 1992.

12. Export-Import Bank Form 87-14, July, 1990, Washington.

13. Export-Import Bank, *1989 Annual Report*, Washington.

14. Board of Governors of the Federal Reserve System, *78th Annual Report*, Washington, 1991.

15. Bank for International Settlements, *Annual Reports*, Basle.

16. "Sec. 224, Brokered Deposits," Financial Institutions Reform, Recovery, and Enforcement Act of 1989, Washington.

17. Ernest T. Baughman, letter of August 21, 1991, Oak Park, Illinois.

CHAPTER 8

Foreign Loans, Foreign Banks

A Chicago Judge on Third World Loans

Retired Cook County (Illinois) Judge Robert J. Collins is a long-time observer of financial institutions. As a young man Collins "lost a few bucks in a bank failure" in the Great Depression of the 1930s, and when he got out of the service he "went straight to Northern Trust Company of Chicago," a venerable, conservative bank. The judge states:

> Recent banking troubles can be attributed to large loans, especially to the third world countries, which would be a great investment if they paid off. However, most of them have a sandy base and default before long. No use in blaming Washington. Although they play a role, it's the banks themselves who have taken a big risk, and by and large, they deserve what they get.[1]

Foreign Loans

When the price of oil was going ever upward just a few years ago and the Organization of Petroleum Exporting Countries (OPEC) had an ever-increasing dollar income for its member countries, several of the major and would-be-major U.S. banks offered their services to the emerging oil empires. Billions of dollars were recycled through these U.S. banks, with many of the billions going to loans to third world, less developed countries (LDCs), as well as to some rather well developed countries. Some gigantic loans were also made to private borrowers in those nations – but the preferred thinking seems to have been that sovereign nations could not, would not go broke.

When the borrowers were slow to repay, banking regulators were slow to condemn, to *classify* (loan *classifications* meaning other than good) such loans. But time, publicity and pressure from Congress and good banking demanded that they be recognized as less than best, covered at least in part by bad-debt reserves.

All sorts of plans have been projected by the U.S. Treasury and others to renew, resolve and rework such credits. The International Monetary Fund lost most of its original purpose when the dollar lost its tie to gold in the 1970s, and the IMF *special drawing rights* (SDRs or paper gold) didn't mean too much either. Both the IMF and sister World Bank (International Bank for Reconstruction and Finance) were encouraged to help foreign nation borrowers in their refinancing of U.S. bank loans. All this has been helpful to nations-debtors, and perhaps even more helpful to large U.S. lenders who without that assistance would have sunk into more serious financial difficulties than they had already experienced, even in some cases gone broke.

U.S. Banks Pull Back Internationally

Perhaps in part due to the terrible lickings that they have taken from the LDC (less developed country) and other poorly paying foreign loans, many large U.S. banks have cut back on their international operations in recent years. Possibly of more importance in their decisions were the heavy costs of attempting to maintain foreign offices. U.S. banks so often have followed the herd. When a few went international, others followed, though results never proved very profitable.

Today, attempting to concentrate on what they know best, leaders in major U.S. banks have pulled back from expensive international operations, trying instead to do good jobs at home while cooperating with experienced foreign banks in serving mutual customers. Wells Fargo & Co., noted San Francisco bank with the stagecoach motif, does its Pacific Rim business through the influential Hongkong Bank.

Foreign Banks Now the Largest

Not so many years ago many of the largest banks in the world were in the United States. California's Bank of America was the largest bank anywhere. Several big New York banks were also top ranked internationally. These same banks remain important today. By the 1990s, of the largest banks, only a minority were in the U.S.

At the beginning of 1990 according to the British publication *The Economist*, the seven largest banks in assets were all Japanese, with No. 8 American, No. 9 again Japanese, and No. 10 French. The one U.S. bank listed No. 8 was Citicorp, the largest in the United States. By mid-1992 *Fortune* magazine reported Citicorp still largest in this country but No. 25 world-wide.[2]

Japanese Banks Lead

The No. 1 bank in the world today in assets is the Dai-Ichi Kangyo Bank Ltd., of Tokyo. In its *1990 Annual Report*, Dai-Ichi stated:

> In the fiscal year ended March 31, 1990, the Bank maintained its position as the world's largest private sector financial institution, as total assets increased 25.5 percent to ¥68,675 billion (U.S. $435 billion).

Dai-Ichi, roughly translated as "Number 1," is today not only

Japan's No. 1 bank, but, as stated above, is No. 1 world wide.

Japan's banks have been more "leveraged" than those of some of the western countries – that is, capital/assets ratio has been lower in Japan. But Japan is working to improve this ratio.

Thomson (Rand McNally) ranking by capital, or net worth, credited Great Britain with the two largest banks, while Citibank of America was third, a Japanese bank No. 4, a French bank No. 5, and numbers six through ten all Japanese.[3] However, this was before Dai-Ichi's increase in capital, and before increases in other Japanese banks' capital accounts.

Any way you look at it, U.S. banks barely get into the running today, with Japanese predominant, and British and French represented. German banks are just slightly smaller, again ahead of many U.S. banks in size today.

It has been extremely difficult for large U.S. banks to raise significant amounts of capital in recent years, with bad reports from the media on asset quality, earnings and dividends. Japan's Dai-Ichi Kangyo Bank Ltd. raised ¥215 billion (U.S. $1.4 billion) in the year ended March 31, 1990 in sales of new common stock, and nearly that much in the previous year. With new funds from the sale of convertible bonds as well, two years' increases in capital-related accounts, only from new securities, was near the equivalent of $4 billion U.S. dollars. The 1992 equity of Dai-Ichi Kangyo Bank of ¥1,986 billion (U.S. $14.9 billion) is far above the capital of any U.S. banks.

In 1990 Dai-Ichi Kangyo Bank Ltd. acquired from Manufacturers Hanover Bank of New York 60 percent interest in the CIT Group, a major U.S. commercial financing company.[4] (Manufacturers at the end of 1991 merged with Chemical Banking Corp. of New York.)

Economic and Banking Problems In Japan

By 1992 Japanese banks had some of the problems of U.S. banks. Pondering what to do about bad loans, Japanese banks and government officials were discussing possible formation of a quasi-public company to buy up bad loans and real estate. (A few U.S. economists appeared to enjoy telling of problems from falling Tokyo stock market prices and the slowdown in Japanese construction.) The *Wall Street Journal* reported that long-term bank lenders were especially hard hit. *WSJ* reporter Clay Chandler said from Tokyo: "The Japanese banks' problems could cause pain in the U.S., where they hold 12% of total commercial bank assets, and especially in California, where they and their affiliates hold nearly a quarter of all bank deposits."

In Dai-Ichi's *Annual Report of March 31, 1992* (Japanese banking companies' years end in March), after discussing economic and business problems, Japanese and world-wide, Chairman Juniji Miyazaki and President Todashi Okuda state "two new management goals: To make return on assets (ROA) our highest priority at all levels of management in our domestic and international operations by maintaining a portfolio with proper risk and return while continuing to provide ever-improving services to our customers. To maintain our capital level well above the BIS standards and to secure a strong operating base that is able to cope with volatility in the financial markets."

Chairman Miyazaki and President Okudo explain that Dai-Ichi Kangyo Bank's capital account is 8.25 percent of the international Basle Committee ratio.

Assets of "DKB" slimmed slightly in 1991 and 1992, to ¥63.2 trillion. At the same time, equivalent U.S. dollars increased, from $435 billion as of March 31, 1990 to $476 billion as of March 31, 1992 – as the U.S. dollar continued to decline in value internationally.

By 1992 each of Japan's five largest banks – Dai-Ichi, Fuji, Sakura, Sanwa and Mitsubishi – had assets and deposits more than *twice* those of any U.S. bank. Japan's banks have led Japan's economic growth. By 1992 Japanese banks also reported certain problems – similar to those of U.S. banks.

Sakura Bank's origin goes back to 1683, when the Mitsui Exchange House was founded in Edo (now Tokyo). Mitsui Bank merged with Taiyo Kobe Bank in 1990. The name was changed to Sakura Bank in 1992. During 1990 Security Pacific Bank proudly announced that then Mitsui Taiyo Kobe had acquired an interest in some of the California bank's operations. In 1992 BankAmerica acquired the balance of Security.

The Japanese bank's 1990 report told of its cultural activities, including the bank's sponsorship of an exhibition center at historic Kyoto, ancient capital of Japan.[5] There the House of Mitsui had participated in the Guion Festival from its early days in Kyoto 300 years ago, beginning in 1686. It was this writer's interesting experience to help coordinate cultural tours of the famous parks, castles, shrines and temples of Kyoto for U.S. personnel in late 1945 while serving with the occupying U. S. Sixth Army.

Japan continues to take the long viewpoint, but at the same time its people adopt the latest techniques, as in manufacturing. See statement from Bank of Japan farther along in this chapter, on the attitudes of the Japanese people. Japan and Germany have also profited from early U.S. post-World War II insistence that they maintain but minimum military establishments and spendings. Instead, the United States carried the major burden in "Cold War" and other international police actions.

Foreign Banks See Opportunities

A naturalized American citizen who had the advantage of coming to the United States after having lived in several other countries sees opportunities in the United States often overlooked by Americans. But he also notes that Japanese and even Canadian banks have been ready to make substantial loans to take advantage of bargain prices on income properties with good potential for appreciation from depressed prices. U.S. banks seem afraid, he says.

Britain's Biggest Bank, Barclays, Continues to Serve

Barclays PLC, Britain's biggest bank in assets, and one of the world's largest in capital accounts, announced in early 1991 that its staff would be reduced 20 percent over the next five to ten years, due to pressures from bad debts and other costs. But Barclays is staying very much alive. Staff reductions were revealed by Barclays' Chairman Sir John Quinton in a London *Financial Times* interview, as reported on this side of the Atlantic by *The Wall Street Journal*.[6] In the bank's *1989 Annual Report*, Sir John had told of continuing loss provisions for LDC loans. Less-developed-country loans have hurt large banks in Great Britain, the United States, Switzerland and other leading western countries. At the beginning of 1990 total assets were £127.6 billion, which at that time equalled U.S. $205.4 billion. Capital was £6.7 billion: U.S. $10.7 billion.

In a February 1991 letter from retired Barclays Group Chairman Sir Anthony Tuke, to this writer, Sir Anthony commented on the relations of his father the late Anthony William Tuke, who also served at Barclays, with U.S. Southwestern financial leader, the late Fred F. Florence, long-time head of Southwest's largest bank, Republic National of Dallas.[7] Sir Anthony noted:

> The recent collapse of banking in the South Western States is very worrying, not least the demise of the Republic bank, which used to have such a high reputation. They certainly appear to have made a big mistake when they merged with their main rivals. As far as the British banks are concerned, they have had a terrible year in 1990, but they have always been better capitalized than the U.S. banks and they are able to show modest profits even after enormous write-offs.

Hongkong

The Hongkong & Shanghai Banking Corporation Ltd. is still another international institution that in recent years is larger and stronger than most large U.S. banks.

In its *1990 Annual Report,* Hongkong Bank doesn't brag of its accomplishments, but voices concern with difficulties where these occur. One difficult area is in the United States, in its Marine Midland Bank, in New York state. Hongkong Bank disposed of its interest in the First Pennsylvania Bank, one of those bailed out by the FDIC and other banks. Rather than exercising its right to acquire full ownership of the Philadelphia bank and attempting to form an interstate U. S. bank with upstate New York Marine Midland, Hongkong Bank allowed Philadelphia National (Core States) to acquire its long-time local competitor.

Hongkong Bank is somewhat concerned with the upcoming takeover of Hongkong by mainland China and what may happen when the Communist Chinese government takes over at the end of the British lease. The bank has created a new controlling entity, chartered in England but operating in Hongkong, HSBC Holdings PLC. Hongkong and Shanghai Banking Corporation Ltd. had assets of HK $1,158.2 billion (U.S. $148.5 billion) at the beginning of 1991, with capital resources of HK $79.8 billion (U.S. $10.2 billion), and earnings for 1990 of HK $3.9 billion (U.S. $497 million).[8]

The bank was established in Hongkong in 1865, and opened offices in Shanghai and London the same year.

Hongkong Bank maintains cooperative agreements with several large U.S. banks that shed most of their foreign operations. (Wells Fargo is one.).[9] In 1992 Hongkong Bank acquired Britain's Midland Bank through its new holding company.

Germany's Deutsche and Dresdner Banks

Deutsche Bank AG, Germany's largest bank, had a capital and reserve account of DM 140 million at the beginning of 1952. At the beginning of 1990 it was DM 12.8 billion (U.S. $7.8 billion). Total assets at the latest date were DM 215 billion (U.S. $127.4 billion). The bank is strong on human resources development with a goal of seeing "promising management candidates assume positions of responsibility as soon as possible . . . an individual development programme for our highly talented young people . . . based on a job rotation scheme which requires the individual to master a wide range of assignments and projects."[10]

Too many U.S. banks failed miserably in training – or interning – their talented young people, contributing to the failures in U. S. banking which wiser European banks have guarded against.

Such belief has long been held in the Deutche Bank. German financier Ludwig Bamberger in 1852 was sentenced in absentia both to prison and to death for his liberal ideas. After 20 years exile in London and in Paris (where he helped found the renowned Banque de Paris and des Pays-Bays) he was allowed to return to Germany. He and Adelbert Delbruck founded the Deutsch Bank. Joseph Wechberg in *The Merchant Bankers* quotes Bamberger on the importance of competent management: "With an efficient manager the supervising board is superfluous, but with an inefficient one it is helpless." It was Bamberger who established the gold standard for Germany.

Dresdner Bank, like West Germany's other banks, welcomed the challenge of unification from East Germany in the 1990s. The bank's *1989 Annual Report* told with some nostalgia that "Dresdner Bank was the first West German bank, indeed the first West German firm, to open an office in its home city of Dresden, followed by other cities in the GDR."[11] The bank drew its name from Dresden, which city for 45 years after World War II was in the totalitarian realm of the German Democratic Republic, whose people finally threw off their Communist yoke.

Dresdner Bank "has more than doubled its equity base over the past 5 years." As of the beginning of 1990, this was DM 7.9 billion (U.S. $4.7 billion). Total assets were DM 142 billion (U.S. $84.2 billion).

It also should be noted that the bank's *1989 Annual Report* had a page of memorial to Alfred Herrhousen, its chairman. Herrhousen was assassinated on November 30, 1989. The Red Army faction claimed responsibility. In 1991, after the reunification of East Germany, Germany's chief prosecutor charged former security officials of the defunct Communist country with aiding the Red Army faction. The memorial page said of Herrhousen, "Commitment was the essence of his life. His gifts and courage enabled him to live by his convictions."

Of reunited Germany, the bank's annual report stated:

> As in the founding year of 1862, today is also a period of German unification and of new hope for people. Today German unification is not being decided in the royal palace of a vanquished neighbour, as in Versailles, nor with blood and iron, but by the free will of Germans who do not wish to establish a new Reich but rather a new federation.[12]

Why the Success of Foreign Banks?

As to the success of foreign banks, let's look at the example of Japan. Why are the Japanese banks so successful? Why are the Japanese successful in other businesses, such as automobile manufacturing and consumer electronic equipment? The Japanese pay tribute to U.S. financier Joseph Dodge, who encouraged them to rebuild their financial institutions at the end of World War II. They also give an annual W. E. Deming Award for quality, for the American quality control expert whose name is hardly known in the United States.[13]

The Japanese take other new world attitudes quite seriously as well. In a book published by the Bank of Japan, *Money and Banking in Japan* (American translation published by St. Martin's Press), these qualities are discussed:

> Finally and fundamentally, the high rate of savings reflects traditional habits, based on such national characteristics as diligence, widespread education, strong desire to raise the standard of living, and so on.[14]

Some of us who were in Hawaii during World War II remember the Honolulu branch of the Yokohama Specie Bank, then under control of the U. S. government. We service men didn't know what they did inside, but we could hear adding machines and typewriters. ("Specie," a word unfamiliar to us in the United States of today, means gold or silver money.) The Yokohama Specie Bank had been organized in 1880 for low interest, government-assisted credit for Japanese businesses in foreign trade. One of the post-war reforms was its 1947 transformation into the Bank of Tokyo. According to *Fortune* magazine, in 1990 the Bank of Tokyo was No. 12 world-wide, its assets equivalent to U.S. $222 billion, just under Citicorp, largest U.S. bank. *Fortune* also listed most of the even-larger banks of the world as being Japanese.[15]

Bank of Tokyo today owns California's Union Bank at Los Angeles. During 1990, Bank of Tokyo acquired the business leasing and non-banking financial services from Bank of New England. Bank of Tokyo Ltd., in its 1990 annual report, told of being the "lead bank and financing coordinator for the $170 million Bosporus Hotel in Istanbul, and the HK$1.55 billion Tate's Cairn Tunnel in HongKong."

Bank of Tokyo leaders "have long recognized the importance of a solid capital foundation and have resisted the trend toward volume-oriented business" which got too many U. S. banks in trouble. The bank is properly "proud of its position among Japanese financial institutions," going back 110 years to the founding of the Yokohama Specie Bank.[16]

Fortune in 1992 reported Bank of Tokyo as No. 15 worldwide with assets equivalent to U.S. $247 billion. *Fortune* reported Citicorp, still largest in the United States, as No. 25 world-wide, with assets of $217 billion.

Concerning the 1992 difficulties of Japanese banks, Michiharu Akimoto of the Bank of Tokyo said: "The Japanese economy is just following the American economy."

Japanese banks are strengthening their capital ratios to bring these up to or above those of the leading banks of western nations, under the new Basle Standards. Until now Japan's gold reserves have lagged below those of western countries. Japan may also be looking to bringing up its gold reserves. (See Gold Holdings table, Appendix C.)

In addition to their large commercial banks, both Germany and Japan have many smaller financial institutions which serve their thrifty populaces. Such concept of service would also seem near-foreign to many regulators and political leaders in Washington, D.C., in the 1990s.

W. Edward Deming is not completely unknown in his native United States. What he said a few years ago to a group of top executives of an American manufacturing company applies equally to U.S. versus Japanese banking. Deming is quoted by Andrea Gabor in *The Man Who Discovered Quality.* "Why can't America compete?" Deming would ask, sputtering with rage. "The *a-a-a-nswer i-i-s* – MANAGEMENT.[17]

The Mysterious BCCI

The 1991 close-down of the mysterious Bank of Credit and Commerce International (BCCI) and its multi-national operations was preceded by questionable revelations going back years, but made more concrete by an audit of the banking company's British operations. Ordered by the Bank of England, the audit by Price Waterhouse showed: " . . . massive bad loans, unrecorded deposits, blatantly phony accounting, and other offenses."

Business Week recounted that by 1987, bank regulators had become so concerned about BCCI that a special "college" of regulators was formed by Luxembourg, Britain, France, Spain, Switzerland and the Cayman Islands (but *not* including the United States.) The Cayman Islands' inspector of banks is quoted in 1991, saying, "It was fraud." *Business Week* also reported that bank clients have included former Panamanian strongman Manuel Noriega and Columbian drug lords.[18]

The Wall Street Journal said that links were being sought between BCCI and the Central Intelligence Agency. *WSJ* stated "It had been clear for months that the CIA maintained accounts at the bank which were used to finance covert activity."[19]

In the United States, Manhattan District Attorney Robert Morgenthau had been digging into BCCI for more than a year prior to its closing. Morgenthau, son of FDR's Treasury Secretary Henry Morgenthau, Jr., told a U.S. Senate committee that "BCCI had an international reputation for capital flight, tax fraud, and money laundering.'' BCCI officials were reported to have received $50 million to ensure their secrecy.[20]

First American Bankshares and the BCCI

A metamorphosis from what had been a movement for "industrial" loans – loans to wage earners and consumers – to that of a six-state and District of Columbia $11 billion bank holding company system, was the changeover from the 1925 "Morris Plan" Industrial Finance Corp. to the more recent First American Bankshares Inc. In the era when many banks would hardly take the time and trouble to make personal loans – an era which, strangely, seems to be returning – Arthur J. Morris (not to be confused with Robert Morris of the American Revolution) pushed the movement for specially organized "industrial banks." These banks would accept savings and checking accounts and make loans to persons of the "industrial class" – wage earners, consumers.[21] Morris Plan Banks appeared in many U.S. cities, often with the cooperation of existing banks.[22]

In 1956 the company that Arthur Morris had established three decades earlier as the Industrial Finance Corporation became Financial General Corp. In 1970 it was renamed Financial General Bankshares Inc., and in 1982 with another change of name to First American Bankshares Inc.[23]

By the late 1950s, Industrial Finance Corp. had begun its acquisition of banks, in 1959 acquiring control of the Second National Bank, Washington, D.C., then renamed First National Bank, later renamed (again) First American Bank, N.A. Banks in Virginia, Maryland, New York, Tennessee, Florida and Georgia were acquired over the years, including reacquisition of the bank for a while controlled by Bert Lance – the National Bank of Georgia.

As Early As 1973 The Federal Reserve Said "No."

Perhaps because it was located in the nation's capital and perhaps also because of its unique multi-state organization of the former Morris Plan Banks, Financial General Bankshares was a sought-for organization. As far back as 1973, Financial General was associated with an organization known as International Bank, which reported interests in off-shore banks in the Caribbean, Europe, Africa and the Near East.

International Bank and Financial General Bankshares shared the same Washington City address and had the same chairman of the board, retired U.S. Major General and Iowa insurance owner George Olmstead.[24] International Bank had a 24.5 percent interest in Financial General, and a 5 percent interest in Central National Bankshares of Iowa. They also had fingers in banks in the Bahamas, Cayman Islands, Trinidad and Tobago, Liberia, the Netherlands and Lebanon.

In September 1973, the Federal Reserve ruled that International Bank must sever its 24.5 percent interest in Financial General before the latter could acquire control of Second National Bank of Richmond.[25] From 1973 to early 1977, International Bank and Financial General sought through various lawsuits to overrule the Fed, even attempting to obtain records of the Federal Reserve under the Freedom of Information Act.

Meanwhile, Thomas Bertram (Bert) Lance had appeared on the scene, acquiring Financial General's 60 percent interest in the National Bank of Georgia. (Ownership of National Bank of Georgia would eventually return to the holding company.) Lance was to go to Washington in 1977 with Georgia Governor Jimmy Carter when he became president, as Carter's budget director. Lance's acquisition was the former Morris Plan Bank of Georgia, chartered in Atlanta in 1933 to succeed the still-earlier Atlanta Loan and Savings Company.

Not long after arriving in Washington, Lance ran into political and financial troubles. Criticized for his mingling of politics and banking back in Georgia, he resigned as Director of the Budget in 1977 and sold his interest in National Bank of Georgia to Saudi tycoon Ghaith Pharaon, just two years after Lance had acquired the bank. Investigative columnist Jack Anderson described it as a bail-out.[26] The Georgia bank under Pharaon reworked a loan to the Carter family warehouse, in which the U.S. President had an interest, saving the Carter family $60,000 in one year on a $830,000 loan.

In 1978, Bert Lance, BCCI founder Agha Hasan Abedi and others tried to acquire control of Financial General, but were rebuffed by the Securities and Exchange Commission. Lance and Abedi were censured for failure to reveal an 18.4 percent interest in the holding company.[27]

By 1980-81 Financial General had new leadership on its board of directors, including retired and semi-retired distinguished political and business figures. New chairman of the board was B.F. Saul II. Also on the board were 82-year-old Armand Hammer, long-time head of Occidental Petroleum and confidante of U.S.S.R. leaders; 74-year-old Clark M. Clifford, Lyndon Johnson's last Secretary of Defense; Stuart Symington (79), former U.S. senator from Missouri whom Harry Truman had appointed as first Secretary of the Air

Force; Elwood R. Quesada (76), retired major general and former head of the Federal Aviation Agency (FAA); and Arch N. Booth (74), former president of the U.S. Chamber of Commerce.[28]

Financial General's 1980 annual report critized the federal government's deficit spending while lauding Financial General's financial picture. The bank was described as having relationships with "key people in the Export-Import Bank, the World Bank, the Inter-American Development Bank, and the U.S. government." The report went on to say that the application of a "group of foreign investors to take over the company" was dismissed by the Federal Reserve after complaints by Maryland, Virginia and Tennessee regulatory agencies. The report said the board of directors would support any tender offer if it complied with the law and was in agreement as to price, terms and conditions.

The 1981 report announced that an agreement had been reached with a group of Middle East investors to buy control of Financial General at a tentative price of $30.08 per share, when the book value was only $19.00. The final agreement was at $33.80 per share. With completion of the deal, the name was changed to First American Bankshares, and Clark Clifford became chairman of the board with Stuart Symington as vice chairman. Other distinguished board members subsequently went on to other pursuits.

As explained in financial shorthand in *Moody's Bank & Finance Manual* of 1983:

> Control: Pursuant to a tender offer of $33.80 per com. sh. expiring Apr. 19, 1982, FGB Holding Co., acquired about 96% of outstg. Co. com. shs. Co. was merged into a subsidiary of FGB Holding Co. in Aug. 1982. FGB Holding is a unit of Credit Commerce American Investment, a Netherlands Antilles concern. These companies are controlled by a group of Mideast investors, Kamal Ibraham Adham, Faisal Saud al-Fulaij and Abjullah Darwaish.[29]

National Bank of Georgia Rejoins First American

In 1987, after a 12-year detour from direct ownership under Financial General-First American, NBC Financial Corp. (National Bank of Georgia) returned to the holding company. Ghaith Pharaon sold his interest in what by then had grown to include a couple of Florida banks as well as the Georgia bank. Part of the delay in rejoining the fold was that Georgia state law first had to be changed to allow National Bank of Georgia to participate in an expanded Southeast region with the other five states (Virginia, Maryland, New York, Tennessee and Florida, and the District of Columbia, to which First American would expand.

In 1991, Manhattan District Attorney Robert Morgenthau's investigators attempted to find out if "huge sums of money were spent lobbying for the bill." Georgia officials and legislators said the "bill proposed by the National Bank of Georgia was unopposed by other state banks and thus no hard sell was necessary."[30]

BCCI's founder Agha Hasan Abedi had been a good friend of former president Carter and had given generously to Carter's charitable interests. *Forbes* magazine reported that Bert Lance was proposed as head of BCCI in 1988 as a compromise between the Saudi and Pakistani factions. However, Abedi's "No. 2," Swaleh Naqvi, instead got the job.[31]

Possibly Misled

Former U.S. Secretary of Defense Clark M. Clifford in his 1991 autobiographical memoir, *Counsel to the President*, speaks of his possibly having been misled as to the exact ownership of the control group that acquired First American Bankshares. Perhaps the BCCI was the real owner.[32] Clifford tells how he served as counsel to the Middle Eastern investors who acquired control of First American in 1982 and how he then served as chairman of the board of the banking company for the near decade following.[33] Vice-chairman of the holding company until his death in 1988 was long-time friend and former U.S. senator from Missouri, Stuart Symington. Both were prominent in Democratic Party circles. Later president of First American was Robert A. Altman, law associate of Clifford, and active member of the Republican Party. Involvement with BCCI was a bipartisan affair.

The Federal Reserve urged Clifford and Altman to resign their bank posts in 1991. Former Republican senator from Maryland, Charles McC. Mathias, fellow board member at First American, put on additional pressure and Clifford and Altman did resign. Successor as head of First American was Democrat Nicholas deB. Katzenbach, Attorney General under Johnson, and subsequent member of the boards of International Business Machines and Southeast Banking Corp. Katzenbach turned down the opportunity to head the reorganization of an ailing insurance company in 1991 to take on instead the perhaps more-challenging job of returning respectability to the First American Bankshares system.[34]

In July 1991, the *New York Times* reported possible "big money and mysteries" for the BCCI.[35]

One year later in July 1992 New York State and Federal grand juries indicted Clifford and Altman on criminal charges of helping to hide BCCI's ownership of Washington-based First American

Bankshares and two other U.S. banks. The indictments told of huge bribes by BCCI to bank regulators and central bankers in 10 developing nations, including Pakistan, Nigeria and Zambia. The indictments also said that BCCI money was used to hide the financial straits of certain nations and to allow them to defraud the World Bank and International Monetary Fund.

Cooperation in the investigation was provided by Saudi Arabian official Sheik Kamal Adham who agreed to plead guilty on fraud charges. With an associate he paid $105 million in fines.

Also charged were Aga Hassan Abedi and Swaleh Naqvi of the BCCI, and Ghaith R. Pharaon and Faisal Saud al-Falaij, named for acting as front men in BCCI's purchase of First American. Messrs. Clifford and Altman pleaded "Not guilty..'[36]

Not until money-laundering investigations against BCCI surfaced did Washington regulators appear to become deeply concerned over First American's ownership.

As a six-state and Washington, D.C. banking company, First American, except for the Middle East complications, had embodied what the regulators had visualized as the future banking ideal for the United States — a large-scale, super-regional banking system.

Foreign Banks Now Control Nearly One-Fourth of U.S. Bank Assets

In its *1991 Annual Report*, the Board of Governors of the Federal Reserve System reported under "U.S. Activities of Foreign Banks":[37]

> Foreign banks continue to be significant participants in the U.S. banking system. As of year-end 1991, 313 foreign banks operated 529 state-licensed branches and agencies, of which 53 are insured by the Federal Deposit Insurance Corporation. These foreign banks also operated 84 branches and agencies licensed by the Office of the Comptroller of the Currency, of which 9 have FDIC insurance. Foreign banks also directly owned 11 Edge Act corporations and 13 commercial lending companies. In addition, foreign banks held an interest of at least 25 percent of 90 U.S. commercial banks. Altogether, these foreign banks control approximately 24 percent of U.S. banking assets.

International Trading Companies — None U.S. Based

Barely known in the United States, trading companies are major contributors to Japan's success in international business. Germany, South Korea, Great Britain and other counties also profit from this business.

The Japanese trading companies of C. Itoh, Sumitomo, Marubeni, Mitsubishi and Mitsui – each did business in 1991 translating to more than U.S.$100 billion. Of the 27 international trading companies listed in *Fortune's* "100 Largest Diversified Service Companies," 15 are Japan based. Three are in Germany, two in South Korea, two in Great Britain, and one each in France, China, Sweden, Hong Kong and the Netherlands. No U.S. trading company is listed.[38]

We of the United States have not understood the necessity for international trade. In years gone by we were pretty well self-sufficient, manufacturing for ourselves and selling to ourselves on this North American continent. Today, large U.S. manufacurers that sell abroad generally do so on their own. Small U.S. manufacturers often have a hard go at international business. The great retailer-distributor Sears, Roebuck & Co. made an effort to organize an international trading company in the early 1980s. The new company, Sears World Trade, did not show quick profits, and the large retailer closed it down. The Japanese explain that trading companies require many years of effort to become truly profitable.

The Japanese take the long view. We of the United States must learn patience as well as persistence if we are to develop in international trade, and if we are to be long-term competitors in international banking and finance.

Through buying and selling products and commodities of the many countries in which they do business, trading companies are able to hedge against fluctuations in the currencies of these countries. When an era of international monetary stability returns, as with a new gold standard, international trading will be even more important to the countries involved.

NOTES

1. Robert J. Collins, Chicago, letter of March 11, 1991.

2. "Survey International Banking," *The Economist*, London, April 7, 1990. *The Wall Street Journal*'s September 20, 1991 survey showed under "Rankings – The World's 100 Largest Banks," that Citicorp and some other large U.S. banks had shrunk slightly while Japanese, German and other foreign banks had continued to grow. Also *Fortune, August 24, 1992.*

3. Thomson (Rand McNally), *International Banking Directory*, Detroit, 1990.

4. Dai-Ichi Kangyo Bank, Ltd., *Annual Report 1990, 1991 and 1992,* Tokyo. Also, Clay Chandler, "Finance Mire," *Wall Street Journal*, October 16, 1992.

5. Mitsui Taiyo Kobe Bank, Ltd., *Annual Report 1990*, Tokyo.

6. Tim Carrington, London staff reporter of *The Wall Street Journal*, quoting *Financial Times*, "Barclays to Cut Its British Staff As Much As 20 percent," February 19, 1991.

7. Sir Anthony Tuke, London, letter of February 27, 1991.

8. Hongkong & Shanghai Banking Corporation, Ltd., 1990 *Annual Report*, Hongkong.

(In the U.S., the 15 million members of the Southern Baptist Convention honor Lottie Moon, early missionary to China, with their annual foreign mission gifts. Lottie Moon, having given her meager salary for many months to help feed starving Chinese during a famine in Shantung Province, died on Christmas Eve, 1912, as the ship *Manchuria* was in the harbor at Kobe, Japan, on her return trip to the U.S. Her modest bank account was with the Shanghai office of the Hongkong & Shanghai Bank.) Source: Catherine B. Allen, *The New Lottie Moon Story*, Broadman Press, Nashville, 1980.

9. Wells Fargo & Co., *1989 Annual Report*, San Francisco.

10. Deutsche Bank AG, *Annual Report for 1989*, Frankfurt am Main. Also Joseph Wechberg, *The Merchant Bankers,* Pocket Books, New York, 1966.

11. Dresdner Bank AG, *Annual Report for 1989*, Frankfurt am Main.

12. Same as above.

13. "The Prophet of Quality," *Business Week*, January 28, 1991, reviews three books published on W. E. Deming in the U.S. press. Deming, long famous and revered in Japan, is hardly known in the U.S., his home country.

14. Bank of Japan, *Money and Banking in Japan*, English translation published by St. Martin's Press, New York, 1974.

15. "Japan is still No. 1," *Fortune*, July 30, 1990. Also "The 100 Largest Commercial Banking Companies," *Fortune*, August 24, 1992.
Not only are Japan's commercial banks larger than those in the U.S., but its investment banking houses are also larger, in capitalization, according to Daniel Burstein. See his *Yen: Japan's New Financial Empire and Its Threat to America*, Simon and Schuster, New York, 1988.

16. Bank of Tokyo, Ltd. *Annual Report 1990*, by Yusuke Kashigawi, chairman; Eiichi Matsumoto, vice chairman; and Tasuku Takagaki, president. Quotation from Michiharu Akimoto from "Financial Mire," October 16, 1992 *Wall Street Journal*.

17. Andrea Gabor, *The Man Who Discovered Quality*, Times Books, New York, 1990.

Looking to the future, noted business and management writer Peter Drucker predicts that leaders of Japanese business are shifting blue-collar manufacturing to other countries, at the same time seeking to keep ahead in new products through access to international brain power. (*The Wall Street Journal*, October 2, 1991.)

18. Mark Maremont in London, Blanca Riemer in Paris, Gail DeGeorge in Miami, Suzanne Wooley in New York, and Catherine Yang in Washington, "The Long and Winding Road to BCCI's Dead End," *Business Week*, July 22, 1991.

19. Peter Truell, "Fed Seeks to Bar BCCI Leaders and Pharaon," *Wall Street Journal*, July 15, 1991.

20. Peter Truell and Nicholas Bray, "BCCI Officials Said to Have Received Payoffs to Stay Silent About Misdeeds, "*Wall Street Journal*, July 17, 1991.

John Greenwald, Jonathan Beaty, S.C. Gwynne, and Alleen Keating, "Taken for a Royal Ride – In the wake of the BCCI debacle, a trustful sheik and more than a million depositors are left holding the bag," *Time*, July 22, 1991.

21. Herbert V. Prochnow, Editor, *American Financial Institutions*, Books for Libraries Press, Freeport, New York, 1951, reprinted 1970.

Prochnow, an authority on banking, headed the First National Bank of Chicago.

22. The Dallas Morris Plan Bank listed J.B. Adoue, Jr. as president and E. L. Flippen as vice president in the 1930s and 1940s. "Tiste" Adoue is described in Chapter 6 for his banking and civic contributions, including playing tennis with U.S. Vice President Henry Wallace. In

addition to being president of the National Bank of Commerce of Dallas, he would later serve as mayor of the city. Edgar Flippen, industrialist and banker, with his brother-in-law Hugh Prather, had established Dallas' fashionable Highland Park. He would subsequently serve as president of the First National Bank in Dallas when that institution was the largest bank in the Southwest. Adoue and Flippen and other board members gave their time and expert knowledge to the Dallas Morris Plan Bank as it served the needs of wage earners of their city. Wilbur Wright was long-time active officer of the bank.

23. *Moody's Bank & Finance Manual, 1983*. Moody's Investors Service, New York.

24. *Moody's Bank & Finance Manual*, 1975, Moody's Investors Service, New York.

Penny Lernoux says in *In Banks We Trust* that International Bank of Washington took a $9 million loss on its investment in Mercantile Bank & Trust Ltd. of the Bahamas when the Bahamian government closed the bank in 1977 because of "sham loans." General George Olmstead had been introduced to the Bahamas bank through noted Miami lawyer-banker Paul Helliwell, whom General Olmstead had known during World War II in the China Section of the Office of Strategic Services (OSS), forerunner of the CIA. Helliwell was Florida paymaster for the 1961 Bay of Pigs invasion early in the administration of U.S. President John F. Kennedy. Lernoux says that Mercantile Bank was used as a conduit for CIA money. International Bank sued Price Waterhouse because its audit of Mercantile failed to show the bank's problems. The accounting firm maintained that it could not be held responsible for the actions of a Bahamian affiliate. See Penny Lernoux, *In Banks We Trust,* Anchor Press/Doubleday, Garden City, 1984.

25. Board of Governors of Federal Reserve System, 62nd Annual Report, 1975, and 63rd Annual Report, 1976. Washington, D.C. Also, telephone conversations with Peter Truell, *Wall Street Journal* staff writer, and with Monroe Kimbrel, former president of Federal Reserve Bank of Atlanta, Thompson, Georgia, September, 1991.

26. Jack Anderson, "Carter scrutinized after BCCI scandal," United Features Syndicate, as published in *The Midland Reporter-Telegram*, September 5, 1991.

27. Gretchen Morgenson, Editor, "Forbes Informer," "Is Bert Lance Back?" *Forbes*, June 13, 1988.

28. *Moody's Bank & Finance Manual*, 1980.

29. *Moody's Bank & Finance Manual*, 1981

30. "BCCI connection to Georgia includes politicians, legislature," Associated Press report in *Lubbock (Texas) Avalanche-Journal*, August 6, 1991.

Andrew Young, U.S. ambassador to the United Nations under Carter and former mayor of Atlanta, was reported to have a $50,000 retainer relationship with Abedi, to introduce Abedi to Third World leaders.

31. Gretchen Morgenson, see Note 27 above.

32. Clark Clifford, *Counsel to the President: A Memoir*, Random House, New York, 1991.

33. Evan Thomas with Bob Cohn, "The Pain of a Power Broker — A bank scandal stains a former elder statesman," *Newsweek*, March 18, 1991.

34. In 1992 Nicholas deB. Katzenbach was again in the news in connection with memorandum that he as assistant attorney general had sent 28 years earlier to Bill Moyers, then press secretary to President Lyndon Johnson, regarding the FBI report on Lee Harvey Oswald and the assassination of John F. Kennedy.

35. Dean Baquet, "BCCI: Big Money and Mysteries," *New York Times*, July 6, 1991.

36. Dean Baquet, "After Plea Bargaining by Sheik, Question Is What He Knows"; also, Steve Lohr, "Indictment Charges Clifford Took Bribes — Broader Inquiry into B.C.C.I. Disclosed," *New York Times*, July 30, 1992.

Also see Peter Truell and Larry Gurwin's *False Profits: The Inside Story of BCCI, the World's* Most Corrupt Financial Empire, Houghton Mifflin, Boston and New York, 1992.

Ghaith Pharaon was also connected with other U.S. financial institutions charged as BCCI controlled. Earlier he was involved in the not-too-successful FDIC bailout of Bank of the Commonwealth at Detroit. See Chapter 14. Bank of America had been a founding shareholder in BCCI. In 1978 the large California bank announced it would sell its BCCI interest.

In August 1993 Robert Altman was found not guilty in New York State court on four felony charges in connection with BCCI's alleged control of First American Bankshares – four charges having been dismissed by the presiding judge. Altman pleaded in his defense that banking authorities had found no fault in a Washington-based, super-regional banking company, that BCCI had not dictated the operations of First American, and that he had received no bribes. Due to ill-health, Clark Clifford had not stood trial.

37. Board of Governors of the Federal Reserve System, *1991 Annual Report*, Washington.

38. "100 Largest Diversified Service Companies, *Fortune*, August 24, 1992.

The *1991 Annual Report* of the Board of Governors of the Federal Reserve System, Washington, stated that no export trading company was approved during 1991 under the Export Trading Company Act Amendments of 1988; though since 1982, 47 bank holding company applications for export trading company have been approved. It would appear that U.S. banking companies' efforts along this line – like that of Sears Roebuck – have not brought forth much in the way of accomplishments.

CHAPTER 9

Strong Banks, Banks That Failed, Good S&Ls

Just a Few Strong U.S. Banking Companies?

For years some of the federal banking regulators, some of the national political leaders and many in the media dreamed of a Utopian situation in which U.S. banking would be gathered into just a few financial institutions. These few strong banking companies could be monitored easily by those in Washington. Size in financial institutions has been equated with strength – perhaps also with wisdom.

In the 1990s it began to dawn upon a few of the regulators, a few politicians and certain of the financial media – perhaps understood better by the American public – that big U.S. financial institutions also get into trouble – and when they do, theirs is BIG trouble.

As the First Republic, Dallas, and Bank of New England Corp., Boston, found – big loans that go bad can mean big problems. As reported in the previous chapter, capitalization of the largest U.S. banks is now below that of large Japanese banks (though U.S. banks have not been so leveraged as Japanese banks). Nor has U.S. bank capitalization been up to the levels of the British banks. In recent years large U.S. banks have found raising new capital difficult, due in part to continuous unfavorable reports in the press and on television and radio. In 1991, America's largest, Citicorp, obtained new capital from preferred convertible stock sold to a Saudi prince and from certain financial funds.

Some Strong Banks – Small and Large

Not too many years ago, a sizable representation of those who worked in banking – not the sage leaders, but some who aspired to importance – derided the smaller banks, especially the country banks, as having but little significance.

The writer well recalls conversations with certain underlings in big downtown Dallas banks, discussing how strong smaller cities and little towns are essential to the growth and income of Dallas and other larger cities. The necessity of bank leadership in these smaller communities was discussed. The little town of Muenster was cited as having a strong bank, a live newspaper, good churches, outstanding schools. Today the former great banks of

Dallas are gone, failed. Portions of their quarters are utilized by out-of-state institutions that provide some banking services. The 150-year-old famed Dallas banking leadership is no longer. What of the bank at Muenster?

The Muenster State Bank – In a Town of 1,500 Population

Of all the towns that he helped, community development specialist John E. Surratt, father of the writer, considered Muenster, Texas to be outstanding. In each town or city, he insisted that the bankers be involved. Muenster bankers cooperated fully. Then a town of 500 people, Muenster is in Cooke County, near the Red River, north of Fort Worth, east of Wichita Falls.

All members of the community were involved in the study of the town and its trade area – their weaknesses, their strengths. Then as now, Muenster had a little oil production but not much. Milk production has traditionally been more important. The milk processing plant added to marketing and manufacturing. A livestock auction was opened. The women of the community were much involved in beautification of the cemetery, in development of the park. The newspaper took a lead in everything good for the community. Better roads were built to serve the farm families of the area. Soil conservation was emphasized. The new community hospital has three doctors and two dentists serving an enlarged trade area. Muenster population has grown to 1,500.

The Muenster State Bank serves the community. It is sound and profitable. Well below the average bank in number of employees, the bank has ten staff members looking after $47 million in assets. But, there is very little turnover among the staff. And while the average bank, large or small, is most happy to have a return of 1 percent on assets, the Muenster State Bank in recent years, when other banks were failing, has earned over 2 percent on assets. Nor is it over-loaned. The customers are well known. When interest rates went sky-high in 1980, the Muenster bank purchased sound but high-earning federal obligations. These proved a most-satisfactory investment. Half a million dollars were paid in a special dividend to the 103 shareholders in 1989, more than had been paid for all the years from the bank's organization in 1923 to 1980.

The community has attractive homes both in town and on the farms. When insurance companies and S&Ls would not finance new homes in the community, the Muenster bank did so as a community service. The Catholic church and the Baptist church have attractive structures. The parochial school and the public school give superior instruction. The community enjoys active year-round civic projects. The annual Germanfest attracts more than 50,000 people to this town of 1,500 people. Bank president Earl Fisher has been with the bank for more than 50 years. His predecessor Herbert Meurer is still on the board of directors. Meurer's predecessor, J.M. Weinzapfel, now in his nineties, remains interested in all that goes on in the community. There are some concerns regarding the national economy. Banker Fisher thinks farm land prices at $700-$800 per acre are too high. He also thinks greed and stupidity put many banks under.[1]

The Muenster bank has grown and prospered as it has helped the community grow and prosper. Such is the key for any bank, of any size – to know and to serve its community – whatever size the community may be.

National Penn Bancshares

The National Bank of Boyertown is a long-time well-run Pennsylvania institution. Established in 1874, the bank and related mortgage and insurance companies of National Penn Bancshares in 1990 acquired area Sellersville Savings and Loan Association. Sellersville Savings was well capitalized, as is the bank and holding company. Year after year the company earns more than 1.4 percent on assets. Year-end 1991 assets were $739 million. Capital was $61.6 million, a good 8.3 percent of assets. The bank serves a five-county area: Berks, Bucks, Chester, Lehigh and Montgomery, northwest of Philadelphia.[2]

The late James K. Boyer was for nearly 30 years the executive of the banking company. Lawrence T. Jilk, Jr. joined the bank in 1977 and became CEO in 1983.

Emphasis is on customer service. The *1990 Annual Report* states:

> High quality customers did not happen by chance. Rather, they must be found, developed and convinced your Company can meet the needs better than anyone else.

In the 1990 report, President Jilk and Executive Vice President Wayne R. Weidner were concerned about the costs of FDIC insurance, saying:

> Our principal imponderable is the unknown cost of FDIC insurance which will likely be increased. We would like to see such premiums vary, based upon the risks of individual banks, but this is unlikely as problems seem to be concentrated in the larger, more politically powerful banks.

NationsBank (NCNB), Banc One, and Team Bank

NCNB, headquartered in Charlotte, North Carolina; Banc One, headquartered in Columbus, Ohio; and new Deposit Guaranty Bank of Dallas had kept their affairs in rather good order, and were able to assume enormous opportunities when federal regulatory agencies decided to close down First RepublicBank Corp. and MCorp, both of Dallas; Texas American out of Fort Worth; and NBC out of San Antonio.

First Republic, MCorp, Texas American and National Bancshares had attempted to spread across Texas and even to go world-wide in their operations. NCNB (renamed NationsBank in 1992), Banc One, and Team Bank have taken full opportunity of their FDIC-sponsored presence in Texas – cutting expenses and personnel – besides having no bad loans from predecessor institutions. They have likewise profited from new service charges on customers they inherited, as well as commissions for collecting old loans, and have been most cautious in extending credit.

Having let go many higher-paid administrative and specialized personnel, they have found it difficult to offer specialized lending and other higher-skilled services. The federally sanctioned Texas takeover institutions are operating to a considerable degree as absentee landlords – giving moderate service, with minimum personnel.

Banc One (Bank One)

Banc One was already a better-than-average-earning banking company before going into its federally assisted expansions. Banc One has consistently earned well above 1 percent on assets, and appears to have avoided many of the difficulties of rapid expansion. Generally good earnings have accompanied generally good service. See Appendix H for details.

NationsBank has seldom exceeded 1 percent net income on assets. Nor was the former NCNB Corp. a top earner before joining the federal regulators in rapid acquisition of banks and S&Ls. Strong on holding down costs, NationsBank has difficulty in achieving a strong lending program in its areas of operation.

In 1991 NCNB, which through FDIC and RTC acquisitions had more Texas deposits than any other institution in the state, and which was benefiting from current and future tax benefits from the takeover of remnants of failed First Republic, announced it would welcome proposed new authority to abolish its one Texas bank charter and make it a branch of North Carolina.[3]

Many of the "failed" smaller banks in the holding companies taken over by the FDIC were in fairly good shape, in spite of previous mismanagement by the home offices.

The success for the investors in Team Bank is related in Chapter 6, in connection with the sell-out to Banc One.

U.S. Bancorp

Over a decade ago this writer had a letter-to-the-editor on banking strengths and earnings published in *Fortune* magazine. This was during the year 1980 when bank earnings seemed to be going ever-skyward, accompanying a prime bank interest rate that had climbed to over 20 percent and ever-upward commodity and real estate prices. Regarding *Fortune's* annual listing of then largest U.S. banks (before foreign banks were considered) this writer recommended that net income be analyzed as a percentage of bank assets. Such would give a better measure of banking profitability and efficiency. Comment was made that reporting of income as a percentage of equity was helpful, but that it did not consider capital strength (capital as a percentage of assets). Quoting the second paragraph of that letter:

> It is not the largest commercial-banking companies that are the most profitable in terms of assets. Ameritrust Corp. of Cleveland, which ranks only 34th on *Fortune's* latest list, and U.S. Bancorp. of Portland, Oregon, which is 48th, both earned over 1% on assets last year. The latter also had capital equal to 7.2% of assets, and the Cleveland Trust group (Ameritrust) has built up its capital to 9.4% of assets. At several of the largest banking companies, capital is less than 5% of assets.

In addition to stating the facts personal bias must be admitted in that letter. Ex-boss from army days Lowell R. Brisbin was cashier and chief operating officer for U.S. Bancorp. Friend Everett Ware Smith had moved from New England to Cleveland to be head of Cleveland Trust (Ameritrust).

U.S. Bancorp has continued to do a good job for its area and was able to expand when opportunity came along. Today it is the largest banking institution in the Northwest. In 1992 Roger L. Breezley, chairman and chief executive officer, announced that $18.9 billion U.S. Bancorp had again earned more than 1 percent on assets – 1.06 percent for 1991.[4]

Sadly, some of Ev Smith's successors went on wild expansion programs. In 1990 Ameritrust even picked up bankrupt MCorp's trust business in Texas, which should have been somewhat profitable but which was way off geographically, and did not help much with improving assets elsewhere. In 1992 Ameritrust, with weaker capital and nonexistent net earnings, was merged into rival Society Bank of Cleveland. Ameritrust still had sufficient strength that its shareholders did not lose all their investment, nor was there a loss to be charged against the completely depleted FDIC Bank Insurance Fund.

What was said of the 1980s regarding bank size as having not much relevancy to bank strength and earnings remains equally true in the 1990s. Too many failed large and small banks in the past twelve years give mute evidence.

A Strong, Large Bank – Morgan Guaranty Trust Company, New York

One of the strongest large U.S. banks is Morgan Guaranty Trust Co. in New York city. The influence of J. Pierpont Morgan continues to guide that institution. Feared as the apotheosis of untrammeled capitalism in the early part of the twentieth century, Morgan had a tremendous influence on business and banking.

Morgan, who was a very private person, reluctantly appeared before Congress' Pujo Committee in 1912. U.S. congressman from Minnesota Charles A. Lindbergh, Sr., who coined the expression "money trust," introduced a resolution in the House to investigate the concentration of power on Wall Street. A subcommittee of the House Banking and Currency Committee, chaired by Louisiana congressman Aresene Pujo, gave the hearing the name. It is ironic that Lindbergh's aviation hero son later married the daughter of Morgan partner Wright Morrow.

Ron Chernow in his book *House of Morgan: An American Banking Dynasty and The Rise of Modern Finance*, recounted that committee attorney Samuel Untermeyer asked J.P. Morgan, "Is not commercial credit based primarily upon money or property?" To which Morgan replied, "No sir, the first thing is character."

Untermeyer then asked, "Before money or property?" To which Morgan replied, "Before money or anything else. Money cannot buy it . . . Because a man I do not trust could not get money from me on all the bonds in Christendom. I have known a man to come into my office, and I have given him a check for a million dollars when I knew that he had not a cent in the world."

According to Chernow, Morgan's statement was neither as cynical as critics thought, nor as noble as friends imagined. It was workable business strategy.

J.P. Morgan and Company was later to merge with Guaranty Trust Co. into Morgan Guaranty Trust Co. (See statement from Guaranty Trust ex-employee Stuart Andrews in Chapter 2.)

In 1989 Morgan Guaranty charged its earnings by $2 billion as an additional loss allowance for loans to developing countries – covering nearly all its risk on such loans, and causing a negative earnings report for the year. Morgan chairman Dennis Weatherstone and president Douglas A. Warner II expressed sympathy for the efforts of the U.S. Treasury and the IMF to work out the lingering loans to developing countries by large U.S. banks but said the Morgan bank had decided that it must do more than to depend upon government. "We were also concerned that the International Monetary Fund, the World Bank and industrialized countries, except for Japan, had not provided adequate financial resources to encourage continuing voluntary participation by international banks in the [U.S. Secretary of Treasury] Brady debt-reduction plan."[5]

At the beginning of 1992, Morgan had $103 billion in assets, with a capital/asset ratio of 5.86 percent – very good for a large bank.[6] Under the proposed new international Basle ratios for large international banks, Morgan also shows up well.

The Basle-based Committee on Banking Regulations and Supervisory Practices is comprised of representatives of the central banks of the leading European countries, Canada and the United States. It proposes a two-tier system for judging capital adequacy of large international banks. "Off-balance sheet" items such as letters of credit would be given some inclusion, whereas cash and other items of little risk would be excluded, or given little measure. Tier One would include equity capital and certain reserves. Tier Two would include additional quasi-capital accounts. Such items would generally not be part of smaller banks' capital accounts, since their capital accounts are largely made up of equity ownerships. As of the beginning of 1992, Morgan had a capital ratio of 6.9 percent of Tier One (equity capital and reserves) to risk assets, plus 3.8 percent for Tier Two (additional accounts), a total of 10.7 percent. Projected U.S. Federal Reserve requirements, in line with the Basle agreement, would be a minimum of 4 percent for Tier One and 8 percent total – which Morgan surpasses, but for which many other large banks were struggling. In 1990 Morgan had the highest earnings of all eastern U.S. banks, In 1991 Morgan's net earnings were highest of all U.S. banks – $1.1 billion – 1.05 percent on assets.[7]

How Well You Train the People to Replace You!

Chernow also cited the statement that Morgan head Henry C. Alexander made to former Guaranty Trust staff when the two banks combined. "I want all of you to know – as the relatively fewer Morgan people here know – that an important element of your career path will be how well you train the people underneath you to replace you."[8] Too many banks failed on this, miserably. Failure to train and to retain competent personnel under corporate leadership has caused hundreds of bank failures, and losses in hundreds of billions of dollars!

Another Good New York Bank

Bankers Trust Co. of New York is another sound institution, earning $667 million on assets of $64 billion in 1991. In recent years it went into branch banking, but more recently sold most branches.

Staying with Sound Banking

While every other old established bank in West Texas cities, in Abilene, Midland, Odessa and San Angelo, either sold out to a distant holding company – with less than completely satisfactory results, as near 100 percent recapitalization – or else went broke, First National Bank of Abilene, Texas survived and prospered. Assets are nearly half a billion dollars for affiliated area banks in a local holding company. Equity to assets is more than 9 percent of which many big city banks could only dream. Retired banker Fred Henry says that the Abilene-based institution is strong and profitable, doing what has been done for over 100 years, serving the local community. Furthermore, it has never missed paying a dividend since the turn of the century![9]

Decatur County Bank

In Decaturville, Tennessee, near the Tennessee River, Decatur County Bank was established in 1899. As of the beginning of 1990, Decatur County Bank's capital account was $3.9 million against total assets of $37.6 million, over 10 percent equity to total assets. No major U.S. bank comes close to such a strong capital ratio. Retired circuit judge/bank director James L. England allows that the bank is doing well and is having growth. The bank has a branch at nearby and larger Parsons. Decatur County Bank is the largest bank in the county.[10] Decatur Bank's secret is service to its area.

A $140,000,000 Bank in a Town of 400 Population

Long-time banker Don Wright in his 1990 book, *The Dynamic Financial Manager*, tells of the amazing "Cow Pasture Bank" of Rio Vista, Texas – a town of 406 population.[11] The First State Bank of Rio Vista has deposits of more than $140 million! The bank, which has been in business since 1920, invites its customers to drive in, fly in, do business by mail, or do business by telephone. (The bank has an airplane landing strip for customers.)

Chief executive Lowell Smith, Jr., like his father before him, knows his customers. The bank subscribes to newspapers from all adjacent counties. Laminated news reports of personal activities of customers and prospective customers are sent to everyone in the area. The *Cowpasture Bank Cookbook* has recipes from customers and wives of customers. It has been re-printed in the thousands. Customers and prospective customers are invited to special events and barbecues. The bank serves its area very well and profitably. Such personal service is beyond the comprehension of many larger financial institutions.

Philadelphia National Bank

A long-time good larger bank is Philadelphia National Bank, which in recent years joined with smaller area banks in CoreStates Financial Corp. Rival First Pennsylvania Bank got into financial difficulties and in 1980 was bailed out by the FDIC with the assistance of various large banks. In the decade to follow, First Pennsylvania was never the outstanding bank of earlier years, and in 1990 it merged with Philadelphia National in the CoreStates organization. (Hongkong Bank sold its interest.) First Pennsylvania claimed through predecessors to have been founded by Robert Morris, financier of the American Revolution and signer of the Declaration of Independence and the U.S. Constitution.

Philadelphia National and CoreStates have been profitable, in spite of difficulties in digesting First Pennsylvania's problems.

First Empire State

First Empire State Corp. in 1991 was a $7.5 billion upstate-New York bank holding company headquartered at Buffalo. The 100-year-old Manufacturers and Traders Trust Co. (M&T) of Buffalo is a major part of First Empire State. The company also has 90-year-old First National Bank of Highland, in the Hudson Valley, and East New York Savings Bank of New York City, organized in 1868 and acquired in 1987 when it converted from mutual ownership to stock ownership.

Morgan Guaranty's 1962 attempt to acquire Manufacturers and Traders was turned down by the Federal Reserve – probably to the benefit of both Manhattan-based Morgan and Buffalo-based M&T. Buffalo is strategically located where the Niagara River leaves Lake Erie on its northward journey via the famous falls to Lake Ontario. Canada is just across the river west of Buffalo. According to a 1986 report in *Forbes*, holding company First Empire, organized in 1969, "ventured far from its hometown and paid dearly. It managed to lose money in real estate investment trust loans and foreign loans that went sour. Its stock sold at less than 50 percent of book value."

Robert Wilmers, formerly of Morgan, went to salvage First Empire with backers that included a Portuguese banker and a Swiss industrialist, and the "Baird family, old-line Buffaloans." *Forbes* told how Wilmers charged off lots of loans in his first years and sold the bank's Mexican and Brazilian loans at a discount. He charged-off a seven-figure loan at First Empire's bank in Highland, New York, which a previous administration had made to Mafia figures who defaulted on their loans.[12]

With capable management, First Empire net earnings rose above 1 percent return on assets, until recent acquisitions temporarily lowered return. Even before the 1991 Goldome acquisition, in 1990 M&T Bank acquired deposits of "approximately $1.7 billion from two failed savings banks that had been seized by regulatory authorities." These included 11 banking offices previously operated by Monroe Savings Bank – and the Western New York Division of Empire Federal Savings of America (no relation to First Empire). M&T took these over with an "initial total of about $800 million in loans, with certain options to return loans on review." First Empire's *1990 Annual Report* said the acquisitions would temporarily depress earnings per asset but should be good in the long run.

Robert G. Wilmers is president and chief executive of First Empire. Paul B. Murray is chairman of the board. Vice chairman is Jorge G. Pereira. Former U.S. Secretary of Defense Frank C. Carlucci is a director of the East New York Savings Bank.

Astute investor Warren Buffett, through Berkshire Hathaway Inc., invested $40 million in First Empire convertible preferred stock in March 1991.

First Empire, which has worked with the Federal Deposit Insurance Corp. and Resolution Trust Corp., and which received FDIC-RTC benefits on its recent takeovers of failed thrift institutions, has words of warning in its 1990 report on the future of U.S. banking and the federal insurance funds. See Appendix O for this excerpt from First Empire's *1990 Annual Report*.[13]

Some Banks That Nearly Failed

Some of the banks that nearly failed should not have gotten into trouble. To their credit, at least two of the big banks that received FDIC and other outside capitalization pulled through – Continental Illinois of Chicago (now Continental Bank) and First Pennsylvania in Philadelphia – though not without problems. First Pennsylvania eventually merged into rival Philadelphia National's CoreStates system.

Franklin National (Chapter 5), like too many other financial institutions, tried to move into a different geographic area, though nearby – from Long Island into Manhattan Island. It also attempted to go international in a hurry, under the mysterious hand of

Michele Sindona.

Great Texas Banks Failed When Leadership Was Gone

With the latest oil boom and bust of the late 1970s and 1980s, 93-year-old First National Bank of Midland grew too fast, in part on brokered CDs, and made too many big loans based on the expectation that the price of oil would go ever upward. The guiding hand of its able pre-boom chief executive, C.J. Kelly, was sorely missed when his health failed.[14]

Not since the onset of the Great Depression was a city so financially devastated as was Dallas after its long-time big three banks, First National, Republic and Mercantile, went through various rapid expansions in their holding companies with an attempted merger of First and Republic – and then went broke. First National, which had become InterFirst, joined with long-time arch rival Republic National in mid 1987 into a holding company with more than 100 member banks. Lasting just over a year, the $38 billion financial company and its 40 remaining banks were declared insolvent in mid-1988.

Long-time leaders Nathan Adams of First National, Fred Florence of Republic, and Bob Thornton of Mercantile had missed the mark in that their successors failed. Nathan Adams had declared his standards years earlier. Once when Adams was speaking on better warehousing for cotton, a banker who had the misfortune of seeing his bank closed asked what Adams knew about farming. Adams said to the assembled crowd, "I may not know much about farming, but so help me God, I never busted a bank."[15]

Detroit Banking Rebuilt in the 1930s
Dallas Banking Leadership Lost in the 1980s

Like Detroit in the 1930s, Dallas lost its leading banks 50 years later. Unlike Detroit – which in 1933 rebuilt its two failed banking systems into the new locally controlled National Bank of Detroit and Manufacturers National – Dallas' two large banking companies were not reborn locally. In 1933, Democrat RFC Chairman Jesse H. Jones put his prestige and that of newly inaugurated President Franklin D. Roosevelt in a challenge to Detroit leadership, to pay off the depositors of failed Union Guardian and First Wayne National banking companies and to organize locally owned successor banks. (This was before the FDIC was established.) Republican businessman Edward Douglas Stair, publisher of the *Detroit Free Press* and chairman of the Detroit Bankers Company, holding company for the First Wayne National Banks, accepted the challenge to "lead Detroit out of the wilderness." President Alfred

P. Sloan of General Motors Corp. committed his company for $12,500,000 in common stock to match the RFC's $12,500,000 preferred stock in a new National Bank of Detroit. A portion of the common stock was then taken by fellow automotive manufacturer Walter Chrysler for his company with other Detroiters subscribing for smaller amounts of stock.[16]

Henry Ford and son Edsel Ford organized a new Manufacturers National Bank on their own, with no RFC funding. The new banks resumed lending to many previous borrowing customers of the failed banks. Depositors in the thousands turned to the new banks. With public confidence restored, the new banks and other, smaller banks that had survived the crash brought back confidence to the people of Detroit. General Motors and the Fords had no desire to be in the banking business permanently and sold off their stock interests to Detroit citizens over the years.

Dallas in the 1980s was a different story. When First Republic and MCorp failed, there was no Jesse Jones from Washington. Nor did local leadership succeed in reorganization of the failed First Republic and MCorp systems (which had grown statewide). During its more-than-100-years history, Dallas had become the financial center of the Southwest. Predecessor banks had always been most prominent in the growth of Dallas and its Southwestern trade area. Dallas banking and business leadership, with the backing of citizens in the smaller cities and towns of the area, had won the location of the 11th Federal Reserve District for Dallas. Dallas banking leadership had tremendous influence on related insurance, wholesale, manufacturing, and retail development in the Dallas area. In the late 1980s all this changed.

Former American Airlines chairman (and former U.S. Postmaster General) Albert V. Casey had become interim chairman of First Republic in its last months of existence. Casey and a group attempted to gain approval from the FDIC to establish a successor bank for First Republic.[17] Former U.S. Sen. John Tower was also with a group that sought to rebuild local ownership of the failed Dallas banking company. Both were turned down by the federal regulators who stated that neither group had banking experience. Perhaps more important to the FDIC and the Comptroller of the Currency and to a lesser extent to the Federal Reserve was a desire to utilize the previously untried powers of Garn-St Germain so as to promote widespread interstate banking. By throwing all 40 First Republic banks into one – state constitution and laws to the contrary – the FDIC et al could utilize the $500 million minimum under Garn-St Germain and give the failed $38 billion banking system to an approved out-of-state banking company, in this case NCNB Corp. of Charlotte, North Carolina, a banking company then smaller than First Republic. With MCorp it was to be BancOne Corp. of Columbus, Ohio. (As for lack of experience, Albert Casey was later chosen to head the subsequently created gigantic federal S&L resolution corporation, the RTC. John Tower died in a commuter plane crash.)

Leadership Lost in Dallas

In more than 100 years of their city's existence, the great Dallas banks had been intimately involved in most everything that happened to the city and its area. The banking headquarters buildings were sought as main offices by leading business companies, by the large law firms and by the accounting firms. Leading specialty retail stores located in the bank buildings. Other large retail establishments were nearby. All looked to these banks for financial assistance and guidance. Said as an excuse for twice keeping Continental Illinois bank of Chicago alive – by the RFC in the 1930s and by the FDIC in the 1980s – was that Continental was a great correspondent bank. First Republic and MBank were also great "correspondent banks." Hundreds of banks in other cities and towns kept accounts in the large Dallas banks. But First Republic and MBank were not kept alive.

Certain of the former bank headquarters buildings of Dallas are near vacant today. Adjacent blocks of office buildings have few tenants. Retail business is near dead in downtown Dallas. Such could be said of other major cities as to retail business, where competition from outlying malls had closed up downtown stores. Dallas has but little going on downtown. Neiman Marcus remains a striking exception in its flagship location – across from vacated bank buildings. Grass is actually growing in cracks of the sidewalks on Commerce Street. Exceptions to downtown decay are the newer self-contained office buildings to the northeast, developed by Trammell Crow and others.

The Federal Reserve Bank of Dallas had outgrown its Akard Street quarters. There was no supportive banking leadership to help the Fed acquire nearby blocks for expansion. A Federal Reserve bank requires access for armored cars carrying currency and coin, as well as quick transit for check clearings. Without considering the consequences, the City of Dallas closed traffic access on Akard Street from the north, placing a plaza at Commerce Street in the pathway of Federal Reserve traffic. Thus in 1992 the Federal Reserve Bank of Dallas moved over a mile away from the existing downtown district, to a new location where the State Highway

Department had created a freeway. The loss of supporting financial leadership is felt again and again in Dallas in the 1990s. This is not just in the central business district but is felt in every area and every phase of the city's existence.

Golden West Financial Corporation — A Good S&L

Out on the West Coast, where many other S&Ls have gone under, Golden West Financial Corp. in Oakland operates successfully through its main subsidiary, World Savings. Husband and wife Herb and Marian Sandler, chairman and president, successfully guide Golden West, with assets of more than $20 billion. When the 1989 S&L reform bill was under consideration by Congress, the Sandlers ran a *Washington Post* advertisement urging Congress to establish strong capital requirements for S&Ls. This fits right in with their operation, with a capital-to-assets ratio of nearly 6 percent — a ratio several times higher than in many S&Ls, and one of which many commercial banks its size would be jealous. Earnings likewise are near or above those of commercial banks its size, approaching 1 percent on assets.

The Wall Street Journal in June 1990 devoted almost four columns to the way that the Sandlers have brought a new meaning to "thrift." There are no corporate jets, and visitors announce their presence by means of a black telephone in the reception area, rather than through a receptionist.[18]

Fulton Savings & Loan

In the middle of Missouri, halfway between St. Louis and Kansas City, is Fulton, county seat of Callaway County. Midwestern Fulton had received attention just before World War II when midwesterner and future President of the United States Ronald Reagan played a major role in the popular motion picture production of *King's Row*, based upon life in Fulton, Missouri. It was at Fulton's Westminster College that Winston Churchill gave birth to the phrase "iron curtain." A few years later, incoming American Bankers Association president Fred Florence, then head of the Republic National Bank of Dallas, presented diplomas and delivered the college graduating class address.

Long-time Callaway County farmer L.F. Books says that the financial institutions in his home town appear to be all right.[19] Fulton Savings and Loan operates the way most S&Ls used to operate. They make home loans and look after the customers in the hometown. As of year-end 1990, Fulton S&L had loans of $51.6 million, savings deposits of $57.5 million, capital of $5.2 million, and total assets of $65.5 million. Regulatory capital to assets was a strong

8.21 percent. Kermit Gehring is the long-time head of Fulton Savings. In the 1990s the iron curtain, like the Communist-erected Berlin Wall, is falling down.

Fulton, Missouri U.S.A. remains strong.[20]

Martin Mayer on "Too Big Not to Fail"

With a play on words on the unofficial policy of federal banking regulators enunciated at the time of the Continental Illinois rescue, that the largest U.S. banks are "too big to be allowed to fail," Martin Mayer gave a 1991 report in *Forbes*, under the title "Too Big Not to Fail."[21] Taking a stand completely opposite to many in the federal government who wish to push big banking still further into nationwide systems, Mayer's subtitle in *Forbes* continued, *Federal policy aimed at saving the biggest banks almost guarantees a repeat of the S&L disaster.* Discussing the weakened condition of many large banks, Mayer blames regulators for poor capitalization of big banks saying they "permitted bank managements to adopt the doctrine that the smaller the equity, the greater the return on equity." He said that stock market values for bank stocks recognize the "see-through office buildings, insolvent Latin American governments, and overleveraged retail chains, all carried on the books (with regulators' permission) as though they were worth face value or something like it."

Mayer states the opposite to what is often stated by supposed experts in banking, that "except in consumer finance and mortgages, there are no economies of scale in banking." He also cites a General Accounting Office study which shows that the "loss to the taxpayers (from the S&L debacle) was equal to about *10%* of the value of insured deposits that existed at the end of 1986." He contrasts the recent period under the now-defunct FSLIC to the era prior to deposit insurance, saying losses to depositors in commercial banks "before the deposit insurance system is estimated to have been *1%* of total deposits."

This writer hopes that Mayer's prediction does not come true – that large U.S. banks are "financial dinosaurs." But this writer agrees with his discernment that the great strength of our banking system is not the giant banks, but in the myriad of middling-size banks – and smaller banks.

Unintentionally, or intentionally it would appear that some of our elected representatives, some of our appointed officials and some in the printed and broadcast media would consolidate banks and S&Ls into a very few, under semi-socialistic government support and control. None would be allowed to fail – any more than the various federal credit corporations listed in Chapter 7 fail. They could just go on and on, year after year, subsidized by federal agencies through special fees and tax benefits – part of the federal debt that has grown so enormous in recent years. Subsidies would come from the pockets of the taxpayers and by printing more paper money. (Or perhaps we should say by creating federal credit – electronic book entry or otherwise – rather than from mere paper money.)

That the super-regional banking companies of the 1990s may be unwieldy, not very efficient, not particularly profitable, not of outstanding service to the communities for which they have been awarded franchises may be a reflection of the unwieldy, not very efficient, deficit financed, federal government that has created them.

This is not to suggest that we do not have some excellent large banks – and some excellent small banks. But banks and other financial institutions should be allowed to excel by merit, not by governmental interference, intervention and favoritism.

Some Other Strong Banks

Sun Trust

A well-run Southeastern banking company is Sun Trust Banks Inc., a combination of Trust Company Banks of Atlanta, Georgia, Sun Banks of Orlando, Florida, and Third National Corp. of Nashville, Tennessee. The banking company attributes success to the autonomy of the three state banking systems that make up the holding company. Brad Kuhn of the *Orlando Sentinel* told of 1991 earnings of $371 million on assets of $34 billion, well above 1 percent.[22]

Fifth-Third

Fifth-Third Bankcorp, headquartered at Cincinnati, Ohio, is still another good banking company. President George A. Schaefer Jr. in an interview with Editor-in-Chief Robert A. Bennett of *United States Banker* told of *benefits* from being in a geographic area that is often in *economic recessions.* (Just the opposite of excuses of many bankers and regulators.) Schaefer says they are used to cyclical businesses and prepare for such conditions. They do not try to have the largest market share, rather "we deliver our products and make a profit and continue to grow at our target rates.... There is plenty of business in our own backyard, we don't need to go to Texas, Illinois and St. Louis, or Pittsburgh."[23]

Fifth-Third has more than 10 percent capital ratio with 13 percent total capital. In a bad year the company earns 1.4 percent on assets, in a good year 1.7 percent. This formula is *hard work and discipline,* according to *United States Banker.*

The bank excels and profits from data processing (which a number of big banks are giving up these days), in addition to its sound lending and trust services, plus service to the deposit customers. Assets are $8.3 billion.

Wachovia

Another good banking company is Wachovia of Winston-Salem, North Carolina. A 1991 merger with renowned but slightly troubled South Carolina National Bank depressed earnings slightly, but $30 billion Wachovia Corp. is in good shape. Shareholders' equity to assets was 7.49 percent at the beginning of 1992. Wachovia has long done a good job in lending to business in its geographic area.[24]

See statement from Wachovia's CEO at conclusion of Appendix A.

Bank South

A 1992 Associated Press report from Atlanta, Georgia told a new series of Bank South radio commercials about "Bob," whose wife had been replaced by "headquarters in North Carolina" with a woman named "Charlotte." Patrick L. Flinn, who had spent more than 20 years with Atlanta-based C&S before becoming Bank South's chief executive says the ad is not to single out NationsBank, but to "pick on everyone because they're all saying bigger is better."[25]

Northwest Corporation

One of the better large banking companies, Northwest Corp. of Minneapolis, Minnesota, is unusual in its emphases on mortgage originations, trust services, agricultural lending, and consumer and commercial finance. Most of its expansion has come from mergers with existing successful banks, rather than from government subsidized acquisitions of failed institutions. Even after digesting difficulties of acquired institutions, net earnings for 1991 were 1.1 percent on assets of $38.5 billion. Chairman Lloyd P. Johnson and President Richard M. Kovecivich allow that "employees are empowered to make decisions locally that enable Northwest to be our customers' first choice for service and solutions."[26] Northwest also avoids concentration of credit to any particular borrower.

Still other banks that continue to do well, and some that failed, are discussed in Chapter 6.

NOTES

1. Telephone conversations and correspondence with President Earl Fisher and Executive Vice President Henry Weinzapfel of Muenster State Bank. See Appendix I for additional information on this outstanding U.S. bank and community. In 1993 after more than 70 years of service to bank and community, J. M. Weinzapfel died at age 98.

2. National Penn Bancshares Inc., *1989* and *1990 Annual Reports,* Boyertown, Pennsylvania.

3. See annual reports of NCNB (Nations Bank), Banc One and Team Bank, also those of the FDIC. In a July 3, 1991 article titled 'NCNB Could Trigger Tax-Benefit Curb Under Its Plan to Acquire C&S/Sovran,'' *Wall Street Journal* reporters Martha Brannigan and David B. Hilder discuss possible additional acquisitions by NCNB in the Southeast, saying NCNB Corp. may possibly risk ''tax benefits it can use to shelter profits in future years.''

The *WSJ* report refers to NCNB's benefits from several federal agencies when it was approved to enter Texas – in the FDIC bridge bank that FDIC originally financed to take over remnants of failed First Republic. Though protected by the FDIC against foreseeable losses, NCNB under special ruling by Internal Revenue (IRS) also received the tax benefits of the failed banks. The *WSJ* report continues:

''NCNB's tax benefits derive largely from its 1988 acquisition of the remnants of failed First RepublicBank Corp. in Dallas and are a major reason why that operation is so profitable.''

4. Telephone conversation with L. R. Brisbin. Also U.S. Bancorp, *1989, 1990, 1991 Annual Reports*, Portland. Also, ''Letters to Fortune'' August 11, 1980 *Fortune.*

5. Ron Chernow, *The House of Morgan: An American Banking Dynasty and The Rise of Modern Finance*, Atlantic Monthly Press, New York, 1990.

Also see Frederick Lewis Allen, *The Great Pierpont Morgan*, Harper, New York, 1949.

Allen also quotes the Pujo Committee statements from J.P. Morgan.

6. J.P. Morgan & Co., *1989, 1990, 1991 Annual Reports*, New York.

7. Robert Mims, ''Corporate Scoreboard,'' *Business Week*, March 18, 1991.

8. Chernow, cited above.

9. Fred G. Henry, Abilene, Texas, Telephone conversations, 1990.

10. James L. England, Decatur County Bank, Decaturville, Tennessee, letter of July 20, 1990.

11. Don Wright, *The Dynamic Bank Manager*, Don Wright Associates, Dallas, 1990.

12. Allan Sloan, ''Gold is where you find it,'' *Forbes*, November 17, 1986.

13. First Empire State Corporation, *1990 Annual Report,* Buffalo, New York.

14. First National Bank of Midland, Texas, *1982 Annual Report*. See also news reports before and after the 93-year-old bank was closed in October, 1983.

15. Nathan Adams, *The First in Dallas,* First National Bank in Dallas, 1942.

16. Jesse H. Jones, *50 Billion Dollars,* (Previously cited.)

17. Albert V. Casey, telephone conversation, 1990.

18. Charles McCoy, ''If only all the S&Ls had been managed like Golden West,'' *Wall Street Journal*, June 19, 1990.

19. L.F. Books, Fulton, Missouri, telephone conversation, August 1990.

20. Kermit Gehring, president, Fulton Savings & Loan Association, telephone conversation, August, 1990. Also, Fulton Savings & Loan's *Annual Report for 1990.*

21. Martin Mayer, ''Too Big Not To Fail,'' *Forbes*, April 15, 1991.

22. Brad Kuhn, *Orlando Sentinel,* January 15, 1992. Also see *Sun Trust Banks, Inc. Annual Report for 1991,* Atlanta.

23. Interview by Editor-in-Chief Robert A. Bennett, *United States Banker, January, 1992.*

24. See *1991 Annual Report* of Wachovia Corp., Winston-Salem.

25. Associated Press reported in *Dallas Morning News,* March 10, 1992.

26. Northwest Corp., *1991 Annual Report*, Minneapolis.

CHAPTER 10

The Insurance Companies

In late 1990, both *Barron's* and the *Wall Street Journal* took up rumors that observers of the financial scene had been repeating for some time: that the insurance companies, like the savings banks, the S&Ls and the commercial banks, also have their problems. Both *Barron's* and *WSJ* began to explore the assets, income and expense, and policyholder's surplus, as well as other capital protection of large life insurance companies.

The Equitable

They opened their series by discussion of the Equitable Life Assurance Society of the United States, a company with assets and insurance in force equal in size to the length of the company name.[1] The *WSJ* questioned how Equitable in New York City, examined by "one of the best of the state insurance departments," could have "veered so far off course." And although it assured the public that there was no immediate threat of insolvency, the venerable journal answered its own question as to how such a company could go so far off course. The *WSJ* explained that Equitable and other life insurance companies had tried to be like banks, with new products such as Guaranteed Investment Contracts (GICs), guaranteeing investors up to "ten-year terms and giving the holders the option of investing more money over the life of the contract at those high rates."

We were told of new subsidiaries that went on spending binges, such as shopping center acquisitions. In the case of Equitable, the *WSJ* criticized conspicuous spending in the "almost six-story-high painting by Roy Liechtenstein and murals by Thomas Hart Benton" in the headquarters building.[2] (In its annual report, Equitable said the New York's mayor Ed Koch had asked that the company acquire and preserve the murals.)

Also mentioned were investments in "junk bonds" and other new types of investments, and slowness in mortgages, a traditional investment for life insurance companies.

The effect of the declining dollar on the psychology of buying insurance was not mentioned in the *WSJ* article – the fact that a $1,000 policy three decades ago was considered a valuable asset at time of death, with desirable cash value build-up against which a bargain policy loan could be made. A $5,000 policy was especially valued. It gave the bread winner assurance that his widow and children would have some protection. Such policies mean little today to the prospective purchaser. The dollar amounts are insignificant in view of the prospective policyholder's expectation that the dollar value will be far less upon death of the insured. In years gone by to belong to the "Million Dollar Roundtable" meant that the insurance agent was a real producer. Now the term is rarely heard.

As with banks, with S&Ls and with other financial institutions, insurance companies have been hard put to know how to invest, how to out-figure the fluctuating interest rates egged on by the U.S. Congress in its unpredictable but ever-greater deficit spendings.

The *WSJ* told of various departed officers of Equitable, leaving chairman Richard H. Jenrette in charge. Jenrette had joined Equitable via its acquisition of the investment securities firm of Donaldson, Lufkin and Jenrette.

Before the news hit the Dow Jones press, Equitable's 1989 annual report mentioned "shedding . . . non-related interests" and returning to its "core business of insurance and investment management."[3]

Equitable reports gave Japan as an example of financial businesses that "still follow the early post-World War II U.S. model which strictly segmented the components of the financial services business." Meanwhile, U.S. deregulation, the reports went on to say, "led to cross-industry competition as regulatory agencies have moved to strike down the traditional lines of demarcation."

Equitable had $44.9 billion in general account assets ($61.7 billion in total assets) at the beginning of 1990, and a surplus of $1.3 billion plus $737 million Mandatory Securities Valuation Account and over a quarter of a trillion dollars in insurance in force. Equitable will probably survive stronger than ever, though it may become a subsidiary of a foreign insurance company.

This won't be the first time it has survived a shakeup. In 1905, the company was shaken by financial scandal and was taken over by wealthy Thomas Fortune Ryan. A board of three trustees headed by ex-president Grover Cleveland (see Chapter 11) brought the Society back into respectability. Ryan subsequently sold some of his interest to railroad emperor E.H. Harriman. By 1909 J.P. Morgan bought their interests, and determined that in case of his death his shares could be acquired by George F. Baker of the First National Bank of New York and James Stillman of the City National Bank. (The two banks would later merge to become First National City Bank—or Citibank.)

In the Pujo investigation (chapter 9), Committee investigator Samuel Untermeyer asked Morgan why he bought the Equitable stock from Ryan when it gave such a meager return on dividends. Pierpont Morgan replied, "Because I thought it was a desirable thing for the situation to do that." Under questioning he finally explained that Ryan was in poor health and Morgan did not know what might become of the stock.[4]

Early in the 20th century, Equitable converted from a stock company to mutual ownership by policyholders. In 1991, in order to replenish its capital reserves, directors of Equitable approved the sale of 40 percent of this large U.S. company to Groupe Axa, S.A., a large French insurance company, and the conversion back to a stock company. The French company lent Equitable $1 billion against secured notes, to be swapped for common stock on approval of policyholders. It was also planned to offer a stock issue to policyholders and the U.S. public to raise additional capital.

A *Wall Street Journal* report stated that Axa's cash infusion came at the same time that Equitable set up $500 million in reserves for "expected losses on real estate investments, mortgages and junk bonds."[5] (See Appendix D for comments in Equitable's *Annual Report*.)

The Prudential

Prudential, another giant life insurance company, also was having trouble in the 1990s. Bache Securities, which Prudential acquired and renamed Prudential Bache, instead of bringing earnings reported losses. Prudential installed new management in the securities affiliate so as to turn it to profitability.

First Executive Corp.

In 1991 First Executive Corp., a high-flying company of the junk bond era, had its subsidiary Executive Life Insurance Co., taken into conservatorship by the California Insurance Department. California Insurance Commissioner John Garamendi said, "The fallout from the junk bond era continued to rain on innocent American investors. One casualty is the Executive Life Insurance Company."[6]

The fallout would hit employees of companies that had funded retirement annuities with Executive Life, also those individuals who had purchased Guaranteed Investment Contracts (GICs) from Executive Life.

Commissioner Garamendi appointed an advisory group of experienced insurance men, investment bankers and other experts to lead Executive Life out of the wilderness.

Kemper Financial

Still another well known company in the industry, Kemper, has continued to perform satisfactorily in insurance and financial service, but took a sizable loss in 1990 for its venture into the securities brokerage business. Acquisition of several unrelated stock and bond dealers did not prove profitable, and $193.5 million was charged against securities brokerage operations during 1990.[7] The securities affiliate was reorganized by Kemper management, so as to gain profitability. Financial companies' attempts to diversify have not always worked out as planned. Kemper Corp., unlike Equitable and Prudential, is a stock company, shareholder-owned.

Financial Companies Buying Insurance Companies

Reverse situations have seen financial companies buying insurance companies. These haven't always worked out well either according to a veteran independent insurance agent.[8]

Japanese Business Can Be Good

A U.S. insurance company, AFLAC Corp. of Columbus, Georgia is unusual in that its business in Japan is greater than its U.S. insurance business. Specializing in cancer insurance, foreign revenues in 1990 were equivalent to more than $2 billion in U.S. dollars, with net before taxes more than $200 million in U.S. dollars.[9] American Family Corp. has a Japanese staff for its operations in Japan and is fulfilling a need in that country for insurance coverage.

Hard Times for Workmen's Compensation

Workmen's compensation insurance goes back many years with the laudable goal of protecting workmen who are injured while employed by someone else. Not all states have insured plans; a few states carry the system, though not always too successfully. In the early 1990s workmen's compensation insurance had become very unwieldy in many states—as widely diversified as Maine and Texas.

In Texas, pioneer Texas Employers Insurance Association went into receivership in 1991. (In 1992 companion company Employers Casualty Co. was put under control of the State Board of Insurance.) The deputy liquidator for the State Board of Insurance, John James, said that on-the-job benefits will stretch out as long as 35 to 40 years, the lifetime benefits to those injured. Texas Employers' liabilities will be assessed on other companies still doing business in the state, and those companies will write off an estimated $248 million over the years, in part against taxes.[10]

Various parties have been blamed for the breakdown in workmen's compensation insurance: attorneys, medical providers, the breakdown in public ethics and the insurance companies. The decline of the U.S. dollar, ever-rising costs, and decline in public morality all play parts in this. As an informed insurance expert points out, workmen's compensation may add premiums of 15 to 25 percent to a company payroll. Such heavy insurance costs can make it most difficult for that company to bid against the services or products of another company, which may choose to pass up workmen's compensation by carrying the risk of operating uninsured.

The Property and Casualty Companies

Regarding property and casualty companies, some of the largest of which are headquartered at Hartford, Connecticut, an independent insurance agency owners says:

1. The consumer movement is so strong as to make it difficult for agents and insurance companies to make a profit.
2. But on the other hand, the safety net, the various state guaranty funds, do give some assurance of the ability of most companies to survive.

The agency owner says there is a "knee-jerk" reaction of insurance companies that often hurts loyal agents and loyal customers. He suggests there likely will be revision in insurance practices – which form, no one yet knows. He thinks that federal regulation would be a mistake and that deregulation would be a mistake. He cites major property and casualty companies' write-downs on real estate loans and real estate investments and says that too many insurance companies have acquired junk bonds.

In both the life and the casualty companies the continuing loss in value of the U.S. dollar creates uncertainty for the policyholder, whether his coverage is too little, too much, or whether or not he can afford premium costs—whether it all is worth the cost and trouble.

Whereas banks are heavily involved in federal regulation, insurance companies have been state regulated, and few big insurance companies have failed. The U.S. Congress in 1991 was investigating the industry, but in view of the fact that federal regulation in other financial activities has not assured total success, members of Congress were reluctant to recommend that the federal government take over insurance regulation. Nor can state consumer protection spokesmen and spokeswomen do consumers much in the way of favors when their browbeating causes insurance companies to refuse to do business in their states.

Federal Judges Cannot Assure Sound Insurance Coverage

Insurance companies are having problems. State Farm, the largest multiple-line insurer, had losses in recent years, caused in part by federal court orders on how they should hire their agents and employees so as to show no partiality. Losses for 1990 were less than the previous year. According to the annual report for the insurance company, "The improvement in underwriting results was due mainly to agent and employee efforts to make sure business was properly classified, to auto insurance price increases and a stabilization of claim losses from property coverages"[11]

Federal judges cannot assure that those hired are capable of doing their jobs. That must come from training as well as ability and education. State Farm's auto company had assets of $37.5 billion in 1990. Investment income of $2 billion kept the underwriting loss of $1.7 billion from depleting the Policyholder Protection Fund (capital) which ended the year with $9.7 billion.

State Farm is a mutual company, belonging to its customers. The company also owns fire, life and health affiliates. The life insurance affiliate paid out $8.2 million on death claims of AIDS victims during the year, which "weren't anticipated when rates were set"[12]

Another Fallout from Insurance Company Collapse – Insured Municipal Bonds

In mid-1991 the collapse of $13.8 billion Mutual Benefit Life Insurance Company of New Jersey hurt life insurance policy holders and owners of Guaranteed Investment Contracts (GICs) issued by the company. It also caused scrambling and confusion in the municipal bond market because of tax-free industrial-revenue bonds that had been guaranteed by the big insurance company as to payment of principal and interest. Favored by many civic promoters and housing authorities, the tax-exempt bonds, issued to benefit industry relocations and real estate developments, lost their ratings in a hurry. According to a *Wall Street Journal* report, "Standard & Poor's Corporation, a major credit-rating agency... downgraded the rating on all the issues backed by Mutual Benefit to NR, or 'not rated' from single A."[13] These were bonds that on their own merits would not carry the "A" rating.

Two very large insurance companies, Metropolitan Life of New York and Prudential of New Jersey, agreed to back future insurance operations of Mutual Benefit. The previous obligations of the company were yet to be resolved.

Continuing unfavorable publicity on Mutual Benefit's real estate loans and failure to accomplish proposed merger with stronger companies had fueled a "run" by ordinary-life policyholders who sought to cash in or borrow against their policies.

Congress and the agencies of government spend for every conceivable reason—or for no reason. Congress seems to have no conception of how to reverse 50 years of deficit spending. Nor can

American financial institutions, including formerly stable insurance companies, counter the effects of the Congressional deficits. To its credit, Congress eliminated some of the income tax subsidies of revenue bonds such as described. Such schemes got into trouble when Mutual Benefit collapsed. Many such bonds were ill conceived and did not make economic sense.

A 1992 report in a journal for older Americans told of the failures of "big-name companies as Executive and Mutual Benefit in New Jersey."

Sounding much like other reports in the media from our national capital that have told of troubles with big banks but that then suggest that salvation is in even bigger banking companies, the report on life insurance suggested that the basic defense is in the largest and strongest companies.[14]

The truth is that a strong company, whatever its size, can offer excellent insurance protection.

NOTES

1. Jonathan R. Laing, "Flawed Policies," *Barron's*, October 1, 1990.

2. Frederick Rose, "Equitable's Troubles Show Mounting Risks Facing Life Insurers," *Wall Street Journal*, December 30, 1990.

3. *1989 Annual Report* of Equitable Life Assurance Society of the United States.

4. Frederick Louis Allen, *The Great Pierpont Morgan*, Harper, New York, 1949.

5. Susan Pulliam, "Equitable Life Sale of Stake Clears Board," *Wall Street Journal*, July 19, 1991. Also, announcement of August 1, 1991.

6. Frederick Rose and David B. Hilder, "Brought to Earth, Junk-Bond Deals Trip Insurer as State Seizes Unit of First Executive" *Wall Street Journal*, April 12, 1991. More than four years earlier, Laura Jereski, under the Title "Funni Muni," had asked in *Forbes* (November 12, 1986) about housing bonds issued by Drexel Burnham Lambert and other security firms that were helping Fred Carr build his First Executive portfolio. The bonds were rated AAA because they were "backed, in effect, by GICs." She asked, "Could anything go wrong?" and answered, "Conceivably, yes," if hard times came along, which they did.

7. Kemper Corporation, *1990 Annual Report*, Long Grove, Illinois.

8. Archie E. Hunter, Jr., Roach, Howard, Smith & Hunter, Dallas, Texas. Conversation of June, 1991.

9. The company's U.S. insurance revenues were just at $600 million in U.S. dollars. American Family Corporation (AFLAC), *1990 Annual Report*, Columbus, Georgia.

July 20, 1992 *Forbes'* report of the "100 Largest U.S. Multinationals" shows AFLAC leading all U.S. companies in percentage of assets overseas, and near the top in percentage of revenue and profits from overseas.

10. Diana Kunde, "TEIA failure may cost Texas $248 million," *Dallas Morning News*, July 9, 1991. As with the Southland Corporation's J.C. Thompson (Appendix N), Texas Employers' founder Homer Mitchell had been a long-time director of Republic National Bank of Dallas and admirer of bank chief executive Fred Florence. The bank and insurance companies had provided strong mutual leadership, which financial leadership was gone with the collapse of Dallas' big three banks.

11. Conversations in 1990-1991 with G.W. Callaway, retired manager, State Farm Companies, Dallas.

12. State Farm Companies, *Annual Report for 1990*, Bloomington, Illinois.

13. William Power and Constance Mitchell, "Seizure of Insurer Roils Bonds," *Wall Street Journal*, July 18, 1991.

14. Richard Janssen "People should be cautious. New look at life insurers," March 1992 *AARP Bulletin*, Washington. (American Association of Retired Persons.) The good suggestion is made in the report of checking with the rating agencies: A.M. Best, Standard & Poor's, Moody's, Duff & Phelps.

CHAPTER 11

A Gold Standard?

Two World Wars and peacekeeping military efforts have been exceedingly costly to the United States and to other countries. Expanding welfare programs have added to the spiraling spendings of government. There is slight comparison of the cost of government today to that of a century ago.

Historians tell us that we were even troubled with treasury surpluses in the nineteenth century – a feat unheard of today. We had no income tax, although it had been tried twice, once during the Civil War and again in 1894. No wonder people refer to "the Good Old Days." We changed all that in 1913 with a constitutional amendment legalizing an income tax that was projected to rise to a maximum rate of six percent.

For more than a hundred years (with a hiatus during the Civil War), we enjoyed a gold standard in monetary systems the civilized world over. After the Civil War, when the United States set out to resume gold payment of the dollar, the argument was not about paper money, but whether we should have a currency tied solely to gold – or a bimetallic gold and silver standard.

The Panic of 1893 coincided with Democrat Grover Cleveland's return to the presidency, the only non-consecutive second term for a U. S. president. By 1895 the situation was even worse, with gold from the U.S. Treasury (before the days of the Federal Reserve) slipping away to Europe. Adding to the difficulties, a remnant of the Civil War Greenbacks, $346 million in United States Notes, could be exchanged for gold as legal tender and, in turn, had to be reissued, thus continuing to draw down the gold supply – contrary to Gold Certificates, which could only be exchanged for specie one time.

Republican J. Pierpont Morgan went to see the President although the Democrat Cleveland was reluctant to receive him. The country's financial situation was so desperate that Cleveland agreed that Morgan, the wealthy August Belmont and the Rothchilds of London should purchase gold for the U. S. government even though the government would be unable to pay them at the time. Morgan and his associates acquired $60 million in gold for the Treasury, assuring President Cleveland, Treasury Secretary John G. Carlisle, and Assistant Secretary William E. Curtis (who carried out the government's end of the necessary paperwork) that the gold would not be returned to Europe. Again, the Treasury's gold supply was above the $100 million reserve limit.

Adding to the confusion, then as now, was the feeling that Morgan and his associates were too powerful – even for good – plus the Populism of that period of a hundred years ago.

William Jennings Bryan, who had been chosen as the Democratic nominee in Cleveland's place to run for president, though he lost the presidential election then and several times later, is remembered to this day for his "Cross of Gold" speech. In it he said: "You should not press down upon the brow of labor this crown of thorns; you shall not crucify mankind upon a cross of gold." Bryan advocated unlimited coinage of silver to gold at a ratio of 16 to 1. He did not advocate a paper dollar.

World War I seriously hurt the monetary systems of all European countries. The resulting hyperinflation of paper currencies made paupers of the wealthy and sent the scions of ancient families into the streets hawking priceless heirlooms for pennies or for the price of a meal or firewood.

The Bank for International Settlements

In 1930 the Bank for International Settlements was created at Basle, Switzerland, to work out reparations for the burden of World War I for Germany and Austria. The United States was a chief architect of the BIS, but didn't join.[1]

The gold standard – free exchange of paper currency for gold – was re-established after the first world war in most nations. With the onset of the Great Depression of the 1930s, the United States and most other leading nations "nationalized" gold, making it illegal for individuals to own gold. The institutions designated to hold or exchange this gold had to be governments, government-controlled central banks, or other government institutions. Thus in the 1930s, in the United States, by Congressional action the gold standard was changed into a gold exchange standard. Only the government was allowed to own gold. Only the government was allowed to exchange gold, with other governments. Even so, in the United States paper currency or credit still remained tied to gold reserves.

The Discipline of Gold on Government

The idea was to keep governments from spending more than the required gold reserves against their paper currency or governmental credit – as with a 25 percent gold minimum requirement in the U. S.

Until 1965, gold certificates were required to back up 25 percent of bank reserves at the Federal Reserve Banks, and also Federal Reserve Notes. As we began to run low on gold, from other nations' drawing on our gold reserves, first we abolished the 25 percent gold requirement against commercial bank deposits with the Federal Reserve Banks. Then in 1968 we did the same with the 25 percent gold reserve requirement against Federal Reserve Notes – the currency that we now use. We also rescinded the requirement for silver reserves to back up silver certificates, as the value of silver went above the value of silver dollars, half-dollars, quarters and dimes.

The IMF – The U.S. Reneges

For a few years our U.S. Treasury attempted to work with other nations' treasuries in setting up a two-tier gold price: a lower one for official transfers and a higher one for the private market for gold. (This would have had no effect on U.S. citizens, who were still forbidden at the time to buy or sell gold!) The two-tier system also finally collapsed when President Richard Nixon's Secretary of the Treasury John Connally refused to sell official supplies of gold at $35 per ounce in August 1971, since foreign claims were in excess of U.S. supplies. The official price was pushed up to $42.22 per ounce in February 1973. By then the market price was going much higher. Finally in 1975, U.S. citizens were again allowed to own and trade in gold, after their government had lost all control of the market.[2]

The Bretton Woods agreement of 1944 was an international effort to stabilize monetary exchange rates by means of a gold exchange standard. Anticipating the end of World War II, a new International Monetary Fund (and related World Bank) at Washington, D. C., was to coordinate this effort toward stability between the dollar, the pound sterling, the franc, the mark and other currencies. (The World Bank was to have additional responsibilities in assistance of reconstruction and development in the various member nations, as implied by its official name of International Bank for Reconstruction and Development.) When the United States ran low on gold in 1971 at the old valuation of $35 per ounce, the gold exchange standard of the IMF was rent asunder.

To Resume Payment in Gold (and Silver) Today?

Returning to a true gold standard today would certainly cause gnashing of teeth – and discipline in spending such as our government has long forgotten. What effect would such stabilization of the dollar have on today's economy, where people could depend on their savings – where they would know that a dollar is a dollar?

We Are the Insurers – We Are the Government

Meanwhile, the American people are gradually learning that they are the government. Scott Burns, columnist in the *Dallas Morning News*, says it best:

> The lesson all of us are learning in the S&L debacle is that we are the Insurers of Last Resort, while the folks in Washington are no more than well-paid intermediaries who redistribute the wealth.[2]

This is true for much of what has been done in Washington in recent years. As the dollar has been increasingly devalued, as debts of government have climbed to astronomical peaks and supposed government insurance funds, as of the FSLIC, have been completely depleted, it is dawning upon us, the citizens, that we are the *Insurers*, we are the *Lenders*, we are also the *Debtors*.

We are the ones ultimately responsible. Those in Washington are, in general, merely "well-paid intermediaries who redistribute the wealth."

Real Statesmen and Stateswomen

Now the burning question is, in this brave new world, will there come forward some real statesmen and stateswomen who are courageous enough to refuse to spend their children's and grandchildren's wealth? Will we be wise enough to recognize them when they come and to follow their lead?

Edouard Balladur, former finance minister of France, is now head of the *Association pour le Liberalisme Populaire*, which the *Wall Street Journal* reports is a group dedicated to free-market liberalism in Paris. In late 1990, the *Journal* asked Balladur several questions on "A Stronger Dollar, a New Money Order."

One of the questions was, "Would you envision a role for gold in a future monetary system?" The former finance minister replied:

> I don't see how a true world system that by necessity must create a new monetary standard could avoid a reference to gold. I don't see either, how we can avoid reform of the banking and credit system. For me, freedom without order is inconceivable.[3]

Old China's Promise to Pay in Gold (or Its Equivalent)

In recent years, a few gold bonds or loans have again appeared – bonds, or notes, payable in gold or its equivalent. With today's fluctuating dollar, mark, franc, pound, yen, what-have-you, it is hard to visualize a fixed value in our various nations' currencies. But that is what we once had, in the golden era before the great wars and rumors of wars.

Just on the eve of the First World War, in 1913 (the same year in which our Federal Reserve System was born), a bond issue of the Government of China promised to pay in gold, or in the equivalent currency of four nations, the sum that it borrowed plus interest at 5 percent. This was considered a good rate in international finance for that time, although low for the confused financial years of the 1970s, '80s, and early '90s.

The Government of China promised to pay in gold, or in the French franc, or the German mark, or the Japanese yen, or the Russian "rouble" (as it was then spelled). This was before two world wars and the Japanese occupation and before the Chinese revolution and the long-time Communist domination of that Asiatic land.

It was also before Imperial Russia fell to its seven long decades under Communism. Interesting, too, is the "radical" suggestion from certain financial leaders in what was the USSR (now the Commonwealth of Independent States). Seeking to have the ruble again convertible into other currencies, as well as to have value at home, these freedom-seeking CIS economists have suggested that the ruble might be backed by gold — a hard problem for emerging free states with their many other problems, as well as for the leaders of the United States and other supposed free nations.

Interestingly, too, the gold bonds of China of 1913 were countersigned by the nearby French-controlled Banque de l'IndoChine. After the loss of Indo-China by the French, by the United States after its Vietnam war, though Communist regimes rule most of Indo-China, that same bank continues today in Paris, as Banque Indosuez. Whereas too many U.S. banks, large and small, have failed miserably in recent years, France's Banque Indosuez survived not only France's loss of Indo-China and of its interest in the Suez Canal, but also political changes in France itself.

These include World War I, the difficulties of the Third Republic through the Great Depression, the fall of France to Hitler in World War II, the Vichy regime and the return to freedom in the Fourth Republic under DeGaulle and his successors. We say again: The people of France know what paper money inflation can and will do and they provide means for themselves to ride it through, hoarding gold and other real assets in times of turmoil.

Sporadic payments were made on the Chinese gold bonds over the years. Assuming the Communist government of China continues for any time, it most likely will again make payment on these bonds if it hopes to receive world-wide recognition as an economic partner in world trade.

NOTES

1. See *Annual Reports* of the Bank for International Settlements, Basle. It was hardly known for many years in the United States, although Owen D. Young and young David Sarnoff were in on its organization.

The BIS was in part an attempt to relieve Austria and Germany of heavy World War I reparation debts which were pressing them as the Great Depression came along. For nearly six decades the BIS remained a mystery, a nonentity, to most Americans. Few U.S. economics textbooks even mentioned this central bank's bank at Basle, which keeps its reserves in gold and gold equivalents, and does its accounting in the *gold franc*.

When the United States refused to join the Bank for International Settlements, shares in the capital stock of the BIS that had been reserved for the United States were temporarily taken up by a few large U.S. banks, and later sold and traded in the Swiss stock market. Owen D. Young was head of the General Electric Co. and David Sarnoff was head of Radio Corporation of America. General Electric, Westinghouse and American Telephone and Telegraph had owned RCA, with GE the larger shareholder. Not long after service to their country by helping organize the BIS, Young and Sarnoff were forced by U.S. anti-trust action to divorce their companies. More than half a century later, with Young and Sarnoff no longer alive, RCA fell behind the Japanese in electronic leadership, and GE was allowed to again gain control of RCA, selling off divisions of the former U.S. electronic giant.

The BIS committee's capital requirements, the projected capital requirements for international banks, are outlined in Appendix G. (Washington's bank regulatory agencies have embraced the Basle requirements all the way, and are requiring U.S. banks of all sizes to report capital ratios under the new international system.)

See Appendix C for per-capita gold holdings of various nations. Switzerland, of course, leads.

2. Scott Burns, columnist, *Dallas Morning News*, October 4, 1990.

3. Interview with Eduard Balladur, "A Stronger Dollar, A New Money Order," *Wall Street Journal*, December 5, 1990.

In 1993 with defeat of France's Socialist Party Balladur was chosen prime minister of that nation. President Francois Mitterand, a Socialist, said he chose Eduard Balladur, a Gaullist, as the most competent to lead in preserving the parity between the franc and the German mark.

CHAPTER 12

What's Happening To The Big CPA And Law Firms? To Big (And Small) Businesses? To Retired Families And Individuals?

The spill-over from closed S&Ls, failed banks and uncertain financial conditions in other businesses is being felt by the accounting and law professions. In late 1990, the seventh-largest CPA firm in the nation, Laventhol & Horwarth, took Chapter 11 bankruptcy and many of its partners left to form local accounting firms. Heavy damage liability suits had been brought against the giant Laventhol & Horwarth because it had audited financial statements of companies that had gone down the drain.

Indeed, the wave of financial institution failures brought on an epidemic of lawsuits against CPA firms across the country because of audits that had been signed by accountants. These lawsuits were followed by a rash of bankruptcies. The problem became so serious that Ernst & Young, the nation's largest accounting firm, ran full-page advertisements in the major financial journals to reassure the public that their firm was not considering bankruptcy court proceedings.

It didn't stop with the CPA firms. Some of the large legal firms dissolved. In the last years of the FSLIC, when it was getting tough on those involved in the S&L fiasco, the federal insurance agency sued "many of the lawyers who counseled" the thrifts which went "belly-up," according to *Forbes*.[1]

The Philadelphia law firm of Blank, Rome, Comisky & McCauley negotiated to pay the FSLIC at least $29 million "to settle charges of counseling a Florida thrift."[2] A small Louisiana law firm was directed to pay the FSLIC $35 million for its negligence in advising a thrift to approve loans violating federal lending limits. Jenkens & Gilchrist of Dallas settled suits with the FDIC, but a former partner, Lawrence Vineyard, who had left the firm in 1983 and who had served as officer and director of two failed thrifts, was sentenced to serve time in federal prison.[3]

What About Businesses (Big and Small)?

With Communist dynasties collapsing in Eastern Europe, should not Western economies be in the best shape ever? What about businesses in the United States? Shouldn't they be most profitable – even though banks have stumbled?

In the early 1990s, major department stores that had survived the Great Depression were in trouble. Two great competitors, Allied Stores and Federated Department Stores, went through Chapter 11 bankruptcy. In part, this was due to an unsuccessful consolidation of the two chains, a leveraged buy-out by Campeau of Canada, financed in part by "junk bonds."

There was the lack of local support, as in downtown Dallas, where department store units closed, as did the major banks that had long supported mercantile efforts in that distributing-center city. Another reason for financial problems for local merchants and for more traditional national chains such as Sears-Roebuck was the aggressive competition from discount houses such as Kmart and Wal-Mart. Widely fluctuating interest rates also contributed to uncertainties for all retailers, wholesalers and manufacturers. Dayton Hudson, one of the more successful retailers operating discount and book stores, in 1991 took on $100 million, 20-year debentures – unsecured debt – costing 9.31 percent. Company Treasurer Karol Emmerich was quoted in the *Wall Street Journal:*

> I don't think interest rates are going to be a lot different in the next 10 to 15 years than they were during the past 10 to 15 years, which means they are going to continue to be volatile and continue to be higher relative to the rate of inflation than they were in the '50s and '60s.[4]

Until congresses and administrations in Washington change their deficit-spending habits U.S. businesses and their work forces, large and small, as well as consumers will suffer accordingly.

What's Happening to Retired Families and Individuals

Families and individuals attempting to live on retirement income are finding it hard to plan on income from CD interest when interest rates fluctuate wildly from one year to the next. Difficult, too, for retirees are ever-increasing costs of living caused by federal deficit inflation.

In addition to what Washington may or may not do, is your bank giving full service to businesses, large and small? Is it serving your family and you individually?

NOTES

1. Dierdre Fanning, "On the Docket – a FSLIC lawsuit against some Dallas Lawyers has lawyers everywhere quaking." *Forbes*, January 9, 1989.

2. Wayne E. Green, "Alleging Negligence, the FSLIC Is Suing Many of the Attorneys of Failed Thrifts," *Wall Street Journal*, March 16, 1989.

3. Michael Totty, "FDIC sues Vernon's lawyers," *Dallas Times-Herald*, March 22, 1990.

Alan Van Zelfden, "Ex-Dallas lawyer pleads guilty to defrauding thrift," *Dallas Times-Herald*, July 19, 1990.

In late 1991 the over-100-year-old *Dallas Times-Herald* also went out of business, in part brought down by heavy buy-out debts from out-of-town ownerships.

Earlier local ownership of the newspaper had looked to Republic National Bank of Dallas for financial backing – which with the collapse of Dallas' big three banks was no longer available.

Dallas' No. 4 bank, formerly profitable Texas Bank & Trust Co., sold out several years earlier to First City of Houston. It was one of the four First City banks whose depositors were subjected to a 20 percent loss on deposits above $100,000 – when the bank was closed by the regulators in late 1992 – less than four years after a bailout by the FDIC.

4. Anita Raghavan and Tom Herman, "Fed May Cut Short-Term Rates on Jobs Data, But Long-Term Yields Are Seen at Their Lows," *Wall Street Journal*, September 3, 1991.

CHAPTER 13
Is Your Bank Safe?

"It stinks."

This comment of a 40-year small business owner on U.S. banking of today accompanied the closure of a federally reorganized and controlled S&L, causing him to lose interest on his account. He also said he didn't think much better of governmentally controlled commercial banks.

Government Will Solve All

At the same time, TV reports and newspaper stories continue to suggest that government is our only salvation — in banking — or for whatever else is needed. The idea of additional government spending as salvation continues to be popular with television commentators and news writers, as well as with many national, state and local political leaders. The dangers that deficit spending poses to the U. S. dollar are passed over — not understood by many. Whatever ails the banking system, many in the media suggest, can be cured by new regulations, or new regulators, or both.

Our ailing, deficit-spending, inflation-fed economy, with more but ever-less-valuable dollars, can be compared to an alcoholic who keeps trying to stop his disease by all sorts of new measures except giving up alcohol. Thus we will never cure our economic problems, including those of banking, by new regulations that fail to include the ending of government deficit spending.

The American people must demand an end to deficit spending. The American people must demand a return to integrity. The American people must be willing to save — to equal the examples of what had been the utterly defeated peoples of Japan and Germany who saved so as to rebuild their nations.

Collapse of the Banking System?

Economist Ludwig von Mises, in discussing the collapse of the monetary and banking system of Germany which took place in 1924, said (translated from German into English):

> What do all the failures of the banks-of-issue and clearing banks matter in comparison with the complete collapse of the banking system in Germany? Everything that has been said in favor of control of the banking system pales into insignificance beside the objections that can nowadays be advanced against state regulation of the issue of notes.[1]

In the 1930s uncancelled postage stamps from the era of German hyperinflation were available to young American stamp collectors for practically nothing – as that was what the stamps and currency of Germany of that previous decade had become – worth nothing. The postage stamps were curios, with over-printing of 10,000, or even 100,000 marks for what had been 1,000 marks.

When Hjalmar Horace Greeley Schacht took over as head of the Reichsbank, he established a new German mark.

The new Reichsmark of 1924 was equal to 1,000,000,000,000 (one trillion) old marks. In 1990, East Germans were allowed to trade a limited number of the state-issue Eastern marks for Western marks at the integration of the eastern socialist state's economy into the western capitalist system.

Like the French whose misadventures with unrestrained fiat currency inflation in the days of the First Republic gave way to iron control under Napoleon Bonaparte, the Germans have been most conscious of the value of money and that paper is seldom of equal value with gold. The gold Napoleon coin is a remnant of the French dictatorship. With the 1920s collapse of the German mark, a new order was offered to the German people by the unknown leader of the National Socialists (Nazis). A decade later, Adolf Hitler had become Fuhrer of the new Third Reich. In less than another ten years, he had created the Second World War. It took the massed might of the Western World finally to stop his madness.

No one in the 1990s expects the U.S. dollar to become completely worthless. However, it is worth far less than it was ten years ago and even less than two and three and four decades earlier.

Government Spending Driving Down Value of the Dollar

To paraphrase von Mises, how can we have sound bank and S&L regulation when deficit government spending drives down the value of the dollar – that threatens the entire monetary and banking system?

Americans don't want a worthless dollar. They expect the Congress and the President to show a new vision – a new courage – to reverse habits of years of deficit spendings. They need a gold standard, with the U. S. paper dollar exchangeable for a gold dollar. They also need for their banks and other financial institutions to be run right.

How Can You Be Protected? What to Look For in a Bank?

To be protected, know your bank. Adequate capital and adequate earnings are important. However, unless the bank tellers, other employees, officers, and bank directors, all are competent, look for another bank. If you ask questions and the bank's personnel do not know the answers, or unless they are willing to admit they do not know, but will find the answers, go somewhere else where you can get essential and safe financial services.

The Financial Condition of Your Bank.

From 'way back, financial statements of national and state-chartered banks have been published in local newspapers, as required by law and through the pride of the banking institutions. Not too many years ago, such reports were on a surprise-call basis, at least three times a year, with a year-end report as of December 31 as well.

Now, all reports are on a uniform quarter-end basis, four times a year. In the early 1970s, under the Freedom of Information Act, Sheshunoff and other bank reporting services began to publish detailed data on financial institutions, balance sheets and operating figures, with various ratios of profitability, capital soundness, etc. These were used by banks and large companies that did business with banks.

Management the Most Important

In recent years, with ever-increasing concerns about conditions of U.S. banks a number of enterprising companies have gone into the business of reporting financial data on banks and S&Ls, for anyone who will pay the cost of the report. Obtaining basic data from the regulatory agencies, these companies give generally recent balance sheet and operating figures on U. S. banks.

Various ratios are presented on earnings, capital adequacy, loan reserves and liquidity. Borrowing from the regulators' CAMEL rating system (Capital, Assets, Management, Earnings and Liquidity), these private reporting companies can give many of the ratios that the regulators have popularized among themselves. They cannot give the one that the regulators reserve to the secret section of their reports – that regarding Management's ability. The ability of management is, of course, a matter of judgement of the observer, but is often the most important consideration.

Character of Banker and of Customer

J.P. Morgan said early in this century that the character of his customer was more important than all other financial considerations. It is still true, of banks and bankers, as well as of bank customers.

Thus, it is up to you to look and learn for yourself, as to the reputation and ability of the people who run your bank. Observe for yourself. Make discreet inquiries of others who may have knowledge.

Consider, too, that the report of the condition of the bank – whether that which appears in the newspaper, that which is posted in the bank lobby, or that which is given via various publications – is always past history. A bank that may show itself to be in good financial condition today, with proper financial figures, but with sorry management it may be down the tubes tomorrow. To try to outguess Congress – or to prepare for the worst that Washington may give – is a challenge for banking as well as the citizenry at large.

Reputation and ability of bank personnel – tellers, new accounts people, loan officers, the bank president and its chairman of the board – are of paramount importance. What to look for in a bank:

1. *Reputation of the bank* – in good times, in hard times, the ability to serve its customers.
2. *Financial condition* – a consistent strength in the bank's financial condition, so important to its reputation and ability to survive the fluctuations in the value of the dollar and of interest rates and prices, caused by government deficit spending.
3. *Competent personnel* – essential to maintaining the bank's financial condition as well as to serving the bank's customers.
4. *Service to the community* – only possible with competent personnel – essential to the bank's financial condition and reputation.

Be Cautious of Supposed Experts

A growth pattern in banking sanctioned by Washington may be helpful or it may be hurtful. Be leery of what is said by supposed experts in government.

In late 1987 a report of the FDIC was published under the title, *Mandate for Change: Restructuring the Banking Industry.* Toward the end was this statement:

> While larger banks may imply higher costs in the event of failures, fewer banks suggest the possibility of fewer failures.
>
> Moreover, fewer banks mean fewer opportunities for banks to slip through the cracks and avoid government supervision that can detect unhealthy activities or behavior.[2]

This was before the failures of First Republic and other major Southwestern bank holding companies, the collapse of the Bank of New England Corp. and the bailout of Southeast Bank – with total assets of over $100 billion. This was before losses pushed the FDIC insurance fund $7 billion dollars into the hole. Was that a slipping through or was it a collapse of the floors? Admittedly, depositors — insured and uninsured, domestic and foreign — in these large banking systems were not allowed to lose — at least not until the 1992 First City bank closures. But what of the shareholders, small and large, and the communities, towns and cities they had served?

In 1992 the *American Banker* reported recently released studies by staff members of the Atlanta Fed and Harvard Business School that showed that most bank mergers fail to bring greater efficiencies and profits — contrary to glowing predictions in the media and official reports, including the U.S. Treasury Department's 1991 voluminous report, *Modernizing the Financial System: Recommendations for Safer, More Competitive Banks.*[3]

Two Reports to the Contrary

The two near-unprecedented reports were issued in early 1992 as "Working Papers," by members of the faculty of the Harvard Business School and by members of the research staff of the Federal Reserve Bank of Atlanta.

Each is described as a working paper, expressing only the view of the authors, and not necessarily the institutions in which they are associated. These were:

> *Bank Mergers: Integration and Profitability* by Jane C. Linder, assistant professor, and Dwight B. Crane, professor, at the Harvard Business School of Harvard University.
>
> *Cost Savings Associated with Bank Mergers* by Arona Srinivasan and Larry D. Wall of the Federal Reserve Bank of Atlanta.

The independent findings of each report were that cost savings in bank mergers are not nearly what they have been touted to be over the years. In fact, much of the opposite was found to be true. The Atlanta working paper researchers concluded: "We have not found any evidence that mergers significantly lower expenses."

The above is heresy against what we have been told for ages by authors of economic banking textbooks, by government spokesmen, by other supposed banking experts — advocates and apologists for bigger banking systems and bigger regulatory agencies.

The findings oppose much of the viewpoint in the 1991 U.S. Treasury Report. Also in regard to the Treasury's plan, Editor-in-Chief Robert A. Bennett commented in *United States Banker*:[5]

> There is little real thought behind many of the proposals in the Brady plan for financial reform. Many of the recommendations would lead to the very problems they are meant to avoid.

We have grown accustomed to presidential commissions, economics textbooks and financial writers glorifying bigness in banking (as well as bigness in government) as the Utopia for all financial ills. We have seen a government fed with dollars borrowed from our children, grandchildren and great grandchildren, spreading ever larger, in efforts to cure all our social ills. It is not necessarily so.

A banker-businessman who served as chairman of the board of a city bank and on the board of directors of a multi-bank holding company that acquired his bank, observed two great weaknesses in financial institutions:

1. Mismanagement
2. Lack of directors' responsibility.

These weaknesses in any bank can affect you whether or not you invest in it or patronize it. The failures of financial institutions erode the trust of outsiders in our communities, our states and our country. Communities with failed banks are less attractive to outside interests. Sooner or later bond ratings go down. Chains of commerce radiating from the failed institution eventually hurt all businesses in the area, some rather quickly. Tax bases decrease but taxes increase. Businesses close.

Jobs are lost.

Demand Integrity

Protect yourself. That is the only way. Demand integrity in government. Demand integrity of the dollar. Demand integrity in banking. Don't look to government for every single thing, as is so often suggested today in television and press.

And talk with each other. It is true, there is safety in numbers, if those numbers are people with names, with faces, with questions and comments that must be answered.

Over and over, as we sought the answer to "What is wrong with U.S. banking?" we have heard the answers: Integrity, principles, the "old-time religion" and reliability. These answers have come from over the country: New England, the Old South, the Midwest, the Southwest and the West Coast. There is a realization that individual integrity is the basis for it all.

Factors and Finance Companies

Factors and finance companies are other financial institutions, often in the past considered somewhat risky by some in banking. Better known to the general public are finance companies, because of their automobile loans and personal loans. Various categories of finance companies exist, including the so-called "captive" finance companies, those belonging to manufacturers. General Motors Acceptance Corp. and General Electric Capital Corp. (formerly General Electric Credit) are very large institutions. Factors, which purchase accounts from businesses at a fee or discount and then collect the accounts, are not so well known. Doyle Kelley and L. D. Crumly, Jr. of KBK Inc., a factoring company in Houston, remarked that a number of years ago some of the area banks rather disdained their company as operating in a risky field. But KBK continues to make a profit, while several of the banks have gone broke. Management is of primary importance in determining success in any and every type of financial institution — as in any business or any institution. Long-term success demands ability and integrity in management.

NOTES

1. Ludwig von Mises, *The Theory of Money and Credit*, translated from German to English by H.E. Batson, Foundation for Economic Education, Irvington-on-Hudson, New York, 1971.

At the end of World War II, Hjalmar H.G. Schacht was charged as a war criminal, to be tried because he had served for a period under Adolf Hitler's regime. Schacht produced a note from David Sarnoff (Ch. 11 Endnotes) praising his cooperation in the organization of the Bank for International Settlements, given to Schacht at the time of the organization of the bank. Schacht remained free and served as an international financial consultant for various middle-eastern and other emerging nations during the latter years of his long career.

Sarnoff served as a general officer with the U.S. Army in WW II, returning to RCA after the war to lead the development of television. It was young David Sarnoff, an expert telegrapher, who early in his career received, via the new wireless, the messages about the sinking of the *Titanic* at the radio receiver on top of Wanamaker's department store in New York city.

2. *Mandate for Change: Restructuring the Banking Industry*, Federal Deposit Insurance Corporation, Washington, 1987.

3. Rich Lane, *American Banker*, (New York) February 13, 1992, and following telephone conversations.

4. Jane C. Linder and Dwight B. Crane, *Bank Mergers: Integration and Profitability*, Working Paper, Harvard Business School, Boston, 1992.

Arona Srinivasan and Larry D. Wall, *Cost Savings Associated with Bank Mergers*, Working Paper, Federal Reserve Bank of Atlanta, 1992.

5. Robert A. Bennett, "Editor-in-Chief comments," *United States Banker*, April, 1991.

CHAPTER 14

What Do We Want? What Should Be Done?

"When Jesse James robbed a bank he walked up to the tellers, pointed a gun in their faces and demanded the money.

"Today our elected officials in Washington are about to pull off a heist on a scale unimaginable to Mr. James. But as befits a more civilized era, their weapon of choice is not a gun, but a piece of legislation." – David Morris, Columnist, *St. Paul Pioneer Press and Dispatch* (See Appendix P).[1]

The Vision From Washington City

The world of the financial regulators in Washington City largely consists of multi-billion-dollar bank and savings institutions. When *Fortune, Forbes, Barron's, Business Week* and *The Wall Street Journal* reported in 1990, 1991 and 1992 that the big banks were troubled this meant the regulators in our nation's capital were also troubled.

Bigger Super-regional Banks – Bigger Trouble?

Not that troubles and failures change the thinking of many in the regulatory agencies nor such thinking as is given to financial institutions by many among Washington's political leaders. Their pet theory continues, that we need bigger super-regional banks – even though too many similar banks have failed or are in financial trouble.

That the Bank of New England Corp. made a terrible failure of attempting to buy up and operate banks in Massachusetts, Connecticut, Maine and Rhode Island has not changed the thinking of many in Washington City, nor their spokesmen in the media. Somehow it is alibied that failure in the effort to build a super-regional financial institution came only because of economic conditions. The fact that individual banks that were acquired had served their communities successfully for 100 to 150 years, in good and bad times, is not mentioned. That the leadership of the Bank of New England failed miserably is hardly mentioned in connection with the effort to build a multi-state banking system. It is seldom admitted that some of the Bank of New England Corporation's worst loans were out of the territory.

Keep the Bank Open?

It would appear that federal banking authorities do not expect and are not prepared for local initiative in trying to keep banks open during trying times. In 1983 when 93-year-old First National Bank of Midland, Texas was facing closure, the examiner in charge was asked if $20 million additional capital from a group of directors could be accepted to keep the bank open. "No," he replied. "It would take $100 million."[2] His mission was to close the bank, not to keep it open. That additional capital had been subscribed a year earlier also was irrelevant; it was all past history.

The FDIC figured that $245 million would cover the loss on the Midland bank when sold to Republic Bank of Dallas, then building its state-wide banking system.[3] By 1990, FDIC's estimated loss in closing First National of Midland had grown to $540 million – more than double its original projection.[4] On top of that, the collapse of the combined Republic and InterFirst holding systems, First Republic, threatened losses of billions more. (With a similar story – the FDIC increasing the initial loss estimate of $2.5 million to $2.9 billion, then adding another $500 million, to $3.4 billion.)

Continental Illinois was kept alive at Chicago with no local capital subscribed – all funding from the FDIC, plus notes from other large banks. Subsequently, FDIC has sold off its shares in that "too large to fail" institution, now renamed Continental Bank.

Somehow, we are told, if we will only create them bigger than ever, perhaps take in many, many states, we will succeed by creating some enormous banking companies, controlled and regulated by men and women of great wisdom and ability. The economies of size, cutting out back-office costs (and front offices too) and sharing the risks with every region – even if the people who are supposed to be leading and regulating do not have much idea of what they are really doing – are repeated over and over.

From time to time it is suggested that the United States could be like other nations that have only a few banking systems with many branches. Germany and Japan are cited, ignoring the fact that each country also has many smaller, strong financial institutions. Or we would model after Australia, also an English-speaking country and like the United States rather new as a nation. Australia has just a few banks and it is reported that they give some service. Along with such concentrations of capitalism have come equal concentrations of socialism.

Australia also has rigid limits on how much money a person can take in or out of the country. Its politicians seek to protect its citizens from investing abroad. Thus, it was an ideal situation for Nugan Hand Bank's illegal currency transactions.

In the early 1990s, when U.S. interest rates had come down at least halfway from the highs of a decade earlier, Australia still had extremely high interest rates. Too, if a customer deposits a check to his or her account in one Australian bank on another Australian bank, you wait for several days for credit. The big Commonwealth Bank is government owned, part of Australia's socialistic system.

We, too, seem to be getting such a system by default when the FDIC takes over the large banks that have been in trouble for months or years, finally turning over the remnants of these banks to government-supported, still-larger banking systems, with the government deposit insurance fund taking the losses. The same happened, even worse, with the S&Ls – some remained under government ownership for a year or more before being sold to new super-financial systems. We observed the complete wipeout of the FSLIC insurance fund, with the public taking the losses.

This is socialism for super-banking. The taxpayers assume the risks – and losses. The new super-banks receive the profits.

Bigness in banking – especially in proposed super-regional systems – is too often coupled with shortness in vision, generally within the beltway of Washington D.C. Such appears to have become a way of thought for regulators, political leaders and the media that report and support that mode of thinking.

What About Trust Services and Other Bank Services?

For many years banks have offered trust services to customers and would-be customers. In its fiduciary capacity a bank looks after affairs for those who put properties in trust for the benefit of themselves or others. Nationally chartered banks were not allowed trust powers until passage of the Federal Reserve Act. Partly to get around this, some of the older trust companies were state-chartered institutions.

Trust department assets are not assets of the bank. Various trusts' cash accounts may be deposited with the commercial side of the bank, which then become liabilities of the bank against which the bank must pledge collateral.

Except in some extremely rare case of employee defalcation within a trust department, a bank would not fail because of its trust operations. Nor in general do trust fees, after expenses of the trust operation, add much to the bank's overall income.

There are exceptions from well operated trust divisions. Morgan Guaranty, through its trust services to individual and corporate customers, adds to the income and stability of that bank. Bank of New York, which claims Alexander Hamilton as its founder, has a significant trust operation, as does Northern Trust Co. of Chicago. Numerous small banks have good trust operations.

Other services offered by banks are collection of funds, as in lock box services, transfer of funds. Still other services can be profitable to banks and to customers. Letters of credit are issued for fees. Credit cards issued by a bank for another bank bring in fee income to the issuing institution, as well as serve its customers.

Mortgage Origination and Servicing Can Be Good for Bank and Customers.

Mortgage loan originations not only serve the needs of the members of the community but also bring fee and interest income to the bank. Residential mortgage loans may be kept by banks or sold to the Federal National Mortgage Association (FNMA – Fannie Mae), to the Federal Home Loan Mortgage Corporation (FHLMC – Freddie Mac), to insurance companies, or to other investors. The Government National Mortgage Association (GNMA – Ginnie Mae) is still another government-sponsored mortgage company. It underwrites FHA and G.I. Loans – Veterans Administration (now Department of Veterans Affairs) guaranteed loans – to poolers who resell interests in these in the financial market. Ginnie Mae facilitates a market for S&Ls, banks and other mortgage lenders who make G. I. and FHA loans. (But there can also be losses, as to the FHA (HUD). (See Chapter 7.)

The local bank may continue to service certain mortgages sold to others for fee income and to benefit from tax and insurance escrow accounts. Service to mortgage customers is also an entrée for additional banking services to those customers.

Deposit Accounts – Fees Charged Customers – Interest Paid Customers

Banks lend customers' deposits to borrowers, who generally are also depositors. (And deposits are created under fractional reserve banking to be reduced when loans are paid.) Banks generally also charge for services on deposit accounts. It can be argued that such service charges have become increasingly onerous in recent years with other bank charges also becoming increasingly heavy. A $20 charge for the same service that used to be $2.50 – was $2.50 too little? Is $20 too much? Banks have also paid customers for deposits in recent years including interest on many accounts that traditionally were considered checking accounts, non-interest bearing, demand accounts. NOW accounts (negotiable order for withdrawal) accounts, as well as CDs (certificates of deposit) became ever more popular. The necessity for paying interest on accounts was a reaction to rising interest rates in the overall marketplace, chiefly caused by Congressional deficit spendings. Merrill

Lynch and other stockbrokers saw the opportunity to get into such financial services and the banks decided to compete.

NOW accounts were pioneered in New England. Collapse of Bank of New England Corp. should not be blamed as much on NOW accounts as on sorry loans made by expansion-crazed management.

Other Charges

A customer at one of the federally-reorganized banks reports a charge of $55 every six months for collecting interest on bonds placed for safekeeping – for which he was formerly charged $3.50. Is this increase of over 15 times the previous charge justified? Is it to help make up other inefficiences? (This government-created bank is not particularly profitable.)

Except for Savings

At the same time that banks are paying interest on various accounts that traditionally had drawn no interest, the long-time staple saving account that had taught youngsters how to save is pretty much forgotten. Many banks don't appear to care much – to feel that savings accounts aren't worth the bank's trouble. Perhaps this is part of modern America, which compares so poorly against Japan and Germany in habits of thrift.

How About these High Rates? What Happened to the Usury Laws?

The U.S. Congress, with its super-abundance of supposed consumer protection laws, put it to the consumer in the *Depository Institutions Deregulation and Monetary Control Act of 1980.* That was at the time when all interest rates went through the ceiling – government, commercial, consumer. Long established state usury laws of 10 percent, 12 percent, were overridden by Congress so as to keep the dollar flowing. Some of the state usury laws are now back in effect. But some consumer rates stay near 20 percent. Are consumers subsidizing the big banks for losses on foreign (LDC), big buy-out (LBO), and speculative real estate loans?

Rescind Glass-Steagall?

Many in banking today say a salvation for sorry earnings is the rescinding of Glass-Steagall's prohibitions against underwriting of securities by banks. Underwriting of general obligation municipal bonds is allowed under Glass-Steagall. Why, then, it is reasoned, shouldn't banks also be allowed to fully participate, once again, in underwriting other bonds, revenue and corporate? Thus commercial banks would be permitted to underwrite bonds of cities, schools, hospitals, states, special districts, which repayments would depend on revenues other than tax collections. Banks would also be permitted to underwrite bonds of corporations, which repayments would chiefly come from corporate earnings. It is also suggested that banks be allowed to underwrite stock issues of corporations. Perhaps judicious participation in such activities might be profitable. But with many banks getting burned on new activities, shouldn't they be most cautious these days?

Consider the difficulties that have hit the big insurance companies that tried their hands at securities underwriting and dealing – and the failures of some of the large investment banking houses, which so strongly went into "junk bonds."

Banks now also want into insurance, even though some of the biggest insurance companies are in trouble. Admittedly, smaller banks have long been allowed to operate as insurance agents in their local communities. But most of them know what they are doing and they know their customers.

Some Recent Questions and Comments

From the holder of shares in a defunct savings and loan who lost her investment:

> Can you explain to me where all these billions voted to "bail out" the S&Ls go? Who is getting the billions? Nobody in the RTC has offered to pay me for my ten shares.

An excellent question. Where did those billions go? With her particular S&L, management and the board of directors had believed that they were receiving wonderful earnings, based on supposed highly profitable $150 millions in investments, made against newly acquired deposits. Within a short time nearly a third of the supposed assets disappeared, evaporated, when too many loans and investments proved to be nearly worthless. Where did the money go? Perhaps some went into insiders' pockets. Probably much more went into wild schemes in distant projects, when Garn-St Germain told S&Ls they could be like commercial banks, but with almost no limit on size of loans and investments or on geographical distribution. Too many S&L managers and directors had no idea of what they were getting into or doing.

Loans to Local Professional and Business People?

From an attorney whose bank went under, deposits now belonging to a bank whose headquarters is hundreds of miles away, most business loans being left with the FDIC:

> Interestingly enough, our current (capital short) situation has arisen solely because of the failure of the banks and the

> desire of the FDIC to get notes repaid, rather than refinancing. This requires not only individuals, but businesses as well, to go on a cash-and-carry basis which certainly will slow the economy and eventually will create a bigger crisis than anything we have seen thus far unless it is altered.

From a mechanic who owns a specialty auto repair garage in a town where the banking authorities turned over control of the bank deposits to absentee owners:

> I have plenty of customers and potential customers, but none of the new banks seems to care about local business loans.

Small Business Served by the Local Bank

A joint study by the U.S. Small Business Administration and the Federal Reserve System is quoted in a February 1991 statement from National Small Business United regarding proposed banking "reforms."[5] John Galles, executive vice president, NSBU, stated:

> The proposed consolidation of U.S. banks will not solve the problems that many financial institutions are now facing.

Referring to the September, 1990 Federal Reserve System staff study, "Banking Markets and the Use of Financial Services by Small and Medium-Size Businesses," Galles said of the study:

> (It) found that the single most important financial institution for nearly every financial product service used by small business is a local commercial bank; almost all firms consider a local commercial bank to be their primary financial institution. Key factors which affect small business selection of financial institutions include proximity, convenience, interest rates, and personal attention and service.[6]

The NSBU executive said it is unfortunate that the U.S. Treasury is "only focusing on large bank consolidation and not on expanding credit availability for business development."

Bankers Should be Serving Small Business – and Large Business

As we rode down the elevator together in late 1990, Stanley Marcus said:

> Bankers got into things which they did not know. Instead, they should be serving small business – and large business.

Marcus was long-time head of world-famous Neiman Marcus Company, leading fashion store.

Banking Troubles, from Greed Run Amuck

From Richard T. Nathan, a retired Massachusetts manufacturer where the old established Third National Bank of Springfield sold out to Bank of New England Corp., Boston:

> The problem results mainly from greed. Greed was allowed to run amuck due to changes in the governing laws proposed by the White House and given the green light by Congress ... As a retiree, I may not be affected significantly by this entire situation, but it will definitely affect my children and beyond.[7]

Referring to outstanding banker J.W. Neal, who saved his bank, before there was deposit insurance, Nathan declares:

> If there were only more of the J. W. Neals in this world! My only recourse is the ballot box and that may be limited power indeed.

A Change in Morals and Perquisites in Banking and Business

From a long-time observer of banking and business: Question – what are the morals of the banking management? When I see the perks and golden parachutes that are common in the industry, I wonder if the leadership of banking and business is anything in which we can be proud?

This question needs to be of deep concern – not only to those who make the laws and who regulate – but to the several banking associations and business chambers, to members of bank boards and to bank officers, to bank employees and to everyone employed in business at every level.

This long time observer on banking and business also asks if it would not be well to have "sunset" provisions on the multiplicity of laws on banking – many of which have worked at cross-currents.

U.S. Depositors Bail Out Foreign Depositors

From Earl J. Fisher of the Muenster State Bank:

> FDIC insurance is unfair to the small banks. We pay FDIC insurance on all our deposits while the larger banks pay no premiums on foreign deposits. For example, Continental Illinois had sixty-some percent of their deposits as foreign deposits. They were 100 percent insured in the bailout, but no premiums were paid. All the big banks are considered too big to fail; hence there is a 100 percent bailout. If that is going to be the policy, then premiums should be charged based upon the exposure.[8]

The obverse of that argument is that large banks, with many domestic deposit accounts over $100,000, are more than carrying their way in that insurance premiums are paid to the FDIC on all their U.S. deposits. But are these also the banks that are not to be allowed to fail?

FDIC Premium to Match Risks

In *The Gathering Crisis in Federal Deposit Insurance,* published in 1985, Edward J. Kane suggested setting FDIC premiums according to risk of the bank's investments – including its off-balance-sheet activities. Kane continues to advocate that federal insurance be modeled after private insurance.[9]

From Gary L. Thurman, a Texas CPA:

> If the FDIC has extended de-facto deposit insurance to half of all bank and S&L accounts and considering the extensive number of federal risk-assumption programs, then one may reasonably inquire if taxpayer-citizens are prospectively liable for total government guarantees in the $5 to $10 trillion range.
>
> At this point, the more important question is: Does anybody know?

(See Appendix Q for Thurman's complete letter.)

Bostonian Paul T. Coulopoulos, whose accounting career included the audit of many U.S. military contracts, said that banks got into trouble by, in effect, paying their loan people a commission for making more loans. He also suggested that it was a mistake to merge the deposit insurance functions of S&Ls and commercial banks into one federal agency – the FDIC. He added that lending in S&Ls and in commercial banks required persons of different caliber, of different ability.[10]

From a long-time chief operating officer of a major bank (regarding acquisition of failed S&Ls and banks in Arizona by out-of-state banks):

> Those biggies are going to have a job to do here in Arizona .... Their systems are far behind. In almost every case, marketing – good customer service – appears to be nonexistent.

A Wise Detroit Banker

Nearly thirty years ago, when asked if the then-$10,000 limit on deposit insurance meant much to the people of Detroit, Rol Fisher replied, "It certainly does. That is the magic number." Rollo G. A. Fisher served Detroit Bank & Trust as head of credit. This was the same bank that had produced Joseph Dodge, who in turn was adviser for the post-world war economic development for Germany and Japan.

Detroit Bank & Trust (now Comerica) had come through the most difficult days of the Great Depression when Detroit's two big bank holding companies, the Union Guardian group and First Wayne group, went under.

It was in Detroit that *Detroit Free Press* publisher Edward Stair was asked by Jesse Jones of the Reconstruction Finance Corporation to lead Detroit out of the wilderness. The automobile companies were all but shut down; America was not buying cars. Thousands of people were out of work, many leaving Detroit. Houses were being abandoned, along with accompanying mortgages. The city government was broke. The big manufacturers were bringing in cash by armored cars to pay such employees as remained on their payrolls. Jones challenged General Motors to back the new National Bank for Detroit (NBD). Henry and Edsel Ford backed the new Manufacturers National Bank. The RFC put preferred bank stock capital, along with GM and Chrysler's common stock ownership, in NBD. The Fords did theirs all alone – their usual style.

In the 1990s, Detroit banks continue to pursue a cautious growth. Comerica even has an operation in Dallas today – picking up pieces and having to digest some losses. Comerica also acquired Bank of the Commonwealth of Detroit, after an unsuccessful bail-out attempt by the FDIC. Commonwealth had suffered under a high-flying ownership takeover. Rol Fisher and successors have continued to be successful, conservative bankers.[11] In Comerica's Annual Report for 1989, the following is stated on opportunities to pick up S&L deposits, as from the RTC:

> As with any acquisition, a thrift acquisition must make sense both strategically and economically.[12]

In 1992 Comerica and equally strong Manufacturers National Bank of Detroit merged into a banking company of $28 billion. (Comerica of Michigan earned 1.21 percent on assets in 1991. Manufacturers of Michigan earned 1.15. Comerica in Texas earned .94. Overall their combined operations in the several states earned 1.08 percent on assets in 1991.) Though Detroit's banks remained strong, automobile manufacturing in Detroit appeared to offer limited growth to that city's economy, against the Japanese and German automotive industries. (And it was Detroit banker Dodge who had helped rebuild Japan's and Germany's financial systems.)

A New Englander asserts:

> Basically, honesty and integrity have gone out of banking. The old banker with the bow tie and the pin-striped suit who welcomed you into the bank, gave you a calendar and made you feel that everything was okay has been replaced with a young MBA with a Mercedes who is looking out for himself.

> Trust, it appears, has been replaced by secondary markets and profits. Our banks offer dozens of rates and terms for CDs and money markets. All people want to do is put their money away safely without resorting to stuffing it in a mattress. I suppose old-fashioned values, simplicity and integrity are the issues that most often surface. They are issues that somehow got away from us in recent times and should be making a comeback soon.[13]

Banker-Newspaper Publisher Truett Smith Observed

"Those guys are stealing things!"[14]

This outspoken comment came from judicious bank founder and newspaper publisher, the late C. Truett Smith in regard to the regulators' closings of the small and gigantic banking institutions alike and awarding of the remnants – deposits and choice assets – to the chosen few.

Smith founded a bank in his hometown of Wylie, Texas helping to bring prosperity back to an area that had been damaged by erosion of the soil and hard times of the Depression. He also founded a hometown newspaper, the *Wylie News.* Smith later served as president of the Texas Bankers Association. He and his businesswoman wife, Rita, gave the public library building to their home community.

Smith was concerned over what is happening to banking in America.

More needs to be heard from the man and woman on the street. These conversations help friends and neighbors – others in the same boat – to realize and to publicize the need for competent management.

Bankers, regulators and congressmen need to take note of these comments from grassroots America. And a college degree is not necessarily the answer. Not that having an MBA is bad; it should be helpful, unless the holder of that degree has too narrow a perspective or is overly impressed with the degree.

After all is said and done, it's still up to you to protect yourself. In spite of conversations and discussions in Washington, D.C. and elsewhere, the $100,000 insurance limit of deposits in banks and credit unions and in such S&Ls as are left – the $100,000 guaranty, or insurance, most likely will stay in effect. Unless you have real confidence in your particular bank or other institution, don't put more than the insured amount in that bank or credit union or S&L. Know your bank, know your credit union, know your S&L. Look at its financial statement. More importantly, look at its management and at its board of directors.

Incorrect Cliches Die Hard

From a book on economics and banking written just a few years ago:

> It is banks with over $500 million in deposits that typically lead the rest in terms of net income after taxes as a percent of equity capital, indicating that the optimum size for a bank is most likely rather large.[15]

Written just before the time that data on all banks began to be released under the Freedom Of Information Act (1977) and collected, studied and analyzed, the above incorrect statement was probably loosely based on the weakness in many large banks, of equity capital to assets of perhaps 4-6 percent, versus stronger capitalization of 8-10 percent in smaller banks. This gave the appearance of greater earnings per size, when it really meant that earnings of whatever amount would appear bigger against a smaller capital base.

Sheshunoff, Ferguson & Co., and other reporting agencies by presenting the facts have shown the fallacy in this assumption.

Has Federal Bank Reformation Benefited Even the Big Banks?

The program espoused by certain supposed banking experts, by some bank regulators, by a number of political leaders and by many in the media is that the United States should have a few very large super-regional banking companies. This would give us a basic banking system similar to that of Australia, or Japan, or Germany, or Great Britain, perhaps also somewhat like that of Canada. This the regulatory authorities have tried to do – in failed Bank of New England Corp., in failed First Republic, in ailing C&S-Sovran, in tarnished Goldome, in discredited First American. Even bigger banking companies have then been Washington's answer: NationsBank, First Interstate, BankAmerica, KeyCorp, Banc One. But do these banking companies always benefit from their federal acquisitions? Except perhaps for the latter, the other companies are not particularly profitable as measured against assets. Picking up FDIC and RTC deposits and assets (even when mostly cash) – with billions and billions of dollars in losses put on the FDIC and RTC and the American public – does not mean automatic good earnings for the federally favored institutions.

(In 1992 First Interstate – which operated in more states than any other banking company – reported its geographical diversification had brought disappointing financial results. See Chapter 6.) Communities need to be served. Loans need to be made – or should be. Talented personnel is required. Lending personnel is needed with local knowledge and overall bank and credit ability. Instead of attempting to create ever larger – sometimes questionable – banking systems along foreign lines, should our government not encourage local ownership and management in banking which can do the job? Managements that were obviously dishonest should not be kept in business. But those with abilities should be encouraged. The cities and towns of the United States must be served in their banking needs if this nation is to compete economically. Prudent lending to individuals and families, to small and large businesses, is at the same time profitable for the banks involved.

Super-regional banks – and smaller banks too – that fail to offer full lending services to the communities they serve will have but mediocre earnings. The most ruthless expense controls cannot create net earnings if there are no earnings to begin with. Loans and investments in the community which the bank serves are the chief sources of bank income. Trust service to the community can also be a source of bank income. The heaviest imaginable charges on deposit accounts and other bank services cannot bring more than marginal income to the bank. A strong lending program is essential, in serving the community, and in creating good net earnings for the bank.

Acquisition of branch operations that had been unprofitable to the previous owners because of heavy built-in overhead is not at all likely to guarantee profitability for the super-regional companies that acquire the systems. FSLIC-RTC-FDIC-created groups of failed financial systems have often continued with too many branches that were uneconomic to operate. Even when personnel is pruned drastically by the new owners and branch office buildings are dumped on the government, with lower lease costs for the new owners, deposits may evaporate as customers seek better service elsewhere.

Too Inefficient To Remain In Business?

Another assumption that had too often been stated in spoken and printed word was:

> Most small banks would be too inefficient to remain in business were a large bank to open up a branch next door.

Unless the larger banks were really out after business, which many are not, the large bank would generally show but little interest in serving the small business needs of the community and would gain only little business other than some deposit business and some consumer loan business.

Veteran Houston banker Don Wigley became chief executive of QuestStar Bank at a tough time just a few years ago. Surviving "increased financial burdens by Congress and the regulators, the bank has found it can have all the good small business loans it wants – as the large super-regional banks don't want them." "We are fulfilling a need," Wigley says, "looking after the small business man. With most banks, there is a sameness in all they do. We try to do a better job."[16] QuestStar is also a very profitable operation. (See Appendix R for outstanding financial data on this small independent bank.)

A New Bank Or Branch Replaces The Old With No Interruption Of Banking Service; The Closing Of the Failed Bank Goes Relatively Unnoticed In The Community.

This may be true with some S&Ls, where so many have failed, and too many have failed more than once; that is, a successor set up by the regulators also fails, with perhaps three successions in the same location. In the case of the commercial or community bank there is a difference if the previous bank has been of any service to the community. The community loses its economic leadership. As a result, local business people can't get loans nor any other service other than the most routine. Higher fees for less service may appear instead. The loss of financial leadership in the community – whatever its size – will most surely be felt.

We Are Opening More Branches To Serve You Better.

Despite ads on TV and in print, few full service branches are being opened in commercial banking (except for those acquired by government subsidy). Full service, with competent lending personnel, is expensive. Most branch bank systems have been cutting back on their full-service branches. Small branches with minimum deposit service are maintained, if necessary. The ATM (automated teller machine) is used when feasible in place of a staffed branch. Several years ago, Bank of America, San Francisco, which had pioneered the largest branch system, announced a 10 percent cutback in brick-and-mortar branches. U.S. Comptroller of the Currency C. T. Conover – who had stated that the largest banks would not be allowed to liquidate – also said that "extensive networks of brick-and-mortar branches are obsolete."

This Presidential Commission On Banking Will Have Far-Reaching Effects On Banking Reform.

It may not be carrying the argument too far to suggest that most reports of presidential commissions and national conferences on bank reorganization are like many new federal laws – well-meaning, but in the long run often creating greater problems than they solve. Several commissions have recommended consolidating the federal regulatory agencies: Comptroller of the Currency, Federal Deposit Insurance Corp. and the Federal Reserve.

One of Eisenhower's commissions recommended the opposite – in connection with the S&Ls – to separate the Federal Savings & Loan Insurance Corp. from the Federal Home Loan Bank Board. This was not done, and there was too much closeness. Both failed, as did many of the S&Ls they were supposed to charter, regulate and insure. Experience has proven the desirability of having the agencies separated.

By giving the savings and loans powers to compete with commercial banks, the savings institutions will be strengthened and will serve the people and business of America.

Several recent books have exposed the villainies of S&L manipulators. Perhaps more disastrous than dishonesty was inexperience and incompetence. The suggestion that savings and loans could automatically convert into commercial banks, via congressional edict, was a mistaken tragedy, which may cost the American public half a trillion dollars or more.

The thrift bailout is a wash

Business Week in 1991 quoted a noted economist: "From a macroeconomic standpoint, the thrift bailout is a wash." The magazine continues along the same line, that the same would be true of any large-scale rescue of the commercial banking industry. "It (money) can be lent out again."[17] The cost to the taxpayers and to the American economy is dismissed as of little consequence. Is no thought given to where the money went? Into poorly constructed condominiums that were never finished? Near worthless? Into a ski resort that was never finished? Into fancy entertainment, including supposedly free services of prostitutes, but paid for by the taxpayers when both the S&L and the FSLIC went broke?

Some economists might understand that with military spending for bullets and bombs there is no financial return on that investment. Do they not see that money wasted by incompetent S&L and bank management is not a "transfer of wealth," but waste – caused by stupidity if not outright robbery – the half a trillion dollars that may be required just to pay off the S&L debacle? Is this burden on the taxpayers merely a transfer of wealth? Who, then, is the beneficiary?

Full Disclosure Will Solve All Problems.

Full disclosure, in general, is beneficial. But repeated unfavorable newspaper stories and other media exposés can hardly fail to cause a run on a bank by its depositors. NO BANK CAN WITHSTAND A CONTINUING RUN. No bank keeps 100 percent of its assets in cash. Banks invest in U.S. government and municipal – state, county, city, school district, hospital district – bonds. Banks also make loans to individuals and to businesses.

Loans cannot be collected immediately. Nor can the U.S. government securities, supposedly risk-free, be sold immediately without possible loss due to market prices.

In its *1989 Annual Report*, strong, well-managed Zions First National Bank of Salt Lake City showed a picture of Orval W. Adams who, as vice president of the bank as it was in 1932, stopped a run on the bank by bringing in a million dollars in cash for all to see and telling everyone in line that they would be served.[18] Instead of continuing to withdraw, the depositors began to return their funds.[19]

This was also true of the First National Bank of Chicago when it had a run in the early 1930s and was likewise true of the First National Bank of Midland at that time. Melvin Traylor and Edward Eagle Brown in Chicago announced that funds were available on the table for all to see at Chicago. In Midland, John Scharbauer, Marvin Ulmer and John Butler made similar announcements, with cash on the table for all who requested it, but with the suggestion that the bank would be glad to have them again as customers.[20]

In the 1990s "runs" became electronic and more hidden and even world-wide, although depositors did physically line up outside in the New England winter of 1991 to help bring down the Bank of New England Corp. A noteworthy international electronic run hit Continental Illinois when a mistranslated wire report to Japan helped kick off the run that was finally stopped by the second bailout of that large Chicago bank.

Financial Reports Can Change

Seafirst Corporation's *1978 Annual Report* pictured U.S. silver dollars (only by then they were not truly silver) sliding along into the bank's vault. The glowing report for the "largest bank holding company in Washington and the Pacific Northwest" told of profitability and loan growth ahead of expectations.[21] Perusal of the report would have caused the reader to believe that almost everything was positive for Seattle-First National Bank. Assets were increasing. Earnings were up. Net earnings were approaching one percent on assets – .85 percent compared with .76 percent for the previous year.

In 1982 Seafirst disappeared as a Washington state-owned banking company. Bad loan participations from much-smaller Penn Square Bank in Oklahoma were blamed – oil loans on which the Washington State bankers had only vague knowledge. There were also bad local loans, at least $7 million to one of the principals in the Queen City S&L fiasco at Seattle.

The FDIC was ready to bail out Seafirst when Bank of America came to the rescue, with a $400 million recapitalization, in the process extending the giant California bank's territory to the Canadian border.[22]

Seafirst shareholders then did not take a complete loss on their investment in the largest bankholding company in the Northwest, as would their counterparts in the largest bankholding company in the Northeast – Bank of New England Corp. In 1991 its shareholders would lose everything when certain "assets," chiefly loans like those at Seafirst, some from out of territory, turned out to be very poor. Stockholders' equity, which Bank of New England Corp. had reported at $1.6 billion at the beginning of 1989, was wiped out completely.[23] An estimated additional $2.5 billion loss was to be charged against the FDIC bank insurance reserve.

Regulators Can Assure Reasonable Risk Management.

Sometime after the second, 1984 Continental Illinois bailout, economist Alan Greenspan, former chairman of the Council of Economic Advisers under President Gerald Ford, who in 1987 would be appointed by President Ronald Reagan as Chairman of the Board of Governors of the Federal Reserve System, stated, in an undated publication from Sears Financial Board (Sears, Roebuck & Co.), titled *Risk, Safety and Bank Deregulation:*

> To be sure, federal insurance of deposits clouds the risk management question for banks by reducing some of the market discipline that characterizes unregulated entities. But regulatory techniques exist to assure reasonable risk management. These techniques, however, do not require that banks continue to be restricted in product diversification and geographic expansion.
>
> Moreover, there is clearly no benefit to a deposit institution's management or shareholders if the institution fails. The only group protected by the deposit insurance are the depositors. Recently, tough actions by the FDIC in a number of instances – such as Continental Illinois Bank – have made it clear that bank managers and boards can lose their jobs and shareholders their stake if they fail to manage risks effectively. In short,

> there are some very effective personal sanctions to assure that federal insurance does not become a license to high-rolling practices.[24]

Since the 1984 Continental Illinois reorganization to which Greenspan referred, bank failures have included other multi-billion dollar institutions. Need for personnel has meant that managers of failed banks were not pushed out of their jobs (except for some blatantly corrupt and some too experienced and highly paid for the successor banks, as well as some who did not want to stay). Many staff members of failed banks have merely been reassigned under new FDIC-financed-and-sanctioned bank ownerships. Admittedly, old shareholders lost all, or nearly all, and boards of directors were out – perhaps even to become defendants in multi-million dollar suits by the FDIC. Many in bank management were kept on – although subject to new out-of-territory owners.

The FDIC, not wishing to build its liquidation division into astronomical numbers, has in recent takeovers of billion-dollar banks assigned collection duties to members of the successor banks' staffs.

NCNB Corporation, acquired what had been over 100 Texas First Republic banks – consolidated to 40 at the time of the failure – and into one by the FDIC – with assets of $38 billion, larger than those of the North Carolina bank. NCNB (later to be renamed NationsBank) – was given responsibility by the FDIC for collecting bad loans and selling foreclosed properties of the failed banks. Except for bringing in certain top management from North Carolina, NCNB kept many former First Republic personnel, not only in the new "good bank" but also in the "bad bank" (collection bank). Former First Republic personnel were assigned to collect poor loans made by First Republic. Those loans which appeared not likely to be fully collected were reassigned to the FDIC, with NCNB reimbursed for the costs of attempted collections and receiving a percentage of proceeds of those loans collected.

The FDIC initially estimated a loss of $2.5 billion on First Republic – later raised to $2.9 billion – still later to $3.4 billion. In late 1991 NationsBank's settlement with the FDIC was for $2.6 billion remaining in sub-par assets. The FDIC allowed NationsBank to keep those for collection, for fee income to the bank.

Likewise, Banc One of Ohio, which received most of the failed MBanks from the FDIC, under a similar arrangement to NCNB's (but without receiving the tax benefits of the failed banks) collected through its subsidiary Bonnet Resources the bad loans that it chose not to take into its own portfolio. As with NCNB (renamed

NationsBank), Bank One was reimbursed by the FDIC for costs of collection efforts plus receiving commissions on successful collections and assets sales.

Thus bank staff members from failed institutions have kept on working, perhaps in the same location, although theoretically and legally in new institutions, both in the "good" and the "bad" divisions of the FDIC-approved takeover banks. Many of the higher-salaried personnel, meaning many of the more experienced, have been let go as the new owners have sought to cut expenses to the minimum.

In 1991 the RTC, which had sold former Bright Banc S&L branches (deposits) to Banc One in 1990, decided that Banc One should not get the whole income from collection efforts of failed Bright Banc assets that the RTC retained, but should share certain of these with NCNB which was also in the collection business for the FDIC. Apparently, ex-bankers were considered more competent collectors than ex-S&Lers by the FDIC-RTC. Also, the "bad bank" (collection bank) operations of Banc One and of NCNB were already in place.

Expansion of S&Ls into low-risk, short-term investments?

In the 1990s Alan Greenspan would likely also amend his statement that accompanied that on discipline of personnel.

> "In recent years, many savings and loans have expanded into short-term investment instruments and their overall risks have accordingly declined."[25]

The sorry commercial loans that the S&Ls stumbled into, the "junk bonds" that they acquired, the development projects that they took on, the "razzle-dazzle arbitrage" that they attempted, were not to be low-risk, short-term investments, but were too often near-total, permanent losses. Admittedly, S&Ls that remained true to their missions have done well.

Greenspan was not alone in his comments. Garn-St Germain, at the time, seemed to be a wonderful idea.

"Core" Banks – A Proposed Salvation for the FDIC and the Banking System?

"Core" banks have been proposed as a means to save the banks and FDIC much as Garn-St Germain was presented as salvation for the S&Ls. It is argued that proposed core banks, sometimes labeled "monetary service companies," should segregate checking accounts, NOW accounts, savings accounts and small CDs and insure these only. At the same time core banks would only be allowed to invest these deposits in federal government securities or other liquid assets. Some proposals would also provide for making business or consumer loans from these funds. All other bank functions would be outside the core banks and would be funded from sources other than insured deposits.

The above suggested reforms sound too much like Garn-St Germain and other changes in laws and regulations of recent years — well-meaning and disastrous.

Assuming the United States went to such a system of "core banks," other countries would then find this land an even-more-fertile field for taking over the most desirable portions of U.S. banking. In recent years as regulators and bankers cut back previous excesses in lending to extremely tight credit, it has been most difficult to obtain loans for small and large businesses and consumers alike. (Congress also encouraged the swing to over-regulating — as in the FDIC Improvement Act of 1991.) Foreign banks have already begun to fill the gap. Do we want to close down U.S. banking and invite Japan, Germany, Canada, Switzerland and Britain to take over completely?

Observations on Bankers

Without having seen the statement from New York businessman Stuart Andrews (Chapter 2), Texas insurance man Frank Norwood makes a similar statement:

> Thirty years ago your banker was your friend, adviser, maybe Sunday School teacher. Also helper (in time of crisis). Someone you trusted. Someone with your best interests in mind. Now...?[26]

An Eastern financial observer has mentioned the tendency of too many in financial institutions to act like the lemmings of Scandinavia, periodically following one another in ever-increasing numbers, in ever-increasing accelerations, until they all drown in the sea. Southwestern banker George Grobowsky talks of the herd instinct. What appears desirable to one financial institution, but may not make sense, is copied by another and still another, until all are in a mad stampede. This banker admitted that before he joined it, his bank made mistakes, of which he is not proud, but he is proud that they stopped their stampede. They worked themselves out, by their own efforts.[27]

REITs — the Herd Instinct of the 1970s — A Premonition of the 1990s

The herd instinct that carried away the reason of some of the large banks in the 1970s came from the Real Estate Investment Trusts — the REITs.

The idea was to let bank customers in on real estate mortgage and investment opportunities, which otherwise might be available only to the banks, or even not otherwise available to the banks. There were two types of REITs: the Mortgage REIT and the Equity REIT.

Edward Kane spoke of the intertwining of banks or bank holding companies with the REITs:

> ...the energy that banks put into keeping allied real estate investments trusts afloat in the face of obvious market values insolvencies brought on by the 1974-75 recession shows their concern for protecting corporations whose names and activities are intertwined with those of the bank.

Some of the REITs came through and are alive today. Others faltered; a number failed.

Won't the Big Bank Mergers Take Care of Problems?

As with every merger announcement of recent years, proposed combinations of two or more large banking companies into supposedly more efficient, even larger institutions have been greeted with enthusiasm.

Spokesmen for the mergers who have been assured of keeping their jobs, at least for certain periods, with "golden parachutes" afterward, have announced the benefits of the mergers – for the community, city or nation. Spokesmen for brokerage houses who might receive commissions for transfer of stock ownership in connection with the mergers or who may otherwise profit from "advice" in the mergers have, in nearly every case, given early approval for such mergers. Statements from federal officials who consciously or unconsciously favor supposed benefits of enlarged banking systems also generally have been favorable. Commentators on national television and radio and reporters in national journals have often told of the benefits of greatness in the proposed institutions to result from the mergers. In some cases, only when the merged institutions showed obvious weaknesses rather than strengths were questions asked.

With the merger of Chemical Bank and Manufacturers Hanover Trust Co., two distinguished, generally strong, Manhattan-based institutions, initial national reports were all to the good. However, questions were beginning to be asked on the local scene. *Newsday,* the Long Island newspaper, had a headline: "Pain but no Gain for City Economy." Speaking of layoff of personnel, closing of offices, withdrawal of outside services, local public officials were quoted about losses to the community with questionable benefits.[29]

In connection with the New York two-bank merger Chemical raised $1.57 billion in new common stock in early 1992. Total stockholders' equity to assets was brought up to 6.34 percent.

An existing bank can cut expenses, including making drastic reductions in personnel and services, but publication of such actions is distasteful. A merger, especially an FDIC takeover, gives a wonderful excuse for reductions in personnel and services, though bad loans and other questionable assets remain – unless these can be dumped on the government.

In the Southwest, combination of the already over-extended Republic Bank system and the already over-extended First International system allowed no benefits. The final combination collapsed just a year after the merger. And the Republic National Bank at Dallas and the First National Bank in Dallas, major predecessor banks at Dallas, and the formerly, equally strong individual predecessor banks at Houston, Fort Worth and smaller cities and towns of Texas had tremendous strengths – before the wild expansions and mergers that accompanied equally erratic federal spendings and associated fluctuations in prices and interest rates.

The mergers in the Southwest gave no credence to the theory that merger makes for strength and efficiency. Unless new capital can be added or perhaps assets and liabilities can be reduced so as to take the strain from over-extension, a merger may be of little or no benefit.

This was also true in New England where well established banks had withstood for over 150 years the vicissitudes of panics, wars, and depressions. When consolidated Bank of New England Corp. got into financial trouble, no new capital was raised, though portions of the company were sold off to thrifty Scotch and Japanese banks.

The experiences in New England and in the Southeast, where mergers have added to weaknesses rather than to strengths, likewise give no evidence to the benefits of mergers – unless new capital funds can be raised to accompany these.

A Challenge for Today and Tomorrow

A former banker, now successful engineer and business man, says:

> The American people must learn that it is not a sin to save. The media – television, newspaper, magazines – must adopt a new philosophy that spend, spend is not the only way in government or in personal living. This must apply to local government and state government as well as to the federal

> government. Parents, schools, colleges must emphasize to the younger generation that it is not possible to make a dollar and to spend a dollar and a half. People have got to want to save. This must be imparted from parents to children, from schools to children.

Rising in less than fifty years from total and humiliating defeat in World War II to formidable positions among the economic powers of the world, the Japanese and German people have shown that saving and production go hand in hand. Their successes in banking, their successes in production are not accidents, but are the results of hard work and thriftiness.

Compete Internationally

At the close of Chapter 8 a report is given on international trading companies and the absence of such U.S. companies. U.S. manufactured products and commodities must compete internationally. U.S. bankers should lead in this.

Where Do We Go For Advice On Protecting Our Retirement Income?

Many have asked: How do I protect myself? How do we as a retired couple protect ourselves? How can my family be protected against the uncertainties of interest income, when interest rates fluctuate so widely?

Where do we go?

Honestly, there is no one answer. Read. Listen. Look for informed publications. Seek the best advice, probably from several sources. Scott Burns, business columnist quoted earlier regarding the American people being the insurers of last resort on the FDIC and the bankrupt FSLIC, says that he does not give individual advice. There are many who advise for a fee or a commission. Some have some knowledge of what they say. For conservative investment income for yourselves or your beneficiaries, consider a bank trust department. Check out its record first, though.

A former resident of Brazil was asked how the people in that terribly inflation-stricken land get by. He said there are several economic classes there. The poor merely exist from day to day. Those better off take advantage, when they can, of the high interest rates of more-or-less-sure short-term investments. Or they hold U.S. dollars or gold. Another former resident told of buying all food immediately after receipt of a paycheck – before prices rise again. At one point in time it appeared more profitable for farmers to speculate than to plant. As in the United States there has at least been talk in Brazil of trying to bring government spending and inflation under control.

Certain of our colleges and universities, particularly denominational and other private colleges and universities, admittedly seeking endowment income, offer suggestions to those wanting to conserve their resources and give to the college at the same time. Some of the programs may have information of value. Along the same line, some of the conservative religious writers of today, such as Larry Burkett, advise caution in personal borrowings and debt creation – good advice.

What, Then, Should We Do?

Several hundred old and new friends and acquaintances, both in the financial world and outside, have contributed information, questions and thoughts to this study on U.S. banking. Several have asked: "How can we make changes? How can we force Congress and the Administration to stop deficit spendings?" Both questions are extremely important. (Independent candidate Ross Perot in the 1992 Presidential Election posed similar, searching, questions.)

How to Force Congresses and Administrations to Stop Deficit Spendings

To stop this ever-heavier burden of debt upon us and on our children and grandchildren, how do we preserve the value of the U.S. dollar – what is left of it? How do we ensure some worth to our savings?

Admittedly, to change the ways of congresses and administrations will be tough. It will be hard to get these governing bodies to see what they have done and are continuing to do to our economic system. It will be difficult to get many in the media to understand what is happening. There must be a new philosophy – a return to self-reliance, a return to freedom – which the peoples of Eastern Europe are seeking but which we, in many ways, have been letting slide away.

A retired president of a Federal Reserve Bank, a very conscientious economic statesman, wonders if "we can rein in the spending proclivities of the U.S. Congress... Maybe shortened and/or less secure tenure for Congressmen would help. A line item veto authority for the President would appear essential."

Perhaps, too, we need the iron discipline of a balanced budget amendment to the U.S. Constitution and the automatic control of government spending of the gold standard.

With his assumption of office in 1993 President Bill Clinton would face heavy responsibilities – to help lead the United States out of its terrible deficit position.

His administration would also have the challenge of helping to return U.S. banking to a strong, safe system that would serve the local communities – small and large – in these United States.

Fire the Regulators?

No, we should not fire the regulators. By and large, they do a good job. However, like the rest of us, they tend to react to what is past, cracking down when it's time to ease up on credit, or being too easy when a boom is on. The regulators are not supposed to run the banks. That isn't their job. On occasions when they are forced into trying to run a bank, the record is generally not too satisfactory. (Several of the FDIC-sponsored bailouts of big banks haven't worked.) Nor should they try to remold U.S. banking along some pet theory of the moment. That isn't their job. Their job is to guard the safety of our banking system.

The idea of consolidating the various federal regulatory agencies into one isn't desirable. Witness the closeness of the Federal Home Loan Bank Board and the FSLIC. Both institutions failed, taking hundreds of S&Ls along with them – to cost the American people perhaps half a trillion dollars or more.

Nor should the 50 state banking departments be abolished in favor of federal regulators. They all can do a good job. Remember the old state bank examiner in Chapter 1.

To continue to attempt to force U.S. banking by federal financial subsidies into a few interstate systems is illogical and unwise.

Go On a Gold Standard?

To return to a gold standard would require discipline – discipline of the American people, special discipline on federal spendings. Nor is it likely that one nation, not even the United States, can do it alone today. Countries that have suffered under hyperinflation appreciate the facts that a fiat paper dollar is merely a piece of paper and that well-meaning people in government can lose their best intentions against inflation. Older, established nations, such as Germany and France, could lead the way. Joining them could be the emerging freedom-seeking countries of Eastern Europe, including the republics in what was the U.S.S.R. Japan will want to join in a better way of economic growth.

Free Exchange of Currencies Between Nations?

With the return of freedom to many of the former communist countries an international gold standard would allow freedom in exchange of currencies between nations. There would be uniformity of values. No longer would there be excuses for pseudo-banks such as Nugan Hand in Australia and the mysterious BCCI. With reductions in federal spendings and burdensome tax collections – and bringing under control international drug smuggling, the IRS would not have to worry the American people with the forms that banks and large cash handlers must now fill out on sizeable cash transactions. The American people should also again be allowed to possess currency, including specie, in whatever denominations they choose.

Join the BIS?

Often people ask, "If it's so important to the central banks of leading European nations to belong the the Bank for International Settlements, why are we (the U.S.) not a member?" When Owen D. Young and other Americans helped to found the BIS, after they had worked out reasonable means for German and Austrian reparations, why did the United States not join? Perhaps the hoped for "isolationism" of that era is the answer. Today, with ever-more important jobs of the BIS, such as the committee that set up uniform capital requirements for all large banks, why aren't we a member? Let's join the BIS, if the other members of the BIS will have us, more than half a century after we helped in its organization. One warning: Other members of the BIS won't be inclined to let us dominate it as we have tried to do with the Washington-based IMF and World Bank. It is not likely that the BIS will cease its diplomatic criticisms of our inflationary ways until our congresses and administrations truly change their profligate spendings.

Return to Integrity and Individual Responsibility?

Edward Sohmer, retired international credit manager for Sears Roebuck & Co., stresses that both cupidity and stupidity have joined to bring down banks and businesses. Behind all banking, all business, all government is individual responsibility.[30]

Ernest Baughman, retired president of the Federal Reserve Bank of Dallas, says we must return to "responsibility of owners/managers of private businesses and, of course, managers of public/government businesses...This has received too little attention in the S&L/Bank holocaust."[31]

Speculative loans should not be made by banks, he says, unless the borrower has enough net worth that he or she can repay the loan when the speculation doesn't work out and the financial institution can tie up the relevant amount of the borrower's net worth to ensure it will be available for debt repayment when needed.

From the Southeast, Monroe Kimbrel, former president of the Federal Reserve Bank of Atlanta, has similar advice:

> It used to be, nothing was as important to the banker as the customer who came in the bank door. Rich, poor, whatever color, the banker knew him. He knew the banker. Each had respect for the another. Unfortunately, or perhaps fortunately, whichever is your viewpoint, today the only thing that seems important is the bottom line.[32]

The truly wise banker, even in the 1990s, will realize that the bottom line can change and quickly. The customer is still most important.

Golden Parachutes

Perhaps better known in connection with large industrial mergers and buy-outs, "golden parachutes" – the sometimes gigantic awards to members of corporate management who may lose their jobs – are also found with financial institutions. Highly paid executives additionally may be rewarded when their institutions merge with other companies – with or without their blessings. Benefits have even included forgiveness of substantial individual loans owed by members of top management to their banking companies when the banks have gone broke.

On occasions, "golden parachutes" were given regulatory blessing – as when a supposedly highly talented banker is hired to try to rescue a foundering financial institution. If the bank survives, he wins. Likewise, if it goes under, even within a short time, he also wins. Some of the big bank mergers that admittedly or otherwise eventually cause hundreds, or thousands, of employees to lose their jobs – at the same time provided large financial rewards, "golden parachutes," for those corporate leaders who helped to set up the mergers – whether these stay or leave.

This is not a subject for additional regulation. We have too many regulations already. (The Crime Control Act of 1990 partly addressed this. Banking institutions that are near to insolvency are prohibited or limited in what can be paid under "golden parachutes" – without regulatory approval. The FDIC Improvement Act of 1991 might also be interpreted as touching on "golden parachutes.") But it is a subject for reflection by the American people. Do "golden parachutes" benefit the bank, the employees, the shareholders, the public? Think it over. Don't be afraid to let your opinions be known.

How Can We Again Have Local Banking Leadership?

A few years ago this question might have been passed off flippantly as applying only to the smallest of communities. Today it applies to some of the largest of U.S. cities. In Detroit in the early

1930s, nationally known businessman-statesman Jesse Jones, representing the RFC, challenged the leadership of that city to rebuild its banking system. Today there is no Jesse Jones and possibly we don't need someone representing a federal agency today to guide us; Washington has shown its ineptitude over recent decades. We have people of ability in every city, every town who just need to be found and challenged.

One of those who helped Detroit rebuild was newspaper publisher Edward Douglas Stair, who, with the leaders of General Motors, Ford and Chrysler, joined other businesses, labor unions and individuals to bring Detroit out of the banking wilderness.

Able bankers were found to head the new institutions. Southwestern cities such as Dallas, which have lost their major financial institutions, could look today to their publishers, their business leaders, leaders in education, and ordinary individuals to re-establish their banking institutions. Able bankers *must* be found to help guide conservatively growing new financial institutions in serving their cities and trade areas.

Cooperation from national and state banking regulators will be expected and should be forthcoming.

Saying the same for S&Ls, in mid-1992 Martin Leary of the Southern Finance Project, Durham, North Carolina, referred to RTC-approved transfers of huge amounts of deposits from what had been locally owned S&Ls to large financial conglomerates.

Leary said the government should return such funds to local ownership and use, rather than promoting transfer of deposits to distant control and use.[33]

Back to the question: What, then should we do? A summary would include:

1. *Demand That Congress and Administration Stop Deficit Spending*

   Demand that your representatives in the U.S. Congress and Administration stop their reckless deficit spending. Their intoxication with spending and inflation of the dollar has caused a reduction in the dollar's value to perhaps one-tenth of what it once was worth and has caused wildly fluctuating prices and interest rates.

   Commend and encourage the few in government — national, state and local — who are beginning to consider economies, rather than increases, in governmental spendings.

2. *Tell Politicians and Regulators We Don't Need More of Their Improvising in Banking*

   Let those who represent you know that we do not need

more, bigger and bigger, super-regional banking systems that would fail, or be propped up by the Federal Government. Let them know that the regulators need to help our system work, as it did in the past, rather than try to re-mold U.S. banks along an Australian, or Japanese, or German system, controlled by a few in business and government.

Provide an example of local leadership if need be. If necessary, organize your own banks. Let those in your state and national capitals know that you expect their cooperation.

3. *Demand a Banking System That Serves the Community*

Tell your Congressmen and Senators that we want a sound banking system, a sound savings and loan industry, a sound system of credit unions and a sound insurance system. Tell them that the banking system should primarily serve the local communities of this country.

Point out the institutions and individuals doing good jobs.

4. *Encourage the Younger Generation to Save – Set an Example*

Set an example and encourage the younger generation to save, to believe in America and its future, based on a sound dollar. We can learn from the people of Japan and Germany who rose from abject defeat to rebuild their nations by thrift and hard work.[34]

Tell our youngsters that the challenge of re-establishing a sound monetary system, based on a gold standard, with a U.S. dollar of real value, is probably too big for us of this generation. But that if they will work for it, a U.S. monetary system based upon a dollar of lasting value, freely exchangeable with the currencies of other nations, is an achievable plan.

5. *Demand Integrity in Banking Business and Government*

Demand integrity in banking, in S&Ls and in other financial institutions. Also expect integrity and personal responsibility in all business and in government, as well as in personal affairs.

6. *Do Your Own Thinking*

Do your own constructive thinking on these problems and opportunities. Don't be bound by what this writer says, or by what any supposed expert may say.

Think for yourself.

NOTES

1. David Morris' column from the *St. Paul Pioneer Press and Dispatch,* as published in the July 31, 1991 *Fort Worth Star-Telegram,* is given in its entirety in Appendix P. Morris is co-director of the Institute for Local Self-Reliance, Washington.

2. John P. Butler, Midland, Texas, conversation in 1990. Mr. Butler was long-time executive with First National Bank of Midland and has served in an advisory capacity with successor institutions.

3. *1984 Annual Report,* Federal Deposit Insurance Corporation, Washington.

4. Maureen E. Muldoon, Financial Analyst, FDIC, letter of August 17, 1990, Washington.

5. *NSBU News Release,* "Proposed Banking Reforms Pose Further Threat to Small Business Access to Credit," National Small Business United, Washington, February 8, 1991.

6. Gregory E. Elliehausen and John D. Wolken, Staff Studies, "Banking Markets and the Use of Financial Services by Small and Medium Sized Businesses," Board of Governors of the Federal Reserve System, Washington, September, 1990. The Small Business Administration joined in sponsorship of this study, conducted by the Survey Research Center of the University of Michigan.

7. Richard T. Nathan, Springfield, Massachusetts, letter of June 22, 1990.

8. Earl J. Fisher, president, Muenster State Bank, Muenster, Texas, letter of January 18, 1991.

Irvine Sprague, long-time FDIC director, in the "Conclusions" of his book *Bailout,* said much the same – "that FDIC assessments should be levied on all deposits, foreign and domestic"

9. Edward J. Kane, *The Gathering Crisis in Federal Deposit Insurance,* MIT Press, Cambridge, 1985. Kane is James E. Cleary Professor of Finance at Boston College. As his predictions continue to come true, Kane is becoming increasingly recognized in the academic, regulatory and political worlds.

10. Paul T. Coulopoulos, Boston, telephone conversation, November, 1990.

11. Rollo G.A. Fisher, statement to author the night before the Annual Conference of Robert Morris Associates, Detroit, September 14, 1963. Subsequent correspondence during 1990 and 1991. See also Irvine Sprague's *Bailout* on Bank of the Commonwealth.

12. Comerica Inc., *Annual Report for 1989*, Detroit.

13. Peter P. Santago, Sr. & Jr., Southington, Connecticut, letter of November 5, 1990.

14. C. Truett Smith, Wylie, Texas, telephone conversation August, 1990.

15. Ritter and Silber, previously cited.

16. Don Wigley, QuestStar Bank, Houston, telephone conversation, and letter of April 13, 1992 to shareholders. See Appendix R.

17. *Business Week,* January 21, 1991.

18. Zions Bancorporation, *1989 Annual Report*, Salt Lake City. Also, telephone conversation with president Harris H. Simmons, 1990.

19. Jesse Jones, *Fifty Billion Dollars*, previously cited.

20. James A. (Buddy) Davidson and John P. Butler, Midland, Texas, conversations, 1990.

21. Seafirst Corporation, *Annual Report for 1978*, Seattle.

22. Irvine Sprague, *Bailout*, Basic Books, Inc., New York, 1986. As late as 1982, just before Seattle-First National Bank was nearly bailed out by the FDIC, with Bank of America coming to the rescue, Sea-First had been given a "green" light rate in a personal financial report publication. Under the title, "Is Your Bank Failing?" the 50 largest commercial banks (U.S.) were listed by size in assets. Sea-First was Number 21. All of the 19 largest banks were coded "yellow." Number 20, National Bank of Detroit, was given a deservedly superior "green" rating, as was Sea-First. The report appeared in *Personal Finance – The Inflation Survival Letter*, Alexandria, Virginia, June 23, 1982. Data was from Veribanc, which

reported as of December 31, 1981 that Sea-First had a 5 percent equity to assets ratio after a profitable 1981. Financial conditions do change and sometimes very quickly, when supposedly good quality loans or other good investments turn out to be of questionable value.

23. Bank of New England Corp., *1989 Annual Report*, Boston, 1990.

24. Alan Greenspan, ***Risk, Safety and Bank Deregulation***, published by Sears Financial Board (Sears, Roebuck & Co.), undated.

25. Same reference.

26. Frank Norwood, Midland, Texas, conversation of August, 1991.

27. George E. Grobowsky, chairman and CEO, First National Bank, Marshall, Texas, telephone conversations 1990 and 1991.

28. Edward J. Kane, *The Gathering Crisis in Federal Deposit Insurance*. In mid-1992 Kane in testimony before the House Banking Committee suggested the FDIC *Bank Insurance Fund*, rather than having a December 31, 1991 net value of *minus* $7 billion, with likely losses may be a *negative* $53 billion. (*Dallas Morning News*, July 6, 1992.)

29. Christine Dugas, "Pain but No Gain for City Economy," *Newsday*, Long Island, New York, July 16, 1991. Also, *Chemical Banking Corp., 1991 Annual Report, and 1992 First* and *Second Quarterly Reports.*

30. Telephone conversations with Edward Sohmer, Richardson, Texas, 1991.

31. Ernest T. Baughman, former president, Federal Reserve Bank of Dallas, letters and telephone conversation, Oak Park, Illinois, 1991.

32. Monroe Kimbrel, former president Federal Reserve Bank of Atlanta, telephone conversation, 1991, Thompson, Georgia.

33. Mark Wrolstad of the *Dallas Morning News* quoted the report of July 8, 1992. Marty Leary of the Southern Finance Project, Durham, North Carolina, wrote the report with the title: "Under New Management: The S&L Crisis and the Rural South." The study was sponsored by the Ford Foundation and the Z. Smith Reynolds Foundation.

The report also stated:

> Local S&Ls that survived the 1980s were more financially sound than the industry as a whole and less reliant on costly, volatile funding sources. They also devoted a larger share of their portfolios to traditional mortgage investments.

34. "Net household savings" were just under 5 percent of household disposable income for U.S. families, according to the *62nd Annual Report* of the Bank for International Settlements. The U.S. savings rate was much less than that of any other major country, even after recent declines in other countries. In Canada and the United Kingdom savings were about 10 percent of family income, double the savings rate in the United States. In France and Japan savings were about 12 percent of income. In Germany and Italy savings were near 15 percent of income, triple the U.S. savings rate. *62nd Annual Report* for year ended March 31, 1992, Bank for International Settlements, June 15, 1992, Basle.

APPENDIX A:

Other Federal Reserve Functions — Congress' Ill-Informed FDIC Improvement Act Of 1991

For List and Map of The 12 Federal Reserve Banks and Their Districts (And the Numbers and Letters That Appear on your Federal Reserve Notes) – See below and opposite page.

Boundaries of Federal Reserve Districts and Their Branch Territories

Source: Board of Governors of the Federal Reserve System

FEDERAL RESERVE BANKS AND STATES SERVED

	District No.	*Alphabetic Symbol*	*States*
Federal Reserve Bank of Boston	1	A	Massachusetts, Rhode Island, Connecticut (except Fairfield County), Vermont, New Hampshire, Maine
Federal Reserve Bank of New York	2	B	New York and New Jersey (northern), Connecticut (Fairfield County)
Federal Reserve Bank of Philadelphia	3	C	Pennsylvania (eastern), New Jersey (southern), Delaware
Federal Reserve Bank of Cleveland	4	D	Ohio, Kentucky (eastern), Pennsylvania (western), West Virginia (northern)
Federal Reserve Bank of Richmond	5	E	Virginia, Maryland, West Virginia (southern), North Carolina, South Carolina, District of Columbia)
Federal Reserve Bank of Atlanta	6	F	Georgia, Florida, Alabama, Tennessee (eastern), Mississippi (southern), Louisiana (southern)
Federal Reserve Bank of Chicago	7	G	Illinois (northern), Indiana (northern), Iowa, Michigan (southern), Wisconsin (southern)
Federal Reserve Bank of St. Louis	8	H	Missouri (eastern), Arkansas, Illinois (southern), Kentucky (western), Tennessee (western), Mississippi (northern), Indiana (southern)
Federal Reserve Bank of Minneapolis	9	I	Minnesota, Michigan (northern), Wisconsin (northern), North Dakota, South Dakota, Montana
Federal Reserve Bank of Kansas City	10	J	Missouri (western), Kansas, Nebraska, Oklahoma, Wyoming, Colorado, New Mexico (northern)
Federal Reserve Bank of Dallas	11	K	Texas, Louisiana (northern), New Mexico (southern)
Federal Reserve Bank of San Francisco	12	L	California, Oregon, Washington, Idaho, Utah, Nevada, Arizona, Alaska, Hawaii

Adjustable Reserve Requirements

Before the days of the Federal Reserve System, "country banks" – banks in smaller cities and towns – kept their reserves with larger banks in "reserve cities." Then as now, local banks also kept a part of reserve needs in vault cash. Checks on the local banks were cleared through their reserve cities' correspondents. Not only was this prudent banking, but from way back state and national laws and regulations had required certain percentages of local bank deposits to be kept as legal reserves with larger banks.

There were also "central reserve cities," the largest cities such as New York and Chicago, where country banks and reserve cities banks kept deposit reserves. The reserve cities and central reserve cities banks provided other correspondent services for their customer banks, including rediscounting local customer loans so as to provide liquidity for the local banks. It was during periods of "financial panic" that such rediscounting of loans stopped near-completely.

The Federal Reserve Act of 1913 (Owen-Glass Currency Reform Bill) changed all that. It required national banks to be members of the new Federal Reserve System and allowed state banks to also obtain membership. All member banks had to keep reserves with the new Federal Reserve Banks, though they could also continue to keep additional deposit accounts with other commercial banks. Until 1933 reserves with the district Federal Reserve Banks were at fixed ratios against deposits in the member banks. Amendments to the Federal Reserve Act in 1933 and 1935 allowed reserve requirements to be varied, supposedly with economic conditions.

Theoretically, and actually, the amount of funds that a commercial bank must have in reserve will limit the amount of loans that a bank can make. A banking economist might point out that loan-created deposits do not take place in just one bank. Deposits and payments will be transferred from a customer of one bank to his account or to his customer's account, or accounts, in other banks. Rather, loans and deposits ebb and flow amongst all the banks in the banking system.

This is the theory of "fractional reserve banking" – which as mentioned elsewhere in this book has bothered certain of the economic "left" and "right" from ages back. "100 Percent Banking" and "Core Banks" are concepts of those who would do away with banking's power to create a portion of the money supply. The substitute would be government fiat creation of whatever amount or percentage of monetary growth that the particular advocate of complete governmental control thinks best.

Check Collections, Wire Transfer, Currency and Coins

Coinciding with serving as depositories for banks' reserves the Federal Reserve Banks also provide the major clearing and collection mechanisms for banks in the United States. Federal Reserve Banks provide wire transfer of funds. They also supply banks and other financial institutions with currency and coins.

In 1980 the Depository Institutions Deregulation and Monetary Control Act brought all banks, also S&Ls and credit unions, under reserve requirements with the Fed, though with Garn-St Germain of 1982-85 exemptions have allowed many smaller institutions to avoid such requirements.

Discount Rate

It was originally conceived that "eligible commercial and agricultural paper" – loans by commercial banks to their customers – would be rediscounted with the district Federal Reserve Bank. In those days most loans to bank customers were "discounted" – interest being collected in advance. (U.S. Treasury Bills are still sold at "discount.") Member banks would then "rediscount" their customers' notes to the Federal Reserve Bank. This "eligible paper" in turn would join with gold to provide collateral for issuing Federal Reserve Notes, thus an elastic currency. Later, U.S. bonds and other security were allowed as collateral for "advances" with the district banks. The Discount Rate is the rate that the Federal Reserve Bank charges for making such loans. Over the years advances and discounts with the "Fed" have not been too great in total volume, but the Discount Rate still is a basic rate in the financial market place. Each district bank sets its own discount rate, subject to review and determination by the Board of Governors. Rates for the twelve banks are generally the same.

Federal Funds Rate

Federal funds are excess funds, such as reserves with the Federal Reserve Banks, which are sold (lent) by banks to other banks on short-term bases. Federal funds are bought (borrowed), generally overnight – only for one day. Supposedly with little risk, generally unsecured, federal funds rates are relatively low.

Reports from the news media indicate that the Federal Open Market Committee sets such rates. But such reports are incorrect. The "Fed" may influence these rates in open market operations, but does not set them.

Certain banks that have gotten into severe liquidity situations, or become known otherwise as problem banks, may not be able to buy unsecured federal funds and may, thus, have to secure these.

Repurchase Agreements (RPs) are somewhat along the same line, a means for providing needed funds, as for banks that sell securities for given, often short, terms with agreements to repurchase these at stated amounts. Repurchase Agreements may be between banks, or between banks and securities dealers, or between various other parties in the financial markets.

Open Market Operations

Open Market Operations – the buying and selling of United States government securities by the Federal Reserve Banks – became more prominent in the 1930s, although of not too much effect until later, after World War II. In the 1950s and 1960, the Federal Open Market Committee set goals expressed as "firming," or "loosening" of the money markets, after discussions on domestic growth, foreign balance of payments, deficits, etc.[1]

In more recent years, as "monetarist" viewpoints have come to the fore, emphasis of the Open Market Committee has been on "monetary aggregates." "Monetarists" are those economists and others who argue that money and its substitutes (in most cases not gold) are most important and that the supply should grow so as to accommodate the growth of the economy. Several categories of monetary aggregates: M1, M2, M3, etc. are itemized. The Open Market Committee is concerned with keeping the growth of the various monetary aggregates from becoming excessive. These "Concepts of Money" in the *1990 Annual Report* of the Board of Governors of the Federal Reserve System included:

- M1 Currency, demand deposits, other checkable deposits, travelers checks.
- M2 M1 plus money market deposit accounts (MMDAs), savings and small denomination time deposits (CDs), retail repurchase agreements (RPs).
- M3 M2 plus large denomination time deposits (CDs), institutions' money market mutual funds, wholesale term repurchase agreements (RPs), Eurodollars held by U.S. residents in Canada and the United Kingdom, and at foreign branches of U.S. banks.

Industrial Loans

A provision for Federal Reserve Banks was that they be allowed under certain conditions to make direct industrial loans, as a means to aid the industrial recovery. Few such loans were requested or made.

Separation of Commercial Banking and Investment Banking

The Glass-Steagall Act's 1933 divorcement of commercial banking – deposit and lending – from securities underwriting and brokering caused changes in a number of the larger banks of the United States, and appropriate Federal Reserve regulations. In recent years, representatives from some large banks, and representatives from some of the regulatory agencies, have argued that times have changed, and this provision of the law should be repealed. Whether the argument is correct is debatable, but the prohibition of intermingling of commercial banking and securities banking caused Federal Reserve regulation.

U.S. Securities as Collateral for Federal Reserve Notes

The Glass-Steagall Act allowed issuance of Federal Reserve notes with United States government obligations as collateral, rather than only against gold and rediscounted bank loans. A percentage of gold was to be required. When the gold tie was broken – firstly, with bank reserve deposits with the Federal Reserve in 1965, secondly, with Federal Reserve Notes in 1968, and finally, with other nations in 1971, near-unrestricted inflationary expansion of currency and credit resulted, as the federal government spent heavily via deficit financing. Not only was there accelerated expansion of the money supply, but also near-unprecedented acceleration of interest rates, pushed up by governmental spending and competition for funds.

Securities Exchange Act

Excessive credit for acquiring securities was one of the alleged causes of the Crash of 1929. Additionally, stocks and bonds issued by companies of questionable financial condition were of concern to the American people and to the Congress. In the new Securities Exchange Act, not only were the stock exchanges and the corporations that issued shares made subject to the new Securities and Exchange Commission, but credit for stock acquisition was made subject to Federal Reserve regulations. The Federal Reserve was to regulate "margin requirements" for individuals as well as for securities dealers.

Wartime Powers

In both of the World Wars and in later Cold War U.S. governmental efforts, the Federal Reserve was heavily involved. Not only were war bonds issued through the Fed, special wartime duties were enacted by Congress. Regulation V continues as part of Federal Reserve Regulations today, based on Congress' authorization for Federal Reserve guaranty of defense plant "V" Loans (as in "V" for Victory).

Restriction on consumer credit was a wartime duty of the Fed, per Congressional order.

International Bank Operations

U.S. and foreign banks may have Edge Act subsidiaries to facilitate international trade. These and foreign bank branches which operate in the United States are subject to Federal Reserve regulation. The Comptroller of the Currency and the FDIC also get involved with the Federal Reserve on international branches and subsidiaries of U.S. banks that operate in other countries. As indicated elsewhere in this book, up till now foreign deposits of U.S. banks have supposedly been exempted from FDIC insurance coverage as well as FDIC premium assessments – though no foreign depositors' losses have been indicated in the bailout of large U.S. banks that had substantial foreign deposits.

Through the Federal Open Market Committee the Federal Reserve from time to time buys and sells currencies of other nations through their central banks and the Bank for International Settlements. These "Swaps" are aimed toward providing international monetary stability – though the efforts do not always work.

As pointed out in Chapter 8, in 1991 foreign banks controlled 24 percent of all U.S. bank assets.[2]

Congress' Ill-Informed FDIC Improvement Act of 1991

Swinging 180 degrees from the utter permissiveness of Garn-St Germain of the previous decade, Congress in late 1991 passed the euphemistically entitled Federal Deposit Insurance Corporation Improvement Act of 1991. Intended as an act to keep the Bank Insurance Fund afloat, the law ended up including peculiar provisions on banking. Janet Novack of *Forbes* quoted former FDIC Chairman L. William Seidman as describing the "FDIC Improvement Act as the Credit Crunch Enhancement Act of 1991 . . . the most oppressive piece of banking legislation that I have ever witnessed."

Similar in mode and hour of adoption to that which saw the approval of deposit insurance to $100,000 at the beginning of the 1980s, the 1991 act with its 158 pages was agreed to by House-

Senate conference committee at 4:57 AM and approved by the two houses of government later that same day. Like the Resolution Trust Corporation Refinancing, Restructuring and Improvement Act of 1991, the FDIC Improvement Act of 1991 was also to become effective over varying times, up to late in 1993. According to *Forbes,* the provisions for the FDIC Improvement Act include:

> How much a bank may pay its executives.
>
> The standards a bank must use when making a loan, and the documentation required.
>
> How fast a bank may expand its asset base.
>
> How much interest rate risk a bank may take.[3]

That Congress is somewhat experienced in setting salaries is shown in Appendix M. Telling banks how to make good loans sounds much like the guidelines given the S&Ls after Garn-St Germain told them they could be like commercial banks – the detailed guidelines spelled out by the Federal Home Loan Bank Board before it was abolished.

Well intentioned in seeking to discourage brokered deposits, this act of Congress also makes difficult requirements of the FDIC in determining what is adequate capitalization for banks. By this "Improvement Act" federal regulators are ordered to close banks that are still solvent but whose capital is depleted – banks that might survive if enough time could be found to raise additional capital.

The banking associations – American Bankers Association, the super-regionals' new Coalition for Interstate and Branch Banking, and the Independent Bankers Association of America – did not greatly oppose the bill. Each was too concerned with other matters, lobbying for recission of Glass-Steagall and for interstate banking, or fighting the Treasury's plan to reduce individual and family coverage in FDIC insurance.

Nor did the President veto the bill, as the Bush administration was involved in its program for pushing super-regional banking and recission of Glass-Steagall, also for centralization of the regulatory system under the Treasury Department. *Forbes* quoted John G. Medline, Jr. chief executive of Wachovia Corp., a long time, well operated banking system in the Southeast at Winston-Salem, who commented:

> In Russia they are trying to move away from this kind of legislation, and instead we're going toward it.

NOTES

1. Federal Reserve Open Market Operations are also supposed to make commercial bank loan expansion easier – as when the FOMC buys securities from banks, it adds reserves available for bank loan expansion. Conversely, when the FOMC sells securities to banks through the open market, reserves are supposedly reduced and loans are less likely to be made.

But congressionally dictated federal deficits overshadow all that the FOMC can do – one way or the other.

2. Board of Governors of the Federal Reserve System, *1991 Annual Report*, Washington.

3. Janet Novack, "Son of Credit Crunch," *Forbes*, May 25, 1992.

APPENDIX B:

Currency — Faces On Our Legal Tender

Currency – Faces on Our Legal Tender

$1 –	George Washington
$2 –	Thomas Jefferson
$5 –	Abraham Lincoln
$10 –	Alexander Hamilton
$20 –	Andrew Jackson
$50 –	Ulysses S. Grant
$100 –	Benjamin Franklin
$500 –	William McKinley
$1,000 –	Grover Cleveland
$5,000 –	James Madison
$10,000 –	Salmon P. Chase
$100,000 –	Woodrow Wilson[1]

All those whose portraits appear on our currency believed in a sound dollar, which would protect the individual. First President George Washington, Federalist and first Secretary of the Treasury Alexander Hamilton, Republican-Democrats Thomas Jefferson and Andrew Jackson, all believed in a sound dollar. Republican Abraham Lincoln and his Civil War Secretary of the Treasury Salmon P. Chase (later chief justice) established the system of national banks and National Currency, reluctantly also allowing "greenback" United States Notes to be issued. (The Confederate government also issued paper dollars. By midsummer, 1864, the Southern dollar was worth two cents on the gold dollar, "fifty for one.")[2]

After the war, former General Ulysses S. Grant, who was drafted by the Republicans and elected President, vetoed efforts of Congress for further inflation, and signed into law the resumption of gold payments by the government in place of paper promises. Benjamin Franklin was the father of thrift. Democrat Grover Cleveland, as President, protected the integrity of the U.S. dollar, as did Republican William McKinley. During Democrat Woodrow Wilson's administration, the Federal Reserve System was established. (The $100,000 bill was to be a means for transferring funds between the several federal reserve banks.)

In the 1960s, U.S. dollars abroad came to be Euro-dollars – deposited, borrowed, and loaned by banks abroad. A U.S. Interest

Equalization Tax was tried, and quickly abandoned. To make international cash transactions more difficult the U.S. bureaucracy cut back drastically on the denomination of U.S. currency printed or in circulation. Since 1969, by agreement of the U. S. Treasury and the Federal Reserve, bills of $500 and larger in denomination have been taken out of circulation, (during which time with accelerated inflation it would have been logical to use much larger Federal Reserve Notes). In addition, all cash transactions of $10,000 or more must be reported by banks, S&Ls and other businesses – purportedly to prevent transactions between drug dealers and other criminals and to collect maximum taxes. The Bank Secrecy Act of 1970 was enlarged in scope in 1988 to include "grossly negligent" as well as "willful" violations. This sought to prohibit American citizens as well as foreigners from having cash transactions of $10,000 or more (unless reported to the federal government). The penalty for failure to report was also raised, from $1,000 to $10,000. Supposedly covering only financial institutions, the U.S. Treasury Department through its Internal Revenue Service has by interpretation extended this reporting duty to automobile dealers and to anyone else in business. (See IRS Forms 4789 and 8300, each of which begins with a statement about the Paperwork Reduction Act.)

The American people are thus instructed by the U.S. Congress to be honest in all their business dealings. And any large transaction of cash must be reported by anyone involved, to the IRS, although keeping in mind that this should be done in such a manner as to reduce paperwork.

The major securities house of Shearson Lehman Hutton has carried out this act to the extent of closing its cashier's offices, thus requiring all customer transactions to be by check. Shearson's business parent, American Express, has long been prominent in the check issuing business.

With increased inflation, the value of the dollar continues to drop, thus causing an ever-increasing number of cash transactions to be reported, and a continuing generation of paperwork – and no bills over $100 allowed to circulate. It is amazing what the American people will put up with from Acts of Congress and subsequent rulings and regulations of the bureaucracy – under the supposed goal of protection from evil-doers and foreign finance. (In 1975, after the international price of gold had gone sky-high, Congress decided that U.S. citizens would again be allowed to own gold.)

One Degree Further in the U.S.S.R. – Which Then Helped Bring Its Collapse

In early 1991, twenty-three years after large bills had been withdrawn from circulation in the U.S.A, U.S.S.R. President Mikhail Gorbachev showed the U.S. one degree further on how to stop citizens' dealings in large currency bills. Gorbachev, also then Chairman of the Communist Party, gave his citizens three days to redeem all currency of 50 ruble denominations or larger. In addition, only 1,000 rubles, or one month's pay, whichever was less, would be exchanged for each citizen for smaller denominations. Since the average paycheck was in the neighborhood of 250 rubles, the banks probably didn't find it hard to stock up on enough small denomination rubles to take care of the demand. Thus the Russian people's cash savings were abolished. Except for those who had been lucky enough to hoard their savings in gold, or U.S. dollars, or other Western currencies, efforts at thrift had proved to be of little value in the Socialist Republics.

The Soviet government's reasoning was also to cut back excess currency, and to catch and penalize those engaged in black markets, that is, private, capitalistic dealings.

These actions against the peoples in what was the U.S.S.R. helped to bring down the seven-decade-old repressive Communist regime and to create the loose Commonwealth of Independent States (C.I.S.).

As the peoples in the newly independent states felt their ways toward free economies as well as free lives, they were also seeking a monetary system, or systems, which would allow freedom. The old ruble had little value internationally, or at home. Discussions even included gold as a base for a new ruble, or whatever each state's monetary unit might be called. Such would place the monetary systems of the new states ahead of that of the U.S.A.

NOTES

1. Board of Governors of the Federal Reserve System, *77th Annual Report*, Washington, 1990.

2. D.W.C. Baker, *A Texas Scrap Book*, New York, 1875, republished 1935 by the Steck Company, Austin. This sometime-humorous report of "the history, biography and miscellany of Texas and its people" told how the Confederate government at Richmond issued an "immense amount of paper money." Also, that "Gold, ever jealous of its own value, and fearful of being depreciated by being brought into contact with this new money, immediately withdrew from the public gaze, and crept into the safe of the merchant, and the stocking and shot-bag of the countryman." Baker also reported that even the merchant manufactured his own "shin-lasters" claiming his small change paper money superior to that of any other merchant's. He reported that taxes, "perhaps exceeding anything recorded in history, amounting to 10, 20, 30 or even 50 percent . . . paid by the people

with a resignation which the ancient patriarch of Uz would have contemplated with profound respect.''

Does this report of the money and economy of the falling Southern Confederacy of the 1860s seem similar to conditions in some countries of the 1990s?

APPENDIX C:
Gold Reserves

Nation	*Fine Troy Ounces of Gold Per Capita Population*
Switzerland	12.42
Lebanon	3.25
Belgium	3.05
Netherlands	2.96
Austria	2.68
Germany	1.55
France	1.46
Kuwait	1.23
Italy	1.16
Luxembourg	1.13
United States	1.05
Libya	.85
Uruguay	.80
Sweden	.71
Canada	.60
Venezuela	.60
Australia	.47
United Kingdom	.33
Saudi Arabia	.32
Israel	.31
Japan	.20
Korea	.13
South Africa	.11
Philippines	.04
India	.01
Mexico	.01
Peoples' Republic of China	.01

Holdings of the then U.S.S.R. and of the Nationalist Republic of China (Taiwan) were not reported, as they were not members of the IMF.
Source: International Monetary Fund, "International Financial Statistics," Vol. XLIII, No. 9, Washington, September, 1990

The chart of 1990 Gold Reserves summarizes the importance of gold holdings in the monetary systems of twenty-seven nations. The significance of a sound currency is evident in Switzerland, where gold reserves per capita are twelve times those of the United States. In total gold reserves, the United States, with 262.03

million ounces, leads the world. Switzerland is second, with 88.28 million ounces. However, the population of the U.S. is thirty-seven times that of Switzerland.

Lebanon, although beset by years of civil war, still maintains per capita gold reserves three times that of the U.S. It is known in banking circles as "the Switzerland of the Near East."

Belgium, the Netherlands, Austria, Germany, France, Italy, and Luxembourg are all strong holders of gold. Could this be due to the long memories of gold-versus-paper troubles?

Kuwait, with its rich stores of oil, was also rich in gold when it was invaded by Iraq.

The Philippines have increased gold reserves tenfold in recent years, while Mexico's have gone down as this neighbor nation to the United States sought to extricate its foreign debts.

It should be noted that per capita reserves do not indicate individual ownership of gold, but include bank holdings. Individuals in the several countries can have tremendous gold holdings without those holdings being reflected in their banking reserves.

We could hardly include a report on gold reserves throughout the world without commenting upon the conspicuous absence of Japan among the leaders. It may be speculated that since Japan's economic thrust is into the future, with micro-technology and space-age industry as its chief assets, gold reserves will also be seen as an urgent priority in giving additional stability to the Japanese yen.

The Peoples' Republic of China, with its many economic problems, continues low on gold reserves per capita. When that Communist government was allowed to join the International Monetary Fund (and the World Bank), the non-communist Republic of China (Taiwan) was expelled from the IMF (and World Bank) but was permitted to purchase its full quota of gold at the old official price of gold. Thus, non-communist China (Taiwan) came out very well in its gold holdings, which, like those of the U.S.S.R., were not reported by the IMF because they were not member countries.

As stated in Appendix B, the mid-1991 falling away of Communist control over the republics of what had been the U.S.S.R. allowed the beginning of new freedoms for the peoples in the republics. Growing economic freedom for a new Commonwealth of Independent States would require a type of "hard" currency, or currencies, possibly based upon gold to replace the U.S.S.R. fiat paper ruble. Gold, like oil, had been a valuable resource produced in the U.S.S.R. A new "ruble," given a value in gold, would place it ahead of the U.S. dollar as a standard of value.

The *Journal of Commerce* (New York), September 25, 1991, quoted a German news agency on what had been the Soviet Gosbank plans to hold onto its gold. What will happen? Anyone's guess.

Chinese Government 5 Percent Gold Bond of 1913

Payable in gold, or the
French franc, or the
German mark, or the
Japanese yen, or the
Russian rouble.

Displayed on the wall of
Little & Co., Midland, Texas

APPENDIX D:
Insurance Companies

The *1989 Annual Report* of Equitable Life Assurance Society of the United States attributes much of the domino-like collapse of the Communist countries of recent years to the "free market, growth-oriented economic policies of Reagan and Thatcher which fueled a worldwide explosion of economic growth." But this country's huge foreign trade deficit and equally huge Federal budget deficit necessitate heavy dependence on other nations.

The report goes on to say:

> These twin deficits actually make many of us feel good in the short run, which no doubt explains why no one seems willing to address the problem . . . but as is the case with any other addiction, the euphoria of borrowed money eventually turns into a hangover for the nation as a whole. There are signs this is happening.
>
> When one considers that stock market values compounded at an 18 percent rate per annum throughout the decade of the 1980s and the bond market returned 12 percent per annum income and capital gains, the logical assumption would be that U.S. financial institutions entering the 1990s would have fattened up their balance sheets and be prepared to take on all challengers. Not so. Whether we are talking about banks, or savings and loans, or insurance companies, or securities firms, it appears that core businesses – be they lending, insuring risks, or buying and selling securities – are either unprofitable or marginally profitable at best. As a result, the equity capital base has not grown proportionately to liabilities in any of these financial industries, and most participants find themselves today with markedly higher ratios of liabilities to capital than at the beginning of the decade – which has been caustically referred to as the "Golden Age of Debt." Moreover, despite eight years of uninterrupted economic growth and strong stock and bond markets, the quality of assets on the balance sheets of most U.S. financial institutions remains a subject of concern, despite massive reserves established by banks for LDC loans (loans to less developed countries), and a federal rescue of the savings and loan industry.

APPENDIX E:

Highly Leveraged Transactions and Leveraged Buyouts

Some of us had trouble understanding the Highly Leveraged Transactions (HLTs) which certain Wall Street and Beverly Hills firms specialized in creating. These allowed outside "raiders" or inside purchase groups to acquire control of major – and not-so-major – corporations, by Leveraged Buyouts (LBOs).

"Leverage" signifies a financial lever, with high credit versus low equity. To pay off the LBOs, some of the assets, or subsidiary companies, or divisions are sold off, so as to pay off the loans. Or bonds are issued – often below investment grade (junk bonds) – with later corporate restructuring or subsequent earnings anticipated as a means of repayment. There are also various combinations of HLT loans and "junk bonds".

A good indication of how little rhyme or reason there was to some of the HLTs is the speed with which the bonds (and loans) went bad. Other HLT's however, worked out rather well, at least for some of those involved. R.J. Reynolds, Safeway, and Owens-Corning all came through highly leveraged buyouts, although divisions and stores were sold off, and long-time employees lost their jobs.

In recent years large and medium-sized banks have had to report their loans of the HLT variety.

APPENDIX F:
Letter From Theodore R. Kennedy

Dear Mr. Surratt:

Your letter of April 2nd came as a pleasant surprise. Concerning Senator Vandenberg's role in formulating the plan for federal bank deposit insurance, I can add only a little beyond what was in the *Wall Street Journal* letter.

Senator Vandenberg had on his senate office wall a framed letter from the first head of FDIC saluting him as "the father of federal bank deposit insurance." [This is from memory; I may not have the words exactly right.]

In 1934 he gave two speeches in the Senate on the subject, the first on January 17 (*Congressional Record,* vol. 78, no. 1, pp. 813-9). The second was on June 9 entitled [in reprints] "Federal Deposit Insurance the Steel Beam of Recovery," (*Cong. Record*, vol. 78, no. 10, pp. 10915-9).

My dissertation footnote indicates you will find in the *New York Times* of June 6, 1933 (p. 1, col. 2) a report of President Roosevelt's threat to veto the Glass-Steagall banking bill if it contained the bank deposit insurance provision. When I mentioned this to Vandenberg's friend, Dr. Smith, he said Vandenberg asked Senator Glass what he thought about the President's threat; Senator Glass said, "Let him veto it – we'll pass it over his veto!" Of course Roosevelt did not hesitate to take full credit for the soundness of banks when he ran for re-election in 1936. If my memory is correct, in a speech at Pittsburg he gleefully pointed out that no bank had failed in one full year.

That is all I can say about Vandenberg and bank deposit insurance. I have not made a study of the Detroit banking crisis but I recall that it was severe and preceded the later national bank holiday.

May I offer you a word of encouragement on your project. The average American, I believe, understands less about the real operation of a bank than the functioning of the pituitary gland. If you can explain this subject in language the man in the street can grasp, you will confer a genuine benefit on our society.

It was a pleasure hearing from you and I wish you smooth sailing on your undertaking.

Yours very truly,

Theodore R. Kennedy
East Lansing, Michigan
April 12, 1990

APPENDIX G:

Basle Committee On Banking Regulations And Supervisory Practices — International Convergence Of Capital Measure And Capital Standards

EXCERPTS

(vi) **Off-balance-sheet engagements**

42. The Committee believes that it is of great importance that all off-balance-sheet activity should be caught within the capital adequacy framework. At the same time, it is recognised that there is only limited experience in assessing the risks in some of the activities; also that for some countries, a complex analytical approach and detailed and frequent reporting systems cannot easily be justified when the amounts of such business, particularly in the newer, more innovative instruments, are only small. The approach that has been agreed, which is on the same lines as that described in the Committee's report on the supervisory treatment of off-balance-sheet exposures issued to banks in March 1986, is comprehensive in that all categories of off-balance-sheet engagements, including recent innovations, will be converted to credit risk equivalents by multiplying the nominal principal amounts by a credit conversion factor, the resulting amounts then being weighted according to the nature of the counterparty. The different instruments and techniques are divided into five broad categories (within which member countries will have some limited discretion to allocate particular instruments according to their individual characteristics in national markets):

(a) those which substitute for loans (e.g. general guarantees of indebtedness, bank acceptance guarantees and standby letters of credit serving as financial guarantees for loans and securities) – these will carry a 100 per cent. credit risk conversion factor;

(b) certain transaction related contingencies (e.g. performance bonds, bid bonds, warranties and standby letters of credit related to particular transactions) – a

50 per cent. credit risk conversion factor;

(c) short-term, self-liquidating trade-related contingent liabilities arising from the movement of goods (e.g. documentary credits collateralised by the underlying shipments) – a 20 per cent. credit risk conversion factor;

(d) commitments with an original maturity exceeding one year (the longer maturity serving broadly as a proxy for higher risk facilities) and all NIFs and RUFs – a 50 per cent. credit risk conversion factor.

Shorter-term commitments or commitments which can be unconditionally cancelled at any time, it is agreed, generally carry only low risk and a nil weight for these is considered to be justified on de minimis grounds;

(e) interest and exchange rate related items (e.g. swaps, options, futures) – the credit risk equivalent amount for these controls will be calculated in one of two ways (see below and Annex 3).

43. Special treatment is needed for the items in (e) above because banks are not exposed to credit risk for the full face value of their contracts, but only to the cost of replacing the cash flow if a counterparty defaults. Most members of the Committee accept that the correct method of assessing the credit risk on these items is to calculate the current replacement cost by marking to market and to add a factor to represent potential exposure during the remaining life of the contract. Some member countries, however, are concerned about the consistency of this method in relation to the rest of the system which only makes broad distinctions between relative risks for on-balance-sheet items, particularly for banks where these off-balance-sheet items currently constitute only a very small part of the total risks. They would prefer to apply an alternative approach consisting of conversion factors based on the nominal principal sum underlying each contract according to its type and maturity. The Committee has concluded that members will be allowed to choose either of the two methods. The details of the two alternative methods are set out in Annex 3.

III. A TARGET STANDARD RATIO

44. In the light of consultations and preliminary testing of the framework, the Committee is agreed that a minimum standard should be set now which international banks generally will be expected to achieve by the end of the transitional period. It is also agreed that this standard should be set at a level that is consistent with the objective of securing over time soundly-based and

consistent capital ratios for all international banks. Accordingly, the Committee confirms that the target standard ratio of capital to weighted risk assets should be set at 8 per cent. (of which the core capital element will be at least 4 per cent.). This is expressed as a common minimum standard which international banks in member countries will be expected to observe by the end of 1992, thus allowing a transitional period of some four-and-a-half years for any necessary adjustment by banks who need time to build up to those levels. The Committee fully recognises that the transition from existing, sometimes long-established, definitions of capital and methods of measurement towards a new internationally agreed standard will not necessarily be achieved easily or quickly. The full period to end-1992 is available to ensure progressive steps towards adjustment and banks whose ratios are presently below the 8 per cent. standard will not be required to take immediate or precipitate action.

* * * * * *

Annex 1

Definition of capital included in the capital base
(To apply at end-1992)

A. Capital elements

Tier 1 (a) Paid-up share capital/common stock
(b) Disclosed reserves

Tier 2 (a) Undisclosed reserves
(b) Asset revaluation reserves
(c) General provisions/general loan loss reserves
(d) Hybrid (debt/equity) capital instruments
(e) Subordinated term debt

APPENDIX H:

Appendix H: Banc One Report On Acquisition Of MBanks

From *Annual Report 1989, Banc One Corporation,* Columbus, Ohio, on assumption of deposits and acquisition of certain assets of former MBanks:

As of December 31, 1989, the Corporation had agreement pending for the acquisition of three banks, a savings bank and an investment banking company. A seven and one-half percent interest in BANK ONE TEXAS, NA, Dallas, Texas (Texas) which the Corporation had been managing since July 5, 1989, for the Federal Deposit Insurance Corporation (FDIC), was acquired effective January 1, 1990 for $34 million. The FDIC invested $416.3 million in the common stock of Texas. Texas also had an unrelated note from the FDIC. The Shareholders' Agreement provided for the acquisition by the Corporation of the remaining 92½ percent interest over a period not exceeding five years at a cost ranging from $303.8 million to $426 million plus an amount approximating the FDIC cost to carry from January 1, 1990 to date of purchase by the Corporation.

This regulatory-assisted transaction will be accounted for as a purchase. The FDIC's assistance begins with the recapitalization of Texas. All assets will be marked to market with the FDIC providing notes to cover any negative capital position. After January 1, 1990, the FDIC will continue to provide assistance. During the first year subsequent to January 1, Texas will be able to segregate an unlimited amount of Texas problem assets into a collection pool subject to credit losses reaching .5% of Texas "non-collection pool" loans. In the second year Texas will be able to transfer up to $600 million problem assets into the collection pool subject to credit losses reaching .6% of "non-collection pool" loans. Throughout the first five years the FDIC will reimburse BANC ONE for the management of and the carrying costs of assets in the collection pool. The FDIC will pay BANC ONE an incentive fee of 5% of net cash collected on collection pool assets during the first two years and 4% during the third through fifth years.

APPENDIX I:

Muenster State Bank Financial Report And Photographs

Above: Muenster State Bank
Upper right: Catholic Church
Lower right: Medical Center
Below: Public School

Condensed Statement of Condition as of December 31, 1991

		December 31, 1991
RESOURCES:		
Cash & Due From Banks ... (Non-Interest Bearing Balances)		$ 2,263,597.32
Due From Banks ... (Interest Bearing Balances)		2,750,000.00
Bonds & Securities		20,582,166.58
Loans & Discounts	$14,479,571.47	
Less: Unearned Interest	301,922.41	
Reserves IRS Rulings	439,336.69	13,738.312.37
Federal Funds Sold		7,125,000.00
Banking House, Furniture & Fixtures		50,001.00
Accrued Interest Income		535,570.79
Other Assets ... (Stock in TIB)	70,000,000	
Less: Reserve for Equity	22,797.00	47,203.00
TOTAL RESOURCES		47,091,851.06
LIABILITIES:		
Capital	1,000,000.00	
Certified Surplus	1,000,000.00	
Profits & Reserves	4,822,178.04	
Total Capital Accounts		6,822,178.04
Demand Deposits	6,268,541.51	
Time & Savings Deposits	33,871,924.96	
Total Deposits		40,140,466.47
Accrued Interest Payable		129,206.55
TOTAL LIABILITIES		47,091,851.06

Condensed Statement of Condition as of December 31, 1991

STATEMENT OF INCOME:

Interest Income From:		
Loans	1,560,921.58	
Investment Securities	1,599,678.69	
Federal Funds Sold	388,250.42	
Certificates of Deposits	242,581.75	
Total Interest Income		3,791,432.44
Other Income		176,850.74
TOTAL INCOME		3,968,283.18
Less: Interest, Salaries, Benefits & Other Expenses:		
Time Deposits	1,900,049.70	
Others	-0-	
Total Interest Expense		1,900,049.70
Salaries & Benefits	370,276.37	
Other Operating Expense	320,195.74	
Total Non-Interest Expense		690,472,11
TOTAL EXPENSE		2,590,521.81
Income Before Income Taxes, Dividends & Expenses		1,377,761.37
Less: Income Taxes Paid		362,532.00
Dividends Paid		400,000.00
Transfer to Reserve For Bad Debts		100,000.00
Transfer to Reserve For Income Tax		-0-
Transfer to Reserve For State Income Tax		18,660.00
NET INCREASE IN CAPITAL ACCOUNTS		496,569.37

MUENSTER STATE BANK

APPENDIX J:

Gross Debt Of The Federal Government

GROSS DEBT OF THE FEDERAL GOVERNMENT
Trillions of Dollars

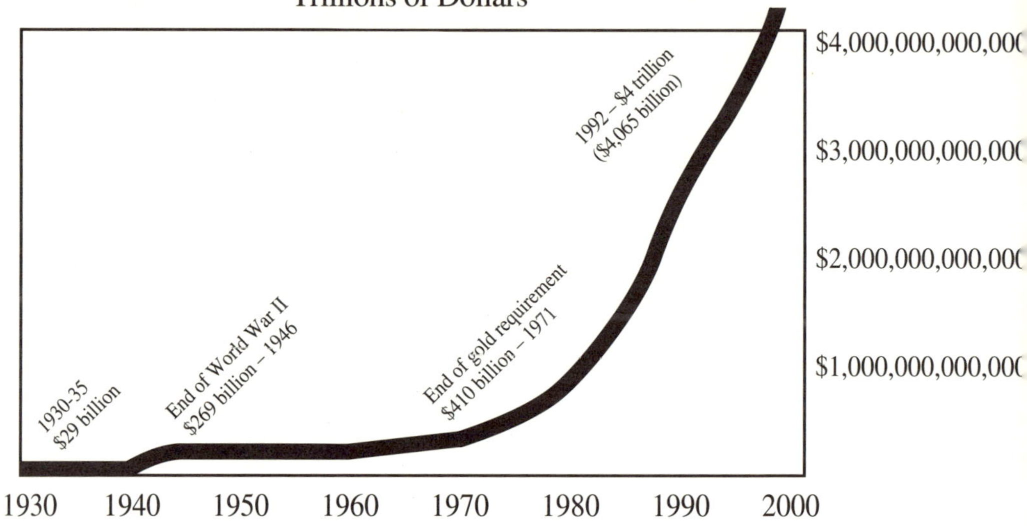

1932
$225 per capita

1992
$16,000 per capita

Since the Nixon Administration severed the international tie to gold in 1971 – after previous Administrations had ended gold requirements on bank reserves and Federal Reserve Notes – there has been little restraint on Federal spendings. 1992 debt was nearly 10 times what it was in 1971 – from $410 billion to nearly $4.1 trillion. Federal debt will continue to go up – until the American people demand that the Congress and the President end out-of-control deficit spending.

Source: Bureau of the Public Debt
U.S. Treasury Dept.

Income Tax and Social Security Tax Burden on the Taxpayer

During the six decades that federal debt has gone up 138-fold, from $29 billion to $4 trillion, federal income taxes have also gone up. When the income tax was adopted by Constitutional amendment at the beginning of World War I, 1913, the top rate set by Congress was 6%, and that on income above $500,000 – which very few Americans had back when the dollar was worth a dollar. Just before World War II only 4-5 million Americans were subject to income taxes, out of 120 million, and total income taxes provided less than 20 percent of the federal revenue. In the 1990s, most employed Americans paid income tax, many at the rate of 28%.

In 1935, when Social Security was approved by Congress, the rate for 1936 was only 1% on employee and 1% on employer, with many persons exempt. Social security tax was slated to go a maximum of 3% each after 1948. Only the first $3,000 of income was included under social security taxes. It had taken six decades for the concept of social security, with old age insurance and other benefits, to reach the United States, from Germany and Great Britain. Originated in 1883 in Prussia, social security was decreed by the "Iron Chancellor," Otto von Bismarck, as a means to pacify his socialist opposition while he was building the military might of what was to become Germany.

After three decades social security spread to Great Britain, and after three more decades to the United States, where it was adopted as an alleviative to the Depression years of the 1930s. As social security has been added to over the years, to include additional programs such as Medicare, and as the dollar has gone down in value with deficit federal spendings, the tax rate for social security has gone up and up. Inflated income has likewise been subject to ever larger tax base. In 1992, employee and employer each paid 6.2% for social security, a total of 12.4% on income up to $55,500. Additional is Medicare tax of 1.45% each for employee and employer, a total of 2.9%, on an even larger income, up to $130,200. Together, social security and Medicare tax rate is 7.65% for employee and employer, a total of 15.3% – contrasted with 6% originally projected as the top social security tax rate!

The March, 1992 *AARP Bulletin* (Washington D. C.) in a report by Eliot Carlson, "AARP Submits health-care reform proposal to members for their review," suggested that Medicare be extended to include all U.S. citizens. This would be financed by increases in taxes on alcohol and tobacco, also an 8% employer payroll tax (with exceptions for employers providing certain insurance coverage) plus an added 5% corporate income tax, and an extra 3% personal income tax or a new 5% federal sales tax (or Value Added Tax). This is from the American Association of Retired Persons, which at the same time announced a 60 percent increase in annual dues from $5 to $8.

Why America Slept

That which editor-in-chief Mortimer B. Zuckerman of *U.S. News & World Report* said in 1990 has become ever more true in this decade of the '90s, with profligate government deficit spending and accompanying inadequate personal and family savings inviting Germany and Japan to take us over. From Zuckerman's editorial "Why America Slept":[1]

> America is happy to have won the cold war. But while we cheer, we are busy losing the hot war for America's economic future . . . .
>
> Our savings and net investment are declining, our national and foreign debt is soaring . . . .
>
> The inflation-adjusted wages of American labor are falling and have been falling for 15 years . . . .
>
> Our sovereign control over our finances, our money supply and our interest rates is weakening, and our foreign markets are declining in industry after industry. There is still an American dream. This is not it.
>
> What has gone wrong? Germany and Japan save and invest two to three times as much as we do per employe. Japan has out-invested America per employe for 20 years. Why? Because real interest rates in the United States in 1989 were three times higher than in Japan. The reason is all too clear: Federal budget deficits . . . .
>
> These deficits use up 75 percent of our savings, push up interest rates, and squeeze out capital investments . . . .
>
> Perhaps the most troubling result of the 1980s is the loss of American financial supremacy just when world financial markets have become more important than ever. Today the top 13 Japanese banks alone have a value that approximates five times the value of our 50 largest financial institutions. Germany and Japan have taken over the longstanding U.S. role as the low-cost, low-interest producer of capital. No wonder that money has become Japan's leading export to the U.S., money that Japan earned the old-fashioned way: Working hard, saving hard, and trading hard . . . .
>
> The villain is not foreign capital which we need to meet our budget deficit. The wickedness lies in our profligacy, which has made us depend on foreign money. The American Esau has

sold his birthright for a mess of consumption, debt and political soft soap . . . .

NOTES

1. Editorial Page, *U.S. News & World Report*, Feb. 20, 1990. Mortimer B. Zuckerman, editor-in-chief, on "Why America Slept." Copyright, 1990, *U.S. News & World Report*.

APPENDIX K:

Cost Of One Ounce Of First-class Mail

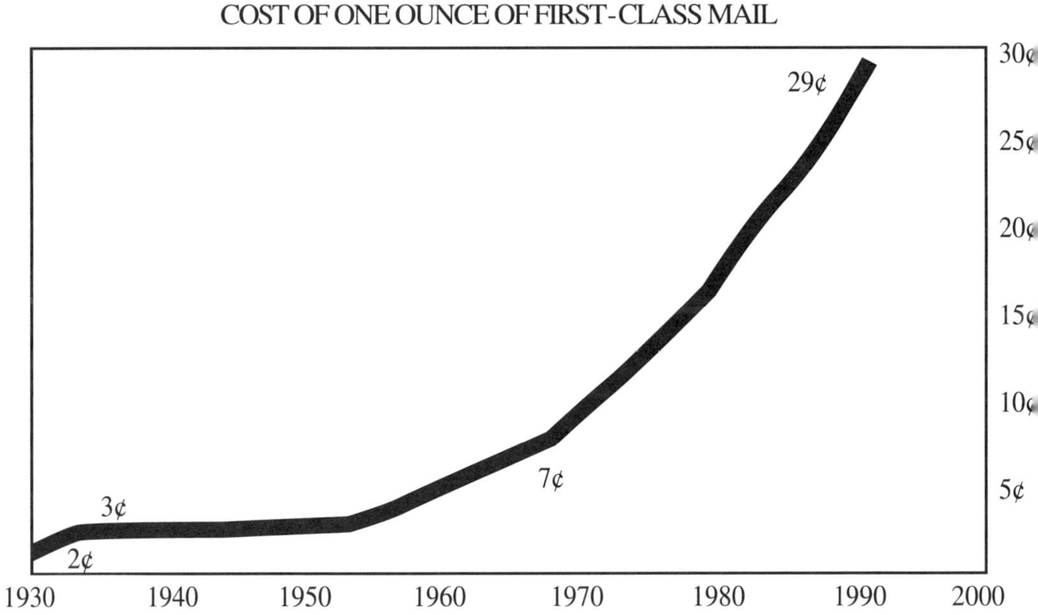

Though often criticized by public and press, the U.S. Postal Service – the Post Office – is probably one of the most efficient of the federal services. It is close to the public and is required to pay its way. Government deficit spendings of the past three decades – especially after the removal of gold reserve requirements of the late 1960s and ending of the tie to gold in 1971 – have pushed down the value of the dollar and caused the cost of first-class mail to go upward and upward.

APPENDIX L:

Decline In Purchasing Power Of U.S. Dollar

DECLINE IN PURCHASING POWER OF U.S. DOLLAR
As Shown In Cost of First Class Mail

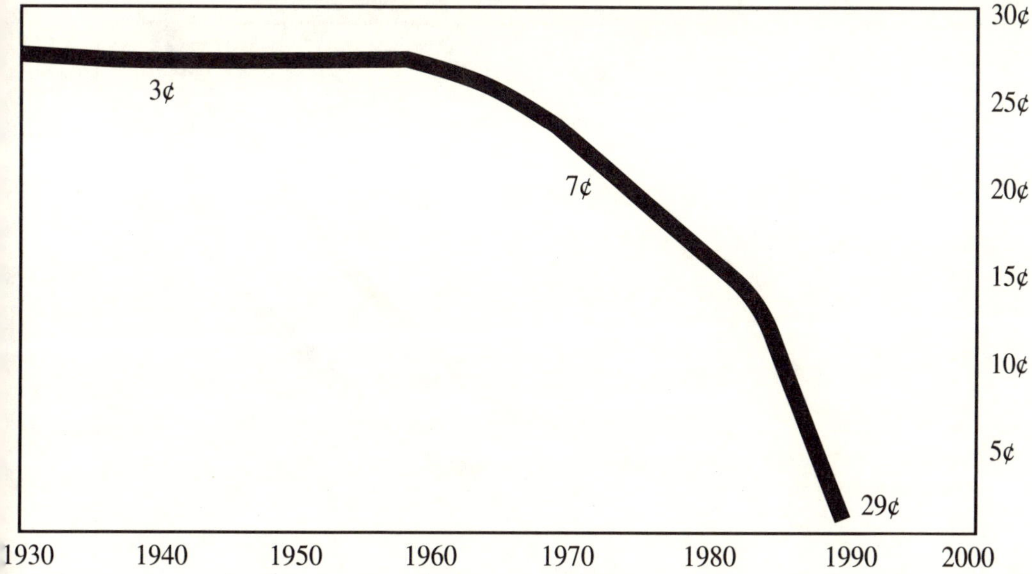

Loss In Purchasing Power – About 90%

Shown inversely from the previous chart the cost of one ounce of first class mail was nearly 30¢ for what used to be 3¢ – ten to one – a loss of nearly 90 percent in the purchasing power of the dollar.

APPENDIX M:

What Congress Pays Itself

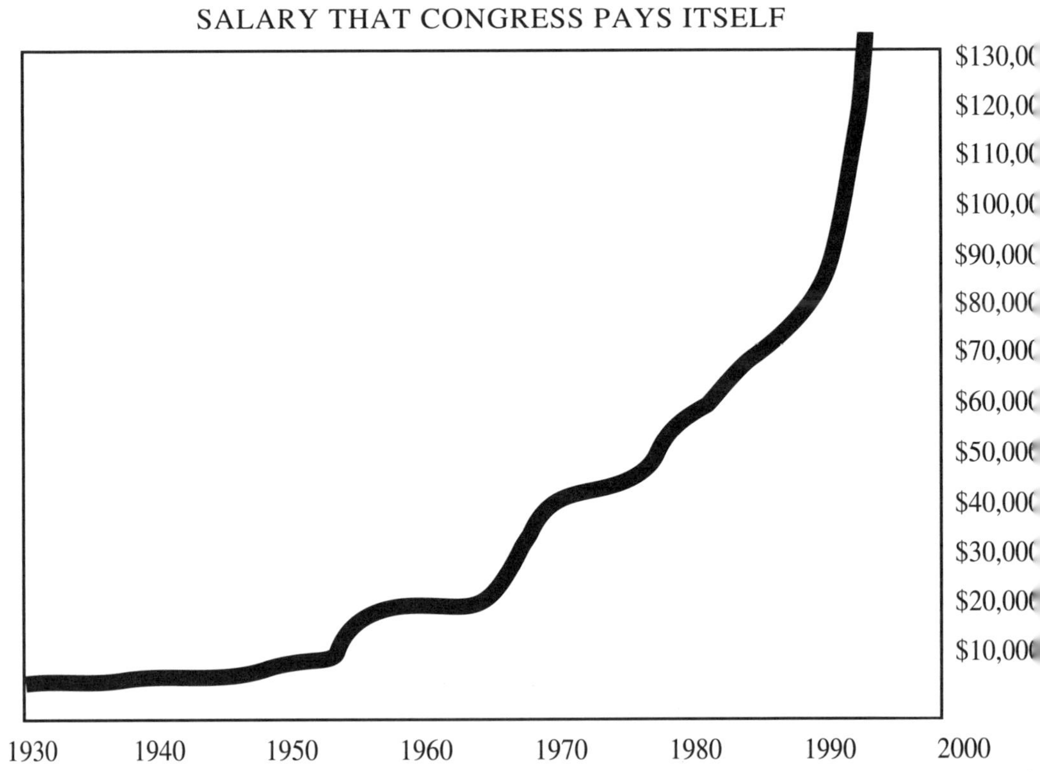

Source: Congressional Quarterly and Associated Press - Karl Tate

When the Depression of the '30s hit the voter, with many out of work and income for others drastically reduced, Congress cut its own salary, temporarily, from $10,000 down to $8,500. By 1935, salary for members of the House of Representatives and the Senate was back to $10,000, where it remained until after World War II. In 1947 Congress raised its pay to $12,500, and then to $22,500 in 1955. After 1960, the last year to balance federal spending with income, as the federal deficit has increased and value of the dollar gone down Congressional pay has gone up.

In the same year that Congress ended gold requirements against bank deposits with the Fed, 1965, it raised its own pay to $30,000. After ending gold requirements for Federal Reserve Notes, it again raised its pay, to $42,500 in 1969. With the end of international convertibility of the dollar against gold in 1971 – before the American people were allowed to own gold – there has been, in effect, no restriction on U.S. debt creation – well intentioned efforts such as Gramm-Rudman-Hollings to the contrary. As shown graphically, Congress in recent years appears to have projected its pay scale on the upward trajectory of a NASA rocket.

During the decade 1981-1991 the cost to mail a letter – the first ounce of First Class Mail – went up from 20¢ to 29¢ – an increase of 45 percent. The Consumer Price Index – the supposed cost of living for most Americans – increased from 90.9 to 136.2 – an increase of 49.8 percent. The official "Threshold of Poverty Level" went up from $9,287 for a family of four persons to $13,924 – an increase of 49.3 percent. That which Congress pays itself went up more than twice as fast as the above, from $60,662 to $125,100 – an increase of 106 percent.

Perhaps Congress works twice as hard as the citizens as a whole. At least it does on its own pay. Additionally, Congress greatly increased the cost of its office operations, and even voted itself a pension – which in the past had been restricted to federal civil service employees, not to elected officials. Most congressional staff operations are exempted from the requirements that Congress puts into law for private employers and employees.

The Federal debt also continued to go skyward during that decade. From just barely above its first trillion dollar mark in 1982 – $1.1 trillion – the debt hit $4.0 at fiscal September 30, 1992 and was increasing a billion dollars a day thereafter. The 10-year increase was 263 percent. Congresses and Administrations appeared to have lost all control over deficit spending that continued to force the value of the dollar ever downward.

Evidence that citizens of the United States resent repeated Congressional pay hikes was the 1992 ratification by three-fourths of the States of what came to be the 27th Amendment to the U.S. Constitution. The amendment prohibits a salary increase for members of the U.S. Senate or House of Representatives from taking place until after the next election of Representatives. The amendment had been introduced more than 200 years earlier by the First Congress as part of the original Bill of Rights.

In 1993, having to wait for Election '82, that which Congress pays itself increased to $133,644 – near 7 percent "cost of living" increases over 13 months.

APPENDIX N:

The Southland Corporation Saga

In the 1930's J. C. Thompson and associates picked up the bonds of Southland Ice Company, Dallas subsidiary of the bankrupt Insull utilities holding empire, at a fraction of the bond's face value. (Ice manufacturing companies, like street railways, were big users of electricity in the early days of electric utilities.) Thompson, manager of Southland Ice, noted the appreciation of customers at one of the ice outlets when the local manager added bread and milk to the ice service. Thus were created the 7-Eleven drive-in convenience stores.

"Jodie" Thompson was to be a long-time director of the Republic National Bank of Dallas. In the early 1960s he and Republic chief executive Fred F. Florence died within a few months of one another. Second generation members of the Thompson family continued to build what had become the Southland Corp., with dairies, auto supply stores, and Citgo Petroleum added to Southland's line of ownership and services. The chain of Southland Corp. convenience stores became nation-wide, then went international into Mexico, Sweden and Japan. Members of the Thompson family served on boards of the holding companies of InterFirst – later to be First Republic – and MCorp – that which had been Mercantile bank.

Southland sought to create a multi-acre home office development just north of downtown Dallas. At the center would be twin office towers with a high-level connecting bridge across Central Expressway. A leveraged buy-out by the Thompsons of other shareholders coincided with Wall Street's "Black Friday of 1987." Perhaps even harder news for Thompson family members was the collapse of First Republic banks and MBanks. These banks had long provided financial strength for Southland Corp. and for other Southwestern businesses.

Southland went into Chapter 11 bankruptcy protection in 1990. In 1991, in spite of opposition from some bondholders and other creditors, the Japanese joint venturer in 7-Eleven Japan, Ito-Yokado Co., bailed out and took control of the Southland Corp. The one magnificent office tower that had been completed was retained. Other vacant land in the proposed office development was sold off. Except in Japan, the international divisions had been sold. U.S. 7-Eleven operations were also cut back.

APPENDIX O:

Extract From 1990 Annual Report of First Empire State Corporation:

To the cloud of recession that overshadows the economy has been added the potential for disruption that comes with engagement in war. While the economic consequences are not the worst of the costs that armed conflict imposes, even on the least pessimistic assumptions they add a further element of uncertainty to calculations which themselves can only be tentative at a time of rising unemployment, low consumer confidence, and fiscal distress at every level of government.

In some earlier eras, circumstances like those now prevailing called forth impressive resources both of finance and of policy leadership from the banking community — national, regional, and local. For reasons well documented in the history of the period, that wasn't true in the collapse of the '30s. It isn't true today, for reasons more intricate in their origin and development but eerily similar in the way they have played out.

A large part of the banking industry in the United States is hurting, its capital wounded, its shares devalued, its self-esteem deflated. The Federal Deposit Insurance Corporation indicates it sees certain failure ahead for 300 to 400 banks, involving combined assets ranging from between $95 billion and $160 billion, depending on the length and severity of the recession. Meanwhile, government officials and central bankers urge banks to counter the recession by providing more credit, and institutions traumatized by deterioration in their loan portfolios and shrinkage in their capital ratios wonder how to respond.

Banking organizations relatively free of the problems that are shaking the industry as a whole are nevertheless concerned at the broader political, economic, and social implications. With public opinion already outraged at the scandals laced through the thrift collapse, and political instincts scenting a target of opportunity in commercial banking, the punitive mood as vented in legislation and/or regulation is unlikely to differentiate among institutions.

As investigations and analyses poke through the aftermath in search of what went wrong, they will find no lack of candidates for blame. High on the list will be the widespread desertion by bankers of their traditional role as censor of their customers' more extravagant ideas. If more bankers had been keeping track of supply and demand in the real estate market as they doled out construction loans, there wouldn't be 500 million square feet of vacant office space in the country today – a glut, incidentally, which by the conventional formula could be cured only by an increase of five million in the number of people working in offices.

Inattention to the borrower's use of the money lent characterized much of bank lending to Third World countries in the 1970s and early '80s. The economic reforms and developments which were supposed to enable the borrowing countries to earn the means of repaying their loans didn't happen, but that didn't shut off the flow of loans as up-front syndication and management fees could be booked into bank earnings.

Obsessive focus on short-range profitability has been denounced as a destructive element in virtually all sectors of American business. It has been especially costly in banking, where it sent loan officers on lending rampages which earned nice bonuses but are remembered now in defaults and restructurings.

Overreaching for the bottom line was matched, and in some cases exceeded, by overreaching for personal compensation. A composite look at seven of the country's largest banking enterprises is illustrative. In 1969 the average salary, bonus, and value of restricted stock awards of their chief executive officers amounted to $270,000. In 1989, the latest year for which data are available, their CEOs received an average of $2.8 million, a better than tenfold increase.

At the 1969 year-end the total market value of the seven companies' common stock was $9 billion. At the end of 1990 it was $25.4 billion, a less than threefold increase, and $2.2 billion of the growth represented new stock issued during the period. Even the much-publicized escalation in the starting salaries of graduates of leading business schools has fallen short of the pace set by CEO pay at the seven sampled banking companies. The median entry-level stipend of Harvard MBAs going to work in 1969 was $14,000. Their 1989 counterparts started at a median $57,000, a slightly more than fourfold increase.

Five of the seven banking companies have adopted "poison pill" defenses making it difficult for dissatisfied stockholders to effect a change in management by acquiring a controlling interest.

More prudent lending, tighter follow-up on borrowers' stated plans for use of funds, a longer-range perspective on profit, and closer correlation between bank performance and the compensation of senior executives – all these are remedies that can come from within the banking industry itself. Other elements of the total problem require action in the realm of public policy and judicial reform.

The biggest and most vexing is deposit insurance. It covers too much. As administered, the system is both unsound and unfair. It gives some depositors more protection than they are entitled to by law and gives others less than they have been allowed to assume they will receive. The doctrine of "too big to fail" has the ironic corollary, "too small to bail."

Worst of all, the present system of deposit insurance removes the single most powerful enforcer of soundness in banking – namely, depositors' concern for the safety of their money. With the government guaranteeing everything, the depositor sees banking as a generic, no fault industry, and every bank is Brand X. Lending, investing, and capital adequacy are free of any constraint imposed by depositor surveillance. That is too much temptation for anyone, depositor or banker, to resist.

Changing the insurance system will not be easy at a time when the sound of bank doors closing is heard in the land. But reform must begin; the size of the commitment must be scaled down. With that change must come greater access by depositors to information on which to base their evaluation of a bank's soundness. Some form of disclosure by bank examiners of their findings, without violation of the confidentiality of bank-customer relationships, should be possible.

The costs incurred by the insurance system are paid by the banks in premiums based on deposits held. Fairness demands that an element of risk-rating be introduced into the premium formula in place of the flat charge per $100 of deposits now applied. Also, if deposits held in foreign offices are to continue to be covered, they should be included in the premium base (as they now are not).

Paying for the losses already incurred by the insurance fund, plus those yet to be suffered, is going to penalize bank earnings for years to come. Meanwhile, a less conspicuous drag on earnings comes from the delays banks encounter when they try to exercise their legal rights under loan agreements or other credit-related contracts. Settlement of claims growing out of defaulted loans or broken contracts is stalled, frequently for years, while income is foregone and assets remain in nonperforming status.

Court reform usually comes only in response to the outcry of an aroused public opinion. Whipping up sentiment on behalf of lenders in confrontation with borrowers is an unpromising cause, but the ultimate losers in the present problems of the banking industry are a large part of the population. They vastly outnumber those who abuse the judicial system to postpone or duck their rightful obligations. They have reasons to support a speeding-up of the sluggish legal system.

To rehabilitate banking, and restore its vital role in the economy along with its constructive influence in the community, will require more than just the passing of the recession. A bounce-back in real estate values will improve the look of balance sheets, but the damage done to the industry's financial muscle and its public standing calls for more fundamental repair.

Attitudes within the industry need to change. It's time to stop the status race in chief executives' pay and insist on a closer relationship between performance and reward. Profit horizons must be lengthened beyond the next quarterly income statement or in the next meeting with security analysts. And, bluntly, professional standards need to be upgraded, especially in the credit evaluation and lending functions.

In the area of public policy, a scaling-down of the obligations assumed by federal deposit insurance is essential. The insurance program should be rolled back to its original purpose of protecting the small depositor who hasn't the means of judging one bank's soundness against another's. It should not be allowed to liberate bankers from the constraints imposed by depositor scrutiny, nor to liberate depositors of large amounts from concern about banks' capital strength and asset quality.

The rules of deposit insurance coverage should be made explicit and binding, with no unwritten clauses in the policy. More meaningful information to use in judging a bank's condition should be available to depositors. The premiums levied for deposit insurance should take into account the relative riskiness of a bank's assets and the adequacy of its capital and reserves.

The industry's sorry current state forms a strange backdrop for proposals to broaden the powers of commercial banks and let them engage in activities from which they now are banned. A case can be made that the historical justification for certain restrictions no longer applies; moveover, as a general rule less restriction is preferable to more. In the industry's present condition, however, any granting of significant new powers should be confined to institutions that meet strict standards of financial soundness and professional competence as judged by the appropriate regulatory authorities.

Not all persuasive is the contention, advanced by some advocates of greater latitude for banks, that existing limitations on their scope and size have been a cause of the industry's present plight. There is no convincing evidence that banks which currently have serious problems would have fewer or less serious ones if they were in more businesses or in more places. The mistakes of the past 15 years didn't happen because the biggest banks in the United States aren't as large or as diversified as some of their foreign competitors.

ROBERT G. WILMERS
President and Chief Executive Officer

PAUL B. MURRAY
Chairman of the Board

One M&T Plaza, Buffalo, New York
February 21, 1991

APPENDIX P:

David Morris On Proposed Financial Institutions Safety And Consumer Choice Act

Columnist David Morris is co-director of the Institute for Self-Reliance, Washington.

The column which follows appeared in the *St. Paul* (Minnesota) *Pioneer Press & Dispatch* and was reprinted in the *Fort Worth* (Texas) *Star-Telegram*, July 31, 1991.

> When Jesse James robbed a bank he walked up to the tellers, pointed a gun in their faces and demanded the money.
>
> Today our elected officials in Washington are about to pull off a heist on a scale unimaginable to Mr. James. But as befits a more civilized era, their weapon of choice is not a gun but a piece of legislation preposterously named the Financial Institutions Safety and Consumer Choice Act of 1991.
>
> Don't let the name fool you. As financial analyst Henry Kaufman warned the Senate Banking Committee this spring, this measure "ultimately puts in jeopardy the fundamental economic democracy of this country."
>
> One of the bill's objectives is to dismantle this country's unique network of community-based banks. Almost 12,000 independent banks serve virtually every city and town. To the Treasury Department, such a multitude of small institutions, and the resulting fragmentation of assets, undermines our ability to compete in a globalized economy.
>
> The proposed law would help centralize financial control in a few dozen national banks.
>
> Those in favor of doing so argue that big banks are more efficient. They reduce costs by eliminating the expense of maintaining individual boards of directors and by requiring only a small central staff to fill out the complicated regulatory paperwork. The backers of big banks also argue that they are more secure. By geographically diversifying their lending portfolios, they insulate themselves from the impact of an economic recession in any one region.
>
> Unfortunately for big bank enthusiasts, the evidence contradicts this sanguine analysis. A recent study by the Durham, N.C.-based Southern Finance Project (SFP) compared banks that focused on their surrounding community to those lending

all over the country.

Banks that restricted lending to local borrowers were more than twice as profitable as those whose loans were geographically dispersed. Those that stayed close to home actually reduced overhead costs and suffered significantly fewer bad loans.

SFP's survey was buttressed by a recent examination undertaken by Federal Reserve economists Stephen Rhoades and Donald Savage, which concluded, "Small banks generally perform as well, or better, than large banks."

Community banks serve their communities better. According to the Federal Reserve, 90 percent of all loans to small businesses are made by community banks. When the National Federation of Independent Business surveyed its members, it found that "firms located in unit branching states (with few branches) rated their bank's performance significantly better than firms in statewide branching states."

The bottom line is that separating banks from their communities may be a costly proposition. In an interview with *Business Week* last year, Charles T. Doyle, mayor of Texas City and chief executive officer of five very profitable community banks in Galveston County, offered one reason that community banks do well:

Sixty percent of Doyle's banks' assets are in personal loans, averaging $7,000 apiece, items such as vacations, medical bills and automobile purchases. The rest help finance Mom-and-Pop businesses.

"These are high-risk loans," Doyle says, "unless you know your customer. You can call it old-fashioned banking, but it works."

One should not romanticize community banks. At times, they can be as aloof and unresponsive to their neighbors as their national brethren. But on the whole, they are solid citizens, a fact that has not escaped the notice of their customers. Almost 7 out of 10 respondents to *American Banker's* 1990 Consumer Survey preferred community-oriented banks; only 23 percent preferred banking with big institutions.

To sum up: There is no evidence that independent, locally oriented banks burden the national economy. A great deal of evidence exists that they strengthen local economies. They are very popular among the general public and the small business community. So why is Congress willfully trying to destroy them?

A decade ago, Congress rushed to sever the link between money and community in the savings-and-loan industry. We will be paying the price for that error in judgment for the rest of our lives. Haven't we learned our lesson?

"Money should never be separated from mission," *Harvard Business Review* Editor Rosabeth Moss Kanter has wisely observed. "It is an instrument, not an end." The U.S. tradition of community banking has been based on that attitude.

Community banks may be popular, but in Washington money talks – and big money screams. Barring an anguished outcry from the public, Congress and the White House are planning to speed the demise of an institution that has served the nation well for many years.

David Morris, an author, lecturer and consultant, writes a column for the *St. Paul Pioneer Press & Dispatch* in St. Paul, Minn.

APPENDIX Q:

Letter From Gary L. Thurman, CPA

Dear Mr. Surratt:

The following is a digest of my observations and conclusions regarding S&L and bank failures:

> In Texas, a significant number of S&L and bank managers abandoned basic balance sheet concepts in order to attract ever-larger deposits and to report maximum earnings. Along the way to the boom-and-bust of the early 1980's, lenders too often lost sight of the need to regularly review the real-world value of assets on the balance sheets required for their credit files. Similarly, it is my opinion that borrowers and lenders basically winked at the disclosures of financial guarantees as "just a contingent liability." Presumably, similar practices were major contributors to S&L and bank failures throughout the country.
>
> As all segments of the nation absorb the economic, personal and other losses resulting from systemic ignorance of basic ethics and banking fundamentals, it is clearly important for individuals with any resources to apply such lessons to the increasingly real-world obligation of taxpayer-citizens for our federal government and its many financial programs and guarantees. If the FDIC has extended defacto deposit insurance to half of all bank and S&L accounts and considering the extensive number of federal risk-assumption programs, then one may reasonably inquire if taxpayer-citizens are prospectively liable for total government guarantees in the five to ten trillion dollar range.
>
> At this point, the more important question is: Does anybody know?!
>
> Having been a tax practitioner in a region severely crippled by bank failures, I can confidently say that very few national priorities are of more immediate importance than getting firm control of banking and financial practices, including government spending and guarantees. Proponents of forced economic redistribution would do well to consider the value of their good intentions in the midst of needless economic impotence caused by irresponsible financial management.

Yours very truly,

Gary L. Thurman, CPA
Midland, Texas
September 30, 1991

APPENDIX R:

Letter To Shareholders, QuestStar Bank

April 3, 1992

Dear Shareholder:

QuestStar Bank had a very eventful year in 1991. Profits were excellent, $1,125,433, which is an increase of 25 percent over the previous year. Total assets, deposits, capital, loans . . . almost every key and significant measure of success was higher. We are very pleased.

Look over the following condensed figures that picture our condition and accomplishments of the past four years. The Bank has outperformed its plans and goals in almost every category, and continues to excel:

	1991	1990	1989	1988
Net income	$ 1,125,434	$ 902,676	$ 701,023	$ 200,203
Earnings per Share	4.50	3.61	2.80	0.80
Earnings per Share (fully diluted)	3.84	3.08	2.45	0.72
Return on Assets	1.61%	1.68%	1.80%	0.67%
Return on Equity	31%	42%	49%	16%
Deposits	$74,617,583	$60,336,498	$39,334,412	$34,944,512
Loans (Net of unearned income)	53,690,693	37,473,362	25,103,181	18,666,211
Allowance for Loan Loss	741,446	745,279	589,696	431,138
Total Assets	79,436,054	64,193,634	42,164,584	36,918,439
Equity Capital	$ 4,157,265	$ 3,031,831	$ 2,129,156	$ 1,428,132
Primary Capital	4,898,711	3,777,110	2,718,852	1,859,270
Book Value per Share	16.63	12.13	8.52	5.71
Book Value per Share (fully diluted)	15.29	11.45	8.38	5.87
Number of Accounts	14,826	13,331	10,250	8,762

Banks are facing increasing financial burdens by Congress and the Regulators. State taxes have skyrocketed and FDIC fees are up. Congress believes that a repeat of the S & L mess can be prevented by increasing regulatory control and procedures of banks. The ''Federal Deposit Insurance Corporation Improvement Act of 1991'' will go into effect this year. Our FDIC premiums have increased almost 300% over the past two years, and are expected to continue to increase. Over forty major compliance programs have been enacted or expanded over the past five years. It becomes increasingly more expensive to operate and compete with non-bank financial organizations. Yet we strive to be more efficient and productive, and constantly try to better serve our customers. We have a very high priority on training our staff.

In spite of the uncertain problems facing banking, we remain optimistic. There are genuine opportunities for small independent banks who have survived the hard times. We understand and are ready to deal efficiently and promptly with small businesses and consumers. We have a local board of directors, local management, and customers have access to decision makers. We have an excellent experienced staff of officers and employees. This is a real advantage to us and we fully appreciate our position to serve small businesses and consumers with loan officers in each of our well staffed offices.

Don't believe those who say the local sources of funding have dried up. We make loans to individuals and small businesses. Last year our loan portfolio increased 43% and roughly 70% of our assets are invested in loans. We plan to continue this philosophy because we understand the needs of our customers and how to serve our community.

Enclosed are shareholder resolutions to increase the number of shares of stock from 300,000 to 1,000,000, and to increase stock options from 50,000 to 83,300.

The Board of Directors is planning to split the stock and additional shares are needed to accomplish this. At this time no new shares are expected to be offered for sale. It is not planned, but should that happen, you would have the right to purchase additional shares on a pro-rata basis.

Additional shares also need to be authorized to increase stock options. These are needed and intended for officer and employee retention, incentive, and compensation, and are granted only with the approval of the Board.

The first quarter earnings have been excellent. With your continued support, we expect to have another record year.

Thank you for your support. You have been most cooperative and helpful. Most of you are customers and we appreciate that.

Yours truly,

QUESTSTAR BANK, N.A.

Don Wigley
Chairman and C.E.O.

1900 West Loop South
Houston, Texas 77027

Acknowledgements

It is impossible to list the several hundred friends and acquaintances, inside and outside of banking, who have given their thoughts, suggestions, questions and constructive criticism to this report. Johnnye Montgomery fought to compose facts into readable phrase. Bill Bradfield gave most helpful copy editing. Erwin Hearne created the cover. Marshall N. Surratt performed diligent proofreading.

Certain close readers may recognize well-informed individuals whom they know, some from service together of decades gone by. Still other knowledgeable Americans quoted are of more recent acquaintance.

A mutual relationship exists. All are concerned for their country, its banking and financial institutions, and its economic survival. They care about their children and their grandchildren and what our U.S. dollar will be worth for them.

Such concern is not new. Texas banker-citizen A. L. Geer calls our attention to Roger Sherman of Connecticut, who sought to protect the people of the United States in 1789 through the new *Constitution of the United States.* A member of the Constitutional Convention, Sherman also served in the Continental Congress of 1776 on the committee with Thomas Jefferson of Virginia, John Adams of Massachusetts, Benjamin Franklin of Pennsylvania and Robert R. Livingston of New York that drew up the *Declaration of Independence.* Still earlier in 1754, Sherman had published the pamphlet titled *A Caveat Against Injustice, or an Inquiry in the Evils of a Fluctuating Currency.*[1] Based on his personal experience with depreciating Colonial currency Sherman warned that "instead of having our Properties defended and secured to us by the Protection of the Government under which we live; we should be always exposed to have them taken from us by Fraud . . ." Sherman also stated: "Money ought to be something of certain value, it being that whereby other Things are to be valued," as with a stated value against "Gold and Silver."

Perhaps we must relearn the hard way certain of these truths in every generation.

Marshall E. Surratt
Dallas

1. Reprinted by Spencer Judd, Publishers, Sewanee, 1982.

Index

NOTES